About the Author

Dr David Tacey is Associate Professor in Humanities at La Trobe University, Melbourne. He is the author of twelve books, including *Re-Enchantment: The New Australian Spirituality* (2000), *The Spirituality Revolution* (2003) and *Edge of the Sacred* (2009). In the 1970s, David studied literature, psychology and philosophy at Flinders and Adelaide Universities, and in the 1980s he completed post-doctoral studies in psychoanalysis and religion in the United States. He was a Harkness Postdoctoral Fellow of the Commonwealth Fund, New York, and his studies were supervised by James Hillman and Thomas Moore. He has taught in various Australian, American and British universities, and is on the editorial boards of several international journals on analytical psychology and religious studies. He is a public intellectual who is often invited to address contemporary issues, including ecological awareness, mental health, spirituality and Aboriginal Australia. His books have been translated into several languages, including Cantonese, Korean, Spanish, Portuguese and French.

Also by David Tacey

The Jung Reader (London: Routledge, 2011)

Uncertain Places: Cultural Complexes in Australasia, edited by Amanda Dowd, Craig San Roque and David Tacey (New Orleans: Spring Journal Books, 2011)

Edge of the Sacred: Jung, Psyche, Earth, Revised International Edition (Einsiedeln, Switzerland: Daimon, 2009)

Re-Enchantment: The New Australian Spirituality (Sydney: HarperCollins, 2000)

How to Read Jung (London: Granta, 2006; W. W. Norton: New York, 2007)

The Idea of the Numinous, edited by David Tacey and Ann Casement (London: Routledge, 2006)

The Spirituality Revolution (Sydney: HarperCollins, 2003; London and New York: Routledge, 2007)

Remaking Men: Jung, Spirituality and Social Change (London and New York: Routledge, 1997)

Edge of the Sacred: Transformation in Australia (Melbourne: HarperCollins, 1995)

Patrick White: Fiction and the Unconscious (Melbourne and Oxford: Oxford University Press, 1988)

Gods and Diseases
Making sense of our physical and mental wellbeing

David Tacey

LONDON AND NEW YORK

First published in English, Australia by HarperCollins Publishers Australia Pty Limited in 2011. This English United Kingdom Edition is published by arrangement with HarperCollins Publishers Australia Pty Limited.

First published in the United Kingdom 2013
by Routledge
27 Church Road, Hove, East Sussex BN3 2FA

Simultaneously published in the USA and Canada 2013
by Routledge
711 Third Avenue, New York, NY 10017

Routledge is an imprint of the Taylor & Francis Group, an informa business

Copyright © David Tacey 2011

The right of David Tacey to be identified as author of this work has been asserted by him in accordance with sections 77 and 78 of the Copyright, Designs and Patents Act 1988.

Every effort has been made to contact copyright-holders. Please advise the publisher of any errors or omissions, and these will be corrected in subsequent editions.

All rights reserved. No part of this book may be reprinted or reproduced or utilised in any form or by any electronic, mechanical, or other means, now known or hereafter invented, including photocopying and recording, or in any information storage or retrieval system, without permission in writing from the publishers.

Trademark notice: Product or corporate names may be trademarks or registered trademarks, and are used only for identification and explanation without intent to infringe.

British Library Cataloguing in Publication Data
A catalogue record for this book is available from the British Library

Library of Congress Cataloging in Publication Data
Tacey, David J. (David John), 1953-
  Gods and diseases : making sense of our physical and mental wellbeing / authored by David Tacey. – 1st ed.
      p. cm.
  Includes bibliographical references.
  1. Mental health–Religious aspects–Christianity. 2. Healing–Religious aspects–Christianity. 3. Spiritual healing. 4. Psychology, Religious. I. Title.
  BT732.4.T33 2013
  201'.7621–dc23
              2012030673

ISBN: 978-0-415-52062-1 (hbk)
ISBN: 978-0-415-52063-8 (pbk)

Typeset in Sabon
by Kirby Jones

for Lisa

The gods have become diseases; Zeus no longer rules Olympus but rather the solar plexus, and produces curious specimens for the doctor's consulting room.
– C. G. Jung, 'Commentary on "The Secret of the Golden Flower"'

'God is dead' – Nietzsche. 'Nietzsche is dead' – God.
– bumper sticker glimpsed in traffic

Nothing that is vast enters into the life of mortals without a curse.
– Sophocles, Antigone

For thousands of years the mind of man has worried about the sick soul, perhaps even earlier than it did about the sick body. The propitiation of gods, the perils of the soul and its salvation, these are not yesterday's problems.
– C. G. Jung, 'The State of Psychotherapy Today'

Contents

Introduction: Return of the Gods	9
1 Gods and Diseases	25
2 The Suffering of Spiritual Rebirth	50
3 The Midlife Crisis as Spiritual Interruption	68
4 Cancer Phobia as a Doorway to Soul	86
5 Sexuality and the Sacred	99
6 Incest, Child Abuse and Alcoholism	121
7 Depression, Self-harm and Suicide	146
8 The Storm Gods and the German Psychosis	167
9 Spirituality, Medicine, Health	192
Conclusion: The Numinous as a Source of Healing	215
Bibliographical Note	240
Endnotes	241
Index	256

INTRODUCTION

Return of the Gods

> I do what logic and common sense and the best-informed research suggests, and then beyond that is something, something strange and unbelievable. The Influences.
>
> Albert Kreinheder[1]

I am sometimes asked, 'Do you believe in gods?' The question is fair enough, since I spend much of my life writing about gods and archetypes – those psychic patterns or forms found in myths, religions, folklore and dreams. I don't believe in gods as discrete entities or beings in space. There are no literal deities out there, and I am repelled by certain kinds of superstitious thinking. I am just as suspicious as anyone else of gods who look like human beings projected into the cosmos. But I do believe that what we might call sacred forces – archetypes found in religious systems and personified as 'gods' or 'spirits' – flow through the human psyche and world, influencing our lives in ways that are transformative and powerful. These forces are transcendental – not visible to normal perception or discernible to reason. It is perilously easy for the mind to mock and berate the notion of 'gods', simply because it fails to understand them. When we take the idea of gods literally, they seem absurd. When we fail to think imaginatively, we are unable to comprehend them at all.

For most modern people, the gods and goddesses of Greece and Rome, the once powerful God of the Judeo-Christian traditions, and the gods, sprites, nixies and fairies of the Nordic, Celtic, Druidic and Saxon peoples are all dead. In some respects, the modern outlook is correct. These deities do not 'exist' in any obvious or recognisable way. They are not objects in space or irrefutable facts. They are not forces that can be discerned by reason and cannot be proved by science or philosophy. To seek these forces by way of intellectual endeavour is to engage in a wild goose chase. These forces can only be experienced in our bodies, hearts and lives. They cannot be tracked by the rational mind.

In the past, defenders of these traditions said the gods can only be understood through faith, not through knowledge. Something like that is still true today, and yet the lack of faith practices or religious observances in most of our lives means our access to these forces is more difficult than ever before. Modern philosophers are to some extent right to assert that the gods are created by culture and are the inventions of human hands. They are indeed, at least in part, anthropomorphic constructs of the imagination. Isn't it right, therefore, to abandon religious and spiritual attitudes altogether? The answer is no, in my view. The gods of any era bear the marks of that era, yes, but that does not mean they are entirely constructed or made up. The gods of any era are intuitive responses to pre-existing forces. These forces are invisible and every culture is forced to 'clothe' them in its own style and national dress. The sceptics continue to argue, however, that God did not make man, but man made God. The fact is that God and man make and remake each other, but both are real, and yet utterly interdependent.

Where we went wrong, as a civilisation, was in assuming that since gods do not exist 'out there' they do not exist at all. We thought our scepticism was a sign of intelligence, but it has turned out to be an expression of stupidity. We may think of gods as metaphors for forces that move through our lives, energising us, animating us, or injuring and afflicting us. The so-called primitive peoples of the past knew more about the reality of the forces that control our lives than we know. In our false enlightenment, we thought ancient peoples were infantile and we knew better. But the modern period of godless rationality is an aberration, and now knowledge of sacred forces is the hallmark of intelligence.

We have gone to sleep at this level and no longer perceive the actions of the gods in the daylight of consciousness. Instead, we witness the gods in our dreams and nightmares, in our hidden or unconscious lives, and in our diseases and afflictions. They are off the radar of our awareness, but that does not mean they do not exist. They are more rampant than before, and the extent to which we are oblivious of their existence is the extent to which they have control over us.

Intuitive thinking

Science is useful for the things that are seen, but for things invisible it is not so helpful. In fact it can be positively harmful if it pretends to speak with authority about the things it does not understand. The gods are best approached not through science but through myth, religion, cosmology, poetry, the arts and music. At the level of individual experience, they are best approached not through reason but through intuition and feeling. Reason and logic will never get us close to the gods, as they make them more unfathomable and removed. Reason makes the gods so distant and improbable that it becomes ludicrous to believe in them.

Only what the Greeks called *mythos* can help get close to the gods. Mythos is a form of thinking which is based on stories, images and intuitions. For many of us, this involves firing up a lost or neglected part of the brain, the so-called right cerebral hemisphere that tends to be holistic, non-verbal, symbolic and imaginative. This hemisphere has been downgraded since the rise of science, but we need to recover it so we can reconnect with our spiritual and intuitive lives. But even with the right hemisphere, we do not 'see' the gods as such, since they do not exist as entities in space. With our intuitive intelligence we see their traces, where they have been and the passages they have trod in our lives. We observe where they have left their mark.

When people ask me about the gods with puzzled looks on their faces, I often try to help them out by saying things that are flippant or humorous – perhaps I use humour to hide my embarrassment for believing in things that are ruled out of bounds by conventional thinking. I might say, 'to see the gods you have to use your imagination', or 'to see them you have to "become as a little child" – because adults can't see them'. Or I might say, 'you must not forget that I come from Irish stock'. This is true, and I often rely on my Irish or Celtic ancestry to explain myself to others. This is easier, and more colourful, than confessing that I am not gripped by empirical science or logic and rely on insights that are drawn from the arts, depth psychology (that is, psychology that takes the unconscious mind into account) and religion. Emphasis on the right brain seems to run in my family, and I am prepared to accept that this could be an inherited trait. Right-brainers can use the left side of the brain, of course, and society and education demands it of us, but it is often experienced as tedious and exhausting.

Although trained in the university system, which is a product of left-brain intelligence, I have never found rational thinking compelling. It does not penetrate deeply enough and always seems to me to miss out on at least half of reality. There is a subtle and spiritual level of reality that mere reason, a blunt tool at the best of times, does not pick up. None of my family members or forbears went to university, and most did not finish high school. They were of peasant or farming stock, and seemed to hold a grudge against education, which I had to fight against in my bid to enter university. Yet they were not unintelligent or stupid but had a religious or mystical view of the world which is not supported by higher education. Although it is discouraged in degree courses, I clung to this worldview, however I was pleased to allow the university to destroy its fundamentalist trappings. I recognised the need to take the best the university could offer – an appreciation of diversity, relativity and common sense – and link it with the 'uncommon' sense of my ancestral line.

Indigenous influence

There was another influence that prevented me from drifting into rationality. I had grown up in the semi-desert regions of central Australia, and in this part of the world I was exposed to the mystical thinking and animism of indigenous peoples. For them the world we see and touch is not even a quarter of reality, and the largest part of the real is invisible, ancestral and spiritual. This meshed rather well with my residual Celtic worldview, although I knew that I could not appropriate their spirituality as my own. Thousands of years, not to mention thousand of kilometres, separated their religious cultures from my own cultural foundations, but I recognised that the Pitjantjatjara, Arrernte and Warlpiri tribes were close to a particular kind of truth that was not valued in the West. I absorbed this Aboriginal legacy at an unconscious level, and I was never prepared to give it up, even though the 'animism' of these peoples was dismissed as primitive thinking by my education. In another book, I have attempted to trace the impact of Aboriginal animistic thinking on my development, and on my society and culture.[2]

As a European-Australian young man at university, I was stuck in an educational system that viewed animistic or mythos thinking as aberrant or infantile. In his 1871 book, *Primitive Culture*, Edward Tylor wrote that the animistic view of the world is 'childish' and typical of what he called 'cognitive underdevelopment'.[3] In the latter part of the nineteenth century, the rational assumptions of Western society were seen as self-evident, and few attempted to critique them. Fewer still could imagine what we are beginning to realise today: that the ancient view of the world has more spiritual value and explicatory power than our rational model. As a white boy recently emerged from the central deserts, I was told that the Aboriginal Dreaming was deluded thinking, projective paranoia and anthropomorphism (giving human form to the non-human). None of my professors or tutors could give it credence, but I refused to abandon their Dreaming to the junk heap of modernity. It always seemed to me to embody a truth that we could not understand: that the world is full of sacred forces which impact on and determine our lives.

The only fine-tuning we have to make today is to see these spiritual forces as symbolic rather than literal or physical. If we take away the literalism of ancient cosmologies, the value of an animated universe remains. We trashed this ancient view before realising what it means to others, or what it could mean for us. We are the primitive ones, the barbarians, the destroyers of what we fail to comprehend. The fact that this destruction continues to be called education or enlightenment indicates to what extent we have succumbed to indoctrination. There must surely come a second enlightenment, where we are able to critique and correct the shortcomings of the first. Some believe that postmodernism is the beginning of a new or second enlightenment.[4] I can only hope that this is the case.

The impact of European colonisation on Aboriginal cultures has been devastating. In my lifetime I have noted some improvements for Aboriginal cultures, partly because the insensitivity of Europeans has been called into question by social justice campaigners, human rights advocates and Aboriginal protest. But a great deal of damage has been done, and it is the rise of such tragic problems as incest and child sexual abuse, alcoholism, depression, psychosis and suicide in Aboriginal communities that has urged me to apply my energies to the study of such problems. Aboriginal people represent the soulful life of Australia, and they also represent my own soul, and thus I have found myself driven to understand what they are going through. Only a spiritual perspective can access their experience, pain and suffering, and the absence of a spiritual perspective in mainstream medicine has prompted me to apply my own spiritual knowledge to the study of pathological behaviours. When the Dreaming is lost, the people get sick, and I feel sure that the same rule applies to all cultures, regardless of race, colour or background. As we read in the Hebrew Bible: 'Where there is no vision the people perish.'[5]

The practical nature of spirituality

The spiritual or mystical point of view is often said to be impractical, remote and otherworldly. To me, however, it is eminently useful. It has a therapeutic value and is a contributor to our long-term sanity. The Western prejudice that it is unrealistic is based on the perspective of the ego, the centre of action and will to which we attach the term 'I'. To the ego, the spirit is a figment of imagination or a product of illusion. It assumes that we are inventing the idea of spirit and there is no such thing in reality. Freud takes this angle in his attack on religion, *The Future of an Illusion*.[6] But what to the rational mind is an illusion is to the soul an important and abiding reality. Eastern philosophies reverse the standpoint of the West, arguing that the visible things of this world are illusory or *maya*, and only the realm of spirit and soul has lasting importance and is fully real.

Fortunately, not all Western thinkers share the Western prejudice. G. K. Chesterton, for instance, has a wonderfully vivid and independent appreciation of the spirit:

> Mysticism keeps men sane. As long as you have mystery you have health; when you destroy mystery you create morbidity. The ordinary man has always been sane because the ordinary man has always been a mystic. He has permitted the twilight. He has always had one foot in earth and the other in fairyland. He has always left himself free to doubt his gods; but (unlike the agnostic of today) free also to believe in them. He has always cared more for truth than for consistency.[7]

This reminds me of something Aboriginal elders once said to me in Alice Springs: that some white fellows are able to 'think like a blackfella'. This involves thinking through mythos – the story, myth or imagination – instead of logos – rational thinking and empirical science. Mythos looks at the whole rather than the part, and the whole is animated by forces which the part can experience but rarely comprehend.

I also like what Chesterton says about mysticism:

> The whole secret of mysticism is this: that man can understand everything by the help of what he does not understand. The morbid logician seeks to make everything lucid, and succeeds in making everything mysterious. The mystic allows one thing to be mysterious, and everything else becomes lucid.[8]

The paradoxical nature of this is impressive. We can understand everything by the help of what we do not understand. When I talk of gods, spirit or soul, these are mysteries and no one fully understands them. They are transcendental concepts and as such they exceed logical thought. They are non-rational but they are far from being 'irrational'. Civilisations have based themselves on these concepts for millennia, and our civilisation will not recover health and balance until it rediscovers a transcendental basis to its outlook.

We are in denial of the sacred today, and as a result we cut ourselves off from the very forces that can provide perspective, orientation and health. Apparently, to develop our logos, we had to cast mythos aside as we progressed in scientific enlightenment. But we are now approaching what could be called the *turning*: we are realising we have thrown out some essential ingredients for a balanced and ordered existence. There is a change of heart and attitude in many areas of knowledge.[9] Much of what we have thrown out has to be recovered and given new value and respect. It is an exciting time in some ways, but the pervasive anxiety felt everywhere is whether we have left this turn too late.

Can the West recover its soul and spirit at this stage, or is this too much to ask of a culture which has made a total investment in logic and reason? My personal view is that it is never too late. We can always pick up what we have lost or abandoned, especially because what we have lost is so much a part of us. The determining factor is whether or not we have the will to move towards a new wholeness. Even if the Western ego continues to deny the need for wholeness, there are non-egoic parts of us that cry out for reconnection and healing.

My path to here

When I was a boy, my mother would disappear at various times and I was never sure where to. 'Hospital,' I was eventually told, 'to help her overcome depression.' I did not know what depression was, nor did anyone explain it to me. It was spoken of in hushed tones and seemed to be one of the tabooed subjects. When I asked my mother, she said it was difficult to explain to a child, but she felt a pressure or force pressing her down, and she was unable to push back against it. She said it made her sad and she felt as if her head were about to explode.

At this same time, when I was about seven years old, I had a recurring dream that she was splashing her face with water at the laundry basin, over and over without stopping. When I would wake in fright and call out she would say, 'Go back to sleep, it is only a dream.' It was more than thirty years later that I realised why I might have been having these dreams. She was desperate for spiritual and emotional rebirth, and the compulsive washing of the face was a symbol of the longed-for renewal. However, this renewal did not occur, despite my dreaming about it, and depression set in and prevented her from living a normal life. As I explore in the chapter on depression and suicide, if rebirth does not take place, the psyche – that part of us that encompasses both the ego and the unconscious – withdraws its energy and we are drawn into a psychic underworld.

My mother suffered from epileptic fits and at various times she would call to someone to fish out her tongue, because she felt she was choking. The tongue had to be held firmly until the fit passed. Later I was fascinated to learn that epilepsy was known in ancient times as the 'sacred disease', because it was felt that sufferers were experiencing visions that were sent by the gods. I think this is what initially sparked my interest in gods and diseases. Towards the end of her life, my mother became demented and had to be hospitalised. When I visited her at the clinic she would accuse me of kidnapping her, abandoning her, and various other heinous crimes. My father suffered from several ailments, including stammering and stuttering, low self-esteem, and a social phobia that prevented him from socialising or attending parties. His condition was later diagnosed as an anxiety disorder, which prevented him from doing many things that normal people did.

My parents were deeply religious in an old-fashioned way. I respected their religiosity but I knew it was not what I wanted for my life. I wanted a closer relationship with the sacred, and not one that was circumscribed by convention and fear. I wanted to bring my critical intellect to bear on religious belief, and this was unthinkable to them. I grew up with an independent mind, and I did not feel that my family's Christian faith was superior to the religious faith of the Aboriginal people we lived alongside in central Australia. I sensed early that the sacred was beyond our direct knowing, and there was no single or absolute interpretation of the sacred. To me, the sacred was a dark mystery, and we should respect all efforts to know it but treat them as culturally limited attempts to engage with an unknowable reality.

I received early instruction in this regard. My grandfather, who spoke about Ireland as home but who had never been there, was a critic of absolutist ideas of the sacred. He told me that any religion that insisted it was the one and only way was not a religion but an ideology. This contradicted what I heard in church, but I felt my grandfather was right.

The Aboriginal people of central Australia never insisted on the absolute nature of truth. Where I lived there were three tribal nations and each had their own stories about the spiritual significance of the place. Heavitree Gap and the MacDonnell Ranges were sacred sites to each of these traditions: to one it was a site of the caterpillar dreaming, to another it was about the dingo, and to another it was about the honey ants. It did not bother any one of these communities that the others had completely different stories about the sacredness of the place. The sacred was complex and varied, with each of these stories forming overlapping or contiguous layers of meaning. This was no city of Jerusalem, where opposing cultures engaged in power struggles and shouted each other down, claiming that only one of the stories is right. In this regard the Aboriginal people were more sophisticated in their understanding of the relativity of truth than those who had come from European cultures.

Intellectual standpoint

My professional training has been multidisciplinary. It has always seemed to me that many views are needed if we are to understand the complexity of the person as an integrated field of mind, body and spirit. In my first degree at Flinders University, South Australia, I read psychology, philosophy and literature. My PhD at the University of Adelaide was in the field of psychoanalysis and literature. Then I moved to the United States after being awarded a Harkness Fellowship of New York, where I conducted post-doctoral studies with James Hillman, a psychoanalyst and Jungian theorist. While working in the United States, I studied with Thomas Moore and Robert Sardello, and the books of these writers, together with those of Hillman, have inspired me to make a contribution to archetypal medicine – therapy of the body and mind based on archetypes – from my own Australian perspective.

Hillman's psychology is polytheistic: many gods, many points of view. Although Jewish by birth, he turned away from monotheism to join other scholars and writers in reviving the gods of Greece. This impacted on me and remains part of my intellectual world. Jung, however, was a different kind of thinker, who combined a polytheistic appreciation of the plurality of the psyche with his inherited Judeo-Christian monotheism. Jung comes closer to my own view of the world since I, too, have been forced to combine a feeling for one God with an appreciation of many gods. As a child I lived between the Christianity of my parents and the Aboriginal Dreaming of my geographical setting. To me, the sacred is larger and greater than any of our constructions. It reveals itself in different ways to different civilisations, and in the course of a lifetime it may even reveal itself in contradictory ways to the one individual.

I have often been encouraged to privilege monotheism above polytheism, or to use the one to debunk the other, but I am unable to do so. We need all the help we can get in understanding the sacred, and at certain times the idea of one God seems appropriate to me, whereas at other times the notion of many gods resonates with the nature of the soul and its multiple archetypes and complexities. There are major examples of thinkers who combined polytheism and monotheism: Socrates offered prayers to the gods while imagining monotheistically about the One, while Petrarch and Ficino were ordained priests of the Church, and yet their imaginations moved along polytheistic lines. Such juggling never pleases religious authorities and it endangered the lives of these thinkers, but it may come closer to the truth.

My sister introduced me to existentialism and psychoanalysis when I was a teenager. She rebelled against our family's religious orientation and became troubled by religious doubts and questions. She took it upon herself to educate herself and me in atheism, agnosticism and modern scholarly thought. In particular, she encouraged me to read Nietzsche and Freud, and by the time I was twenty I had devoured most of the writings of these two great atheists. As a boy I recall being asked what I would like to do when I grow up – my answer was that I would like to combine the insights of Freud and Nietzsche into a new religious understanding of human nature. At that stage I had not yet heard of Jung, who had done precisely that. When I first encountered Jung, I was struck by the similarities between his depth psychology and the spiritual cosmology of Aboriginal peoples.

For me, Jung acted as a much-needed bridge between Aboriginal religions and Western knowledge. He inhabits a curious yet vital intermediate position. Naturally he risks being dismissed as a 'primitive' thinker by those who prefer a more rational and empirical form of psychology, but for those of us who value the mysteries of soul and spirit he is an invaluable resource and reliable guide. Jung was one of the first of the psychologists to recognise that invisible factors in the psyche play a major role in creating disease and shaping behaviour. Although these factors could not be seen, they were present and real. He never visited Australia, but there is a keen interest in Aboriginal cultures and religions found in his writings, including in his autobiography, where we find references to the tribes I grew up alongside in central Australia.

Jung's reputation in academia is controversial to say the least, and professional trainings in psychology and psychiatry tend to dismiss his ideas as the speculations of a mystic. Yet I press on regardless, noting that the scriptures affirm that the stone rejected by the builders can become the cornerstone of the new order.[10] My independence of mind caused me not only to reject my parents' simple faith but also to be critical of the education I received at university. I refused religious and secular fundamentalisms alike, and see both as missing the mark.

Author's note

This is my tenth in a series of books which explore spiritual meaning in today's world. This book supplements but does not replace my earlier writings. For a survey of the landscape of spirituality in the modern world, see *The Spirituality Revolution: The Emergence of Contemporary Spirituality* (Sydney: HarperCollins, 2003; and London and New York: Routledge, 2004). For a study of Australian culture and spirituality, see *ReEnchantment: The New Australian Spirituality* (Sydney: HarperCollins, 2000). For an account of Jung as a religious thinker see *How to Read Jung* (London: Granta, 2006; New

York: W.W. Norton, 2007). For a study of the appropriation of Jung's thought by the New Age movement, see *Jung and the New Age* (London: Routledge, 2001). For an exploration of the impact of the unconscious on gender and sexuality, see *Remaking Men: Jung, Spirituality and Social Change* (London: Routledge, 1997, Melbourne: Viking, 1997). For more on the relation between Jungian psychology and ecological awareness, see *Edge of the Sacred: Jung, Psyche, Earth* (Einsiedeln, Switzerland: Daimon, 2009).

An earlier version of Chapter 6 appeared as 'Incest, Society, and Transformation: An Australian Perspective' in *Psychological Perspectives* (Los Angeles, Issue 23, November 1990, pp. 16–31). An earlier part of Chapter 7 appeared as 'Spiritual Perspectives on Suicidal Impulses in Young Adults' in Richard H. Cox, Betty Ervin-Cox and Louis Hoffman (eds), *Spirituality and Psychological Health* (Colorado Springs: Colorado School of Professional Psychology Press, 2005, pp. 107–28). A version of Chapter 9 was published as 'Spirituality and Mental Health: The Mystery of Healing', in Marian De Souza, Leslie Francis, James O'Higgins-Norman and Daniel Scott (eds), *International Handbook of Education for Spirituality, Care and Wellbeing* (Dordrecht, Heidelberg, London and New York: Springer, 2009, pp. 275–90).

I thank the editors of these works for their editing of the original essays, which has been retained in the present volume.

CHAPTER 1

Gods and Diseases

Something strange or foreign, something that
does not 'belong' nests within illness.
Alfred Ziegler[1]

Archetypes and subtle forces

There is more to life than what we can see at the surface. There are vast, swirling depths which underlie our existence and constitute our hidden nature. Some of us prefer to leave these depths to poets and prophets, and as T. S. Eliot reminded us, 'human kind cannot bear very much reality'.[2] Indeed these depths are shielded from many of us so long as all goes well and we adapt successfully to society and its conventions. Those of us who manage to do so will have the advantage of a relatively smooth-running life, but we will also miss a great deal of its meaning. For while the depths are dreadful and frightening, they are also beautiful and sublime. If we do not face them, we miss out on most of life.

Illness and disease have the peculiar ability to plunge us into the watery depths of the unconscious, and there we have to 'sink or swim'. What we discover is that there are enormously powerful forces down there. These forces were called gods or spirits in former times and were believed to be 'up there' in the heavens. Today we experience them 'down below'. What can we call them in our godless time? Jung referred to them as 'archetypes', but I think 'gods' are nevertheless what they remain. 'Archetypes' suited Jung's scientific project, but I am more interested in truth than scientific logic. Unlike Jung I do not see myself as a scientist, but as a cultural analyst in search of meaning.

It is astonishing that these 'gods', normally obscured from our vision, come into the horizon of our awareness when we are gripped by ill health. It seems that in our time suffering is the royal road to the sacred. Perhaps it was always so, but in our society, where talk of the gods has been banished and those who discuss this subject are thought to be crazy, the breaking apart of the personality that comes with illness or suffering is necessary for such an encounter. We have been manipulated into believing that there are no gods or spirits, and such things are figments of our imagination, but when our normal selves are changed by illness or suffering, we have to put this attitude to one side and engage in dialogue with forces that are stronger than we are. Our inner world is spiritual, even mystical, to a surprising degree, especially where illnesses are concerned.

Diseases of the spirit

Spiritual forces and subtle factors can trigger diseases in the body to an extent that conventional medicine has not been able to recognise. The fact is that most of our medical practitioners are trained in the bio-psycho-social model and are not able to identify the more subtle factors that fail to appear on the radar of scientific investigation. They will appear on the medical radar of the future, but at the moment we live in a kind of spiritual dark ages, created by a rationality that kills off mystery and denies its existence. This is not a criticism of doctors or an attack on their work, but a shortcoming of our Western knowledge system. Anyone who diagnoses a spurned god at the heart of a medical complaint might be regarded as either a 'witchdoctor', a throwback to medieval times, or a lunatic with a poor relationship with reality. Such is our conditioning in the materialistic worldview that we erect all kinds of defensive barriers and prejudices against other points of view.

In my view, many of the pathologies I explore in this book – neurosis, sexual dysfunction, incest and child abuse, cancer phobia, alcoholism, depression, self-harm and suicidal impulses – are primarily *diseases of the spirit* and only secondarily diseases of the body. This is why the medical model as it stands can do little to heal these problems. It can reduce symptoms in some cases and alleviate suffering, but it cannot resolve or transform these pathologies unless it introduces the dimension of spirit or soul into the equation.

In some areas of medicine, this change is already underway, as I will explain in Chapter 9. But running parallel to Western medicine is the field of 'archetypal medicine'. This tradition has always interested me, not because it is rebellious or anti-establishment but because it is a medicine based on the gods. I have felt a resonance with it, and think it is overdue for a renaissance and public airing. I would like to think that I can contribute in some way to this renaissance. I do not intend to engage in labelling, in attributing a particular deity to a specific disease. Rather I seek to bring out the broadly spiritual element in the complaints and afflictions that have claimed my attention.

Archetypal medicine

The master exponent of archetypal medicine is C. G. Jung, the Swiss psychiatrist and psychoanalyst. I will be drawing on Jung's psychology throughout the book, but it is important to recognise that archetypal medicine is not his personal invention. It is a persistent and age-old tradition, found wherever the spirit is recognised as an active and potent ingredient in human health and wellbeing. Thus in a history of archetypal medicine we would have to include every ancient and pre-modern culture, from the late medieval period back to the Stone Age and beyond. Every 'spiritual' culture has recognised the central role of subtle or hidden forces in disease, including the indigenous cultures with their shamanistic practices and the god-centred healing arts of Greece and Rome. It is only our modern civilisation that has decided to throw out the spiritual factor, because it cannot see it or test it in a laboratory. Yet if we fail to recognise the gods or make allowance for them, they express themselves more readily in pathological form – they seek outward expression whether we assist them or not.

In ancient Greece, a defiled god would turn wrathful and fierce; further back, in the Stone Age, a friendly spirit would turn demonic and hostile. Not much has changed in this regard. Since we make no room for the gods and do not respect them or invest energy or interest in their wellbeing, the situation we face is difficult. In 1929 Jung announced 'the gods have become diseases',[3] because they seem to have no other option in our lives than to become factors of disturbance. Since our minds ignore them, the only place they have left to make themselves felt and draw our attention is in our bodies – in sufferings and sexual disturbances. Then we might listen, but even then, we might not. Some of us seem more prepared to suffer blindly, mutely, than admit that the world might be enchanted by forces beyond ourselves. We are fearful of the spirit and will do anything to avoid it. Many of us would sooner die than have to come to terms with a divine presence. Our conditioning has made us enemies of the spirit, and our present culture makes us even less likely to turn towards the spirit with interest because it has become wrathful at our neglect.

We do not feel like opening the doors of our awareness to forces that have turned against us, and yet we must do so. This is the odd modern predicament we face: the savage gods have to be befriended. Jung's original announcement about the gods becoming diseases needs to be set in context:

> We think we can congratulate ourselves on having already reached such a pinnacle of clarity, imagining that we have left all these phantasmal gods far behind. But what we have left behind are only verbal spectres, not the psychic factors that were responsible for the birth of the gods. We are still as much possessed by autonomous psychic contents as if they were Olympians. Today they are called phobias, obsessions, and so forth: in a word, neurotic symptoms. The gods have become diseases. Zeus no longer rules Olympus but rather the solar plexus, and produces curious specimens for the doctor's consulting room, or disorders the brains of politicians and journalists who unwittingly let loose psychic epidemics on the world.[4]

Jung contrasts the 'phantasmal gods' of the ancient past with the 'psychic factors' that were responsible for their formation. We live in a time where the old forms and names are dead, and yet the eternal and ongoing spirits themselves have not been recognised or given new names. A sense of nameless dread hangs over our civilisation and this anxiety is related to our failure to name or appease the gods.

At least some of our modern diseases can be converted back into gods, as this book will explore, but each person has to make this spiritual journey in his or her own way. Society at large is not going to help us, and the medical world is no friend of spirituality either, although there are signs that this is changing.[5] But if we can find the key metaphors for some of our diseases, we can lead the energies back to the spiritual world from whence they came.

In some ways, this is like healing in the manner in which Jesus practised it, as reported in the gospels. We need to cast out 'demonic' forces by turning towards the sacred with an open and receptive heart. If we reject the widely held assumption that the world is not enchanted, that there is no 'spirit' in the universe, that existence is meaningless, there can be a sudden conversion at the heart of our lives. Turning towards the sacred is itself the healing act, as this releases us from the grip of complexes and neuroses, those nervous disorders that can generally be traced back to a split or dissociation in the psyche. As Jung has said, 'the numinous is the real therapy'.[6] 'Numinous' means possessing divine power, but this can be understood as a spiritual transformation within *this* world, not an intervention from another world. Spirit is the mystery element in creation, and although it may be metaphysical in itself, it sits closely beside or within the physical world, waiting for our attention. If we can find the metaphor in our illness, we are halfway there. We may not receive a cure, or some miraculous turnaround, but we may receive healing.

The problem of credibility

The gods return in our time not as sublime figures on Mt Olympus or a trinity of gods in heaven, but as fierce psychological forces in the human psyche. Perhaps the gods have always come from within, and we only now discover this when the cults of the gods have fallen into disrepair. As Jung puts it:

> All ages before us have believed in gods in some form or other. Only an unparalleled impoverishment of symbolism could enable us to rediscover the gods as psychic factors, that is, as archetypes of the unconscious. No doubt this discovery is hardly credible at present.[7]

He is right; it is hardly credible to most intellectuals and scientists. It takes an intuitive sensibility to understand Jung's argument. Our 'unparalleled impoverishment' of religious symbolism forces us to deal with the gods as naked powers of the psyche, except that these are not limited to the human psyche, but extend far beyond it. Jung's argument points in the direction of our need for a new religious awareness, if not a new 'religion' as such. We cannot afford to have these powers thrashing around inside us without the dignity of a name, a cult, a tradition, a symbolic container.

We are helpless before the spiritual forces and do not know where to turn for wisdom or orientation. A new search must develop, so that we can recover our relationship with the forces that govern our lives. The collapse of cosmologies in our time has perhaps served one positive purpose: we can no longer rely on old, hackneyed or clichéd images of gods. If we want to befriend them, we have to use new vision and imagination. The old certainties have been lost and propping up derelict beliefs does not serve us well. As Jung wrote: 'We moderns are faced with the necessity of rediscovering the life of the spirit; we must experience it anew for ourselves.'[8]

It is the task of future cultures to provide new forms to help us relate to the gods. Spiritual ideas and forms last for a certain time during which they convince those who fall under their suggestive spell, but they have a limited lifespan. When religions treat their gods too literally or with too much familiarity or presumption, the best minds in society see through the lie and announce the death of the gods. The gods are then exposed as the work of human hands, having no relation to reality. Then the whole cycle starts over again. This takes place whenever a religious system collapses, such as with the fall of the Greco-Roman world. When a new cosmology is established, the new gods are not seen as the mere inventions of fantasy but represent an intuitive response to a once convincing reality.

Seeing through to the metaphor

This book explores the root metaphors in a number of mental illnesses and self-destructive behaviours. In self-harm and suicidal ideas, for instance, the persistent metaphor is that of harming or destroying the conventional self as a prelude to a transformation of personality. Tragically, if this metaphor is lived out at the literal level, there can be no transformation, only death. The metaphor of killing the old self to allow a new one to be born is as old as humanity. But in our ever-increasing material world, with its literal-minded interpretations, this metaphor can seize hold of us from within and destroy us. The impulse to transform, which is often expressed initially as an impulse to destroy, can eat away at the individual's health and peace of mind until it is realised. If the transformative impulse is not realised at the level of mind and spirit, it will fall into the body and act destructively. If we think literally, we are destroyed, and if we think metaphorically, we are saved – that is, saved from literalism.

The same can be said for incest and child sexual abuse. Here the root metaphor is that of connecting with the 'child within', because the child carries the possibility of transformation. 'Unless you change and become like a little child',[9] as the scriptures say, one cannot overcome the present burnt-out, exhausted, adult condition and achieve new life. This metaphor is sometimes taken literally by our instincts, and we find ourselves compulsively attracted to incest, sexual abuse of minors, and child pornography. In this way, the desire to be reborn to a new self is profaned and pathologised. The aim of archetypal medicine is to encourage the sufferer of addictive, perverse or pathological behaviours to 'see through' the compulsion and enact the instinctual impulse at a spiritual level, as ritual, liturgy or realisation, not at a literal level.

This change cannot be initiated by the intellect alone, but must be a real effort of the total personality, engaging the feelings and emotions. Albert Kreinheder has pointed out that many of us overestimate the impact that 'intellectual' knowledge will have on our diseases and suffering:

> Psychotherapists sometimes explain to a suffering patient that migraine, for instance, is caused by their perfectionism, and if only they would be more easy going and relaxed, the headaches would go away. Or the cancer patient may be informed that her disease comes to 'nice' people who never get angry and who take too much of the blame for everything that goes on around them. Then she might be advised to be a little tougher toward others, a little kinder toward herself, and to live more for pleasure and less for duty ... The trouble is that knowing such facts seems to have little or no effect on the physical condition of the patient and may, in fact, even make it worse.[10]

'Knowing' what the problem is in terms of conceptual knowledge is not enough. Things will only change if there is real commitment and dedication rather than passive listening to intellectual ideas or attending a weekend workshop. It is typical of our Western culture that it would imagine that cognitive knowing can do the trick and achieve the work of transformation. But the soul and body have to be engaged, listened to and encountered in an attitude of complete receptivity and openness. To effect change at this level involves areas of our experience that are not normally activated in our daily existence. The old words 'conversion' and 'rebirth' are closer to what is required than simply accumulating facts in a detached manner.

Seeing the spiritual metaphor, or god, in a disease is not normal 'seeing', not an act performed by the retina in association with the mind. As Alfred Ziegler writes: 'In archetypal medicine, seeing is not observing but perceiving, a perception similar to the mysticism of the Middle Ages, the vision of the twilight.' This seeing 'requires "blinking" to make sight hazy'.[11] Our vision needs to be blurred, and that is how we can 'see' the activity of the gods. Normal vision cannot see it, which has led to the suspicion that the gods are illusions and this kind of seeing is a form of madness.

The medical profession continues to be preoccupied with tracing diseases to chemical imbalances and physical causes. But the archetypal approach reads our illnesses as statements about what has failed to happen in the realm of the spirit. Something 'spiritual' wants to manifest in our lives, but it cannot do so. An energy or force is present, but if it cannot be expressed in a spiritual form it gets trapped in the body and leads to sickness. Archetypal medicine looks for the obscure in the revealed, the esoteric in the exoteric, the metaphor in the depraved. The somatisation of our spiritual impulses, absorbing them into the body, becomes a real problem in secular times, when society provides few outlets for spiritual needs. An important need of the spirit is to connect with a source beyond itself and be reborn through this encounter. The spirit cannot survive within the container of the ego but must be joined to something greater. This is the rite of transformation that is enacted in all the initiation ceremonies of major religions and indigenous cultures. If this impulse has no way of fulfilling itself in ceremony it might instead express itself in a variety of pathological disorders, such as alcoholism and depression. By becoming aware of the spiritual content of our desires, we help to rid the body of its suffering and return the spiritual impulse to its rightful place.

'It's only psychological': popular approaches and positive thinking

What I am describing in these pages may sound a little like 'psychosomatic medicine' insofar as it deals with somatic or bodily disturbances that trace their origin to the psyche. But as it has been used in the past, the term 'psychosomatic' is no longer useful because it ignores the workings of the unconscious and assumes the patient has brought the disease upon him or herself. The concept of the psyche in this tradition is far too narrow, and assumes that the psyche is essentially conscious and under the individual's control and willpower – if only he or she could awaken to various self-destructive patterns, all would be well. When some people say that a sickness or disease is 'only psychological', they have no idea what they are talking about. The sickness-making factor is invariably unconscious, a fact that is frequently overlooked or ignored in attempts to popularise the notion that there is a psychological element in sickness and healing.

For instance, the books, audios and lectures by Louise Hay, Wayne Dyer, Gay Hendricks, Jerry Hicks and others tend to misunderstand the nature of the sickness-making (or pathogenic) agent. These works are well-meaning, and I do not doubt that many have benefited from them, but they simplify the pathogenic factor to 'negative thoughts in the mind', or 'negative views of oneself', which – they claim – cause illness and disease. But the root cause of the sickness may be extremely difficult to access, and only after a great deal of reflection, self-analysis or analysis with a therapist may the underlying cause become known, if at all. In her bestselling *Heal Your Body*, Louise Hay claims that we conspire against ourselves and that our 'thoughts' create our lives.[12] If we can change our thoughts we can transform our lives and cure our diseases. Hence such popular systems come up with the idea of remedying the situation with 'positive thinking', 'spoken affirmations', 'mind over matter' and adjustments to behaviour. This is a form of mental reprogramming which has little to do with the approach I am adopting in this book.

By failing to understand the complexity of the mind and overlooking its unconscious dynamics, these approaches, although with the best intent, seem to have the reverse effect of making the suffering person more burdened with guilt than ever. Those of us who fall sick are already 'guilty' enough for not being able to function in the normal way, and by arguing that each of us is personally responsible for our diseases or afflictions heaps another load of guilt upon the person. This can create the worst kind of attitude for mental and physical healing to occur. However, there is an element of truth in the populist systems, which is why they enjoy such commercial success, often across decades. The general public is intuitively alert to the meaningfulness of disease, and so long as the medical system is unable to explain this or make it known, we fall prey to commercial ventures which take up this theme and develop it in a sensational way.

Wrestling with our demons

Archetypal medicine is not trying to suggest that the patient is deliberately subverting his or her health. Rather, something utterly unknown to the conscious mind is making its presence felt in a symptom or disease. Whereas psychosomatics seek to destroy the symptom to restore the person to a normal life, the Jungian approach seeks to understand the symptom in order to transform the patient. As Jung put it: 'We should not try to "get rid" of a neurosis, but rather to experience what it means, what it has to teach, what its purpose is'.[13] To destroy the symptom might be to destroy our god or guardian angel, or, as some would say today, our true self.

The Jungian approach does not moralise against the patient but in favour of the symptom. Something not yet conscious is expressing itself in a symptom, and we had better find out what it is so we can live the life we are meant to be living. 'We should even learn to be thankful for [the neurosis], otherwise we pass it by and miss the opportunity of getting to know ourselves as we really are,' says Jung again.¹⁴ The archetypal approach assumes a meaningful end point or goal in the treatment of disease. It can only do this because it assumes that the body and mind together are an intelligent whole which is directing the personal life toward a more integrated state. The mechanistic medical approach does not assume a guiding hand behind the disease, and hence to kill off the disease is about as far as its imagination can reach. The Jungian approach works subtly and sensitively with the symptom so that a deeper meaning is revealed and the person can be encouraged to experience a larger life. In clinical psychotherapy it is the transference of the psychological contents to the analyst that allows the unconscious to speak and reveal its mystery.

The discovery of the metaphor in an illness is a moment of liberation and release. Instead of allowing the illness to take hold of the body, steps are taken to mitigate this by understanding what the metaphor wants. To approach the metaphor in the right spirit is to humanise and weaken the force that is trying to destroy us. If we can listen to the metaphor and discover what it seeks, the body might be protected from its devastating impact. Jung called this the 'intuitive method' and he practised it during his own difficult period of mental confusion after his break with Freud, when the contents of his unconscious seemed hell-bent on destroying him. He said that the only way to 'endure these assaults of the unconscious' was to 'find the meaning of what I was experiencing in these fantasies'.¹⁵ He spoke about finding meaning by translating the raw emotions into images or metaphors that he could befriend:

> To the extent that I managed to translate the emotions into images – that is to say, to find the images which were concealed in the emotions – I was inwardly calmed and reassured. Had I left those images hidden in the emotions, I might have been torn to pieces by them.¹⁶

The image in the emotion has to be coaxed out and revealed, and by so doing the psychic content can change from destroyer to friend. The image tells us who or what in the psyche is launching the attack, and this gives us a chance to know our assailant for the first time. When we grant it this respect and autonomy, it is able to turn towards us in a new way. In medieval language, the content can shift from demon to guiding spirit.

In the Hebrew Bible, the story of Jacob wrestling with the angel of God is an example of the process I am describing (Genesis 32:22–31). The fight with the angel by the ford of the river Jabbok is said to have lasted all night, until the symbolic dawn of the morning light. As morning approaches, the attacking angel asks Jacob: 'What is your name?' Jacob answers, but says he will not stop fighting until the angel has blessed him. The angel blesses him and declares that his name is no longer Jacob but *Israel*, which means 'one who wrestles with God'. This is a central story in the Western tradition and it reveals a number of things.

The angel of God attacks Jacob because it did not know his name (32:27). If the spirit remains alien and we have not yet attempted to befriend it, it will assault the ego with force and violence. The enmity between spirit and ego originates from the fact that the one does not know the other. When the ego has sustained the assault and asks to be blessed, the angel changes from avenging demon to holy spirit and bestows riches upon Jacob and blessings upon his descendants. The messenger of God often appears as a vengeful figure in sacred stories, and only after the human figure has accepted the divinity of the intruder can transformation take place. This pattern runs throughout scripture, myth, religion and depth psychology. The divine *other* interrupts our lives, and only when we have made the necessary readjustment is a higher integration of body and spirit possible.

In terms of our surviving the disruptive forces arising from the unconscious, Jung insists that the main way to protect ourselves is to personify the invading contents:

> The essential thing is to differentiate oneself from these unconscious contents by personifying them, and at the same time to bring them into relationship with consciousness. That is the technique for stripping them of their power. It is not too difficult to personify them, as they always possess a certain degree of autonomy, a separate identity of their own. Their autonomy is a most uncomfortable thing to reconcile oneself to, and yet the very fact that the unconscious presents itself in that way gives us the best means of handling it.[17]

Although pop psychology might refer to these forces as 'negative thoughts' and dismiss them as mental garbage, an archetypal approach understands that at the core of these negative thoughts is a god or angel. Something larger than us is causing the disturbance, and to treat this influence with reverence and awe is the most appropriate response. As Jung makes clear, it is worth our while to treat these forces as autonomous and separate to us if the alternative is to be torn to pieces by them.

This is the way that Jung dealt with the psychotic episodes he suffered from between 1913 and 1919, thus enabling him to survive this potentially fatal period. Recently, the aesthetic and intellectual products of his struggle with the unconscious have been published as *The Red Book*, a remarkable record of his attempt to discover meaning in his mental disturbance during this time.[18] By personifying the forces that assailed him as Philemon, Salome, Soul and a cast of other characters, Jung was able to learn a great deal from his mental chaos and eventually transform it into the basis of his own analytical psychology: 'To the superficial observer [the contents of this book] will appear like madness. It would also have developed into one, had I not been able to absorb the overpowering force of the original experiences.'[19] In this way, the wounded Jung restored the savage forces to dignified gods, and he could turn his attention to healing others. This is something we are all capable of, if we are able to face the sources of our own suffering.

The spiritual roots of healing

In some ways archetypal medicine provides a direct link to the historical roots of medicine. In the temples devoted to Asclepius, the son of Apollo, priests were engaged not only in the tasks of worship but in the healing of diseases. Patients were invited to enter dream-incubation chambers, where they were expected to have a dream that would indicate what spiritual impulse or god might be responsible for their malady. In this paradigm, the clue to the illness was discovered in the products of the unconscious, and to that extent the archetypal approach seeks to revive this practice. Medicine has forgotten these ancient roots of the healing sciences, mainly because the techniques of the past make little sense to the rational patterns of modern thinking. The caduceus or rod of Asclepius, the snake-entwined staff, may remain a symbol of medicine, but not much remains of the wisdom that was attached to the god of healing and his dream-interpreting priests.

Moving from ancient Greece we find spirituality and disease linked in every shamanic tradition of every indigenous or tribal culture. But as with the Asclepian traditions, these practices have been almost universally discredited and are now viewed as part of an archaic, pre-scientific model of the world. In my view, we need to recover respect for these systems of healing and regret our failure to appreciate their value and worth. For me personally, spiritual insights gleaned from Aboriginal cultures have helped me to access the deeper dimension of some of our modern epidemics. Perhaps we will recover respect for these traditions once we recover respect for spirit in our worldview.

Metaphor as illness

By way of contrast with archetypal medicine, it is worth referring to Susan Sontag's classic work *Illness as Metaphor*. Sontag's book is a sustained criticism of the idea that metaphor, myth and meaning play a role in the formation of diseases. This 'psychologising' tradition, which 'starts with Freud and Jung', is, she claims, a dehumanising attack on our dignity and freedom:

> My point is that illness is *not* a metaphor, and that the most truthful way of regarding illness – and the healthiest way of being ill – is one most purified of, most resistant to, metaphoric thinking. Yet it is hardly possible to take up residence in the kingdom of the ill unprejudiced by the lurid metaphors with which it has been landscaped.[20]

Hers is a humanist attempt at 'liberation from metaphors' and from the belief (which she downgrades to a superstition) that disease has its roots in the psychology of the person. She sees this 'superstition' as the persistence in modern times of a morbidly archaic and moralising tendency of the human mind. She wishes to 'rectify' the experience of disease by eliminating its metaphoric content and thus to 'de-mythicise' illness.

Sontag's polemic against reading illness as metaphor appeared in 1977 and was republished in 1990 with a large added section on AIDS.[21] Her impassioned plea to the world to stop interpreting illness and disease as having imposed deeper meanings struck a massive chord with my own generation, and it virtually silenced mainstream attempts at this discourse for thirty years. Her attack was so stinging that no one dared to contradict her stance, which seemed to be based on a desire to support the ill in their suffering and protect them from moralising interference in their experience of illness. Indeed, it stopped me in my tracks as well, and caused me to hesitate for some years about going into print with my own thoughts on diseases.

Her work for me is always close at hand, as a kind of a check on my own impulses, and I am not immune to her position. But her main contention is that finding metaphors in illness perpetuates the cycle of blame in the experience of illness. She claims:

> Psychological theories of illness are a powerful means of placing the blame on the ill. Patients who are instructed that they have, unwittingly, caused their disease are also being made to feel that they have deserved it.[22]

More daring still, in relation to her experience of cancer patients, Sontag goes on to assert:

> Nothing is more punitive than to give a disease a meaning – that meaning being invariably a moralistic one. Any important disease whose causality is murky, and for which treatment is ineffectual, tends to be awash in significance.[23]

But her concern for those who suffer is misplaced. For a start, why does 'meaning' have to be negative and persecutory? If we can find a meaning in our illnesses and diseases, this gives us hope and purpose in the midst of our suffering. It does not grind us into non-existence as she contends, but on the contrary elevates our suffering and gives us a direction for the future. As Nietzsche said, men and women can tolerate any how if they can find a justifying why to their suffering.[24]

But just as importantly, Sontag has misunderstood the intention of finding meaning in illness. It is not to lay a burden of blame or to moralise against the patient. The moralising, if that is how it can be labelled, is in favour of the affliction – giving dignity and importance to what is otherwise seen as a nuisance and a personal rebuke. Admittedly, she may be thinking of the old-style 'psychosomatic' diagnosis, which operated in a moralistic way, preaching to patients and haranguing them for bringing afflictions upon themselves. But to claim, as she does, that Freud and Jung indulged in this kind of moralism is incorrect and unfair.

What we find in Sontag's attack on metaphorical medicine, however, is the workings of a secular, humanist mind, and how it can misinterpret the experience of the sacred. For such a mind, the sacred is nothing more than a burden and a humiliation. It takes away our dignity and freedom, and even stops us from seeking health and recovery: psychological approaches, she says, 'not only weaken the patient's ability to understand the range of plausible medical treatment but also, implicitly, direct the patient away from such treatment'.[25] Rather than seeing illness as metaphor, she claims it works the other way around: metaphor is the illness. Concern with metaphor and myth, she claims, is what takes people away from pathways of physical recovery. This bizarre and improbable argument is underpinned by a hatred of the sacred and a belief that connecting our suffering with a larger story about ourselves is demeaning, eating up our dignity. In this regard, Sontag's attack on metaphor is an attack on the gods and on God: God can bugger off because, in my already demoralised state, I have no desire to have the fingers of moral authority pointing at my diseased condition.

Susan Sontag's attitude to myth and metaphor, or her stance against them, reminds me of Mircea Eliade's depiction of the 'demysticised' state of the non-religious person. Eliade writes:

> The non-religious man refuses transcendence [and] accepts the relativity of 'reality'... Modern non-religious man ...

makes himself, and he only makes himself completely in proportion as he desacralizes himself and the world. The sacred is the prime obstacle to his freedom. He will become himself only when he is totally demysticized. He will not be truly free until he has killed the last god.[26]

What begins in Sontag's case with a stance of supporting the suffering patient ends up as a god-killing exercise. She seeks to eradicate a spiritual sensibility as a sham and fraud, an affront to common sense. She wants us to suffer in silence and in the dignity of our existential aloneness and absence of meaning. In her view, we are absurd subjects living in a random and nihilistic universe. How that position can pose as humanistic care for suffering patients strikes me as far-fetched.

The theory in plain language
In the final stages of preparing this book for publication, I came across a moving work by a Jungian analyst who wrote about his experience of cancer in the final days of his life. What struck me about his book was not only the poignant and honest nature of its reflections, but the simplicity of its language and approach. In *Body and Soul: The Other Side of Illness*, Albert Kreinheder puts the difficult archetypal approach to illness in non-technical language, for the general reader. It made me realise how important simple communication is in this field, and that much can be conveyed without using psychological jargon or difficult terms. To convey the archetypal approach in this way one must be prepared to risk poetic and even florid language about the gods and spirit. Kreinheder shows courage in this task, which can be difficult for educated people who prefer to write in a complicated fashion. The fact that this Jungian analyst dies even as he is 'understanding' his own cancer diagnosis is an indication that healing, or coming to terms with the meaning of a disease,

does not necessarily lead to cure. Healing can mean dying with dignity and peace of mind.

In the opposite vein to Susan Sontag, Kreinheder writes:

> Every illness is an onslaught upon us as we are. Somehow we get so alienated from the whole of life that a very extreme invasion is necessary to break in upon the hardened formation of oneself. We must be weakened and crushed so that we will finally be so loosened and liquefied that the life spirit can flow into us again.[27]

The primary assumption is that illness and disease have a purpose, they are not random, no matter what the medical profession might tell us. 'The symptoms are the crying out of the body, telling you it has had enough'.[28] Therefore, working with symptoms or diseases from the inside requires an ability to remain with these problems and not to get rid of them:

> We shouldn't be too eager to get rid of the symptoms. The symptom isn't really the problem. It is merely the visible manifestation. The problem is in the total way of thinking and feeling and acting. The symptom is a kind of indicator that something has gone wrong with the total mechanism. Most ordinary people cannot face such a possibility, the possibility that their whole life and their perceptions of life up to this point have been erroneous. It is hard for them to contemplate the idea of killing off their old self and starting all over from scratch with totally new assumptions. Yet that is just about what needs to be done.[29]

This requires a new way of looking at illness, and a new way of looking at yourself, facing the fact that you may not have been living as your true self for a long while, perhaps not even for the whole of your lifetime. It is difficult to live the truth of your being, especially if that being does not fit in with those around you. We have such a strong desire to fit in that our own selves may be injured or hurt in this adjustment to social reality. The 'violence' with which symptoms and afflictions assail us may be seen as the psychic response to, and the energic equivalent of, the violence we have done to our own nature.

Getting to the first step can be a challenge for many people. The fact is that many of us do not want to change, as Kreinheder again explains:

> When people are sick, they want to get well. They don't want to change their personalities or their attitudes or any of their habits. Such people ask, 'What if I like the way I am?'[30]

Related to this are several other questions: Who says I need to change? Why should my symptoms tell me how to live? Aren't I the best judge of how I should live and be? This resistant and all too conventional attitude must be overcome if change is to occur. The fact is that the idea that diseases could be speaking to us in this way is not part of our culture, our ordinary knowledge. It is extraordinary knowledge and uncommon sense, and suggesting it is to risk being told that you are crazy. The whole process hinges on the willingness of the suffering person to recognise wisdom in illness. To discover the 'other' side of illness is to meet your true self, and it is impossible to discover the meaning of illness without at the same time being prepared to undergo a change in identity, philosophy of life and values. There can be no change without sacrifice.

There can be no change unless you are prepared to grant a secret wisdom in the illness itself. There is an intelligence at the back of disease, as Kreinheder puts it: 'Every disease is like an invading force trying to destroy our rigid forms and make us more whole'.³¹ Inside the disease is not just an intelligence but a particular kind of power which is tired of being neglected:

> The life-threatening diseases seem always to have a god or an archetype behind them. These words – god, archetype, symbol, the sacred – are for all practical purposes synonymous. We've been shutting them out, and they want to get in. They break down the doors, forcing their way in, and in doing so cause terrible wounds and disabilities.³²

In the analysis of disease, the difficult task is to discern what archetypal power is assailing one's life and attacking the body: 'With every invading symptom there comes also a symbolic content, and it is the task of the soul to expand itself so it can include the invading images and symbols.'³³ Kreinheder understands that the last thing most of us want is to befriend the disease and ask it what it wants, but this is exactly what we have to do:

> When you stop cursing the symptoms and get deeper into the images instead, then the healing comes. But the healing never starts at the place of the symptom. Your foot does not get better. Maybe later, but not as the first thing. First you have to be healed in your soul. The paradox is that the wound, the illness, is also the treasure. The physical misery gets your attention. But then if you go deeper into it, there is much more to it, memories and imagination and worries that will come. That's where the treasure is, in the psychic images that come with the symptoms. The symptoms open you up. They literally tear you open so that the things you need can flow in.³⁴

It is not getting rid of the symptoms that is important but understanding them. This does not have to be intellectual or rational, as if one is researching an essay. They could be understood, for instance, intuitively rather than rationally, or indirectly rather than directly. We might need to feel them rather than think them, but whatever way we decide to approach it, some inner work has to be done so that we engage the forces behind the symptoms, and learn to respect and love them. When we love rather than curse them, the healing can begin. But healing is not the same as cure, as Kreinheder makes clear. Healing is about the 'depth work' that has to be done, 'having it out with' the alien forces and opening ourselves up to them, so they are no longer excluded. Then comes the next stage: integrating the invading forces into a renewed image of ourselves.

Kreinheder puts it this way: 'Now what one ought to do is to go about developing a relationship with these powers. That is the only solution'.[35] The key is to recognise that these alien forces are part of our psychic reality, and we have to expand to include them in our identity. This is one of the most difficult parts of the process. Most people think of themselves as merely an ego – a conscious being – not as a field upon which forces play and have their sport. If we can only move from the idea of ourselves as a hardened ego, to the idea of ourselves as an open field, a great many things can shift and transformation can take place. 'Either the gods consume and demolish us, body and soul, or else we keep our sanity and are able to enlarge ourselves to include these new realities, and thus we flower into a greater soul,' says Kreinheder.[36] The golden rule appears to be expand and include the other will, or bust under its violent assault. 'You've got to be open to be cured. Yet some people will never open up. They just keep their teeth clenched and won't change one iota, and they just let it kill them. That's how afraid they are of the images'.[37]

So the challenge ahead can be summarised in this way:

1. Stop cursing and get used to the fact that forces are at work in our lives and diseases.
2. Befriend the alien impulses and attempt to understand their shape and character.
3. Integrate the lost or rejected aspects of your being that these forces represent.
4. Allow them to change your life so that their will can be fulfilled.

This theory might sound crazy to some, but all I can say is that it appears to work. It is based on some obscure logic that we can hardly fathom. I have to admit that sometimes my own rational mind struggles to comprehend the process, because it goes beyond our capacity for logical thought. But it is less important that we rationally comprehend it than that we do something about it and act on these intuitive steps.

CHAPTER 2

The Suffering of Spiritual Rebirth

The induction into spirit

Spiritual rebirth and suffering appear to go together, something that is found in all major religions and indigenous traditions. While some of us find the idea morbid and would like to think the sacred could be experienced in joyful not negative ways, the emergence of the sacred appears to demand a certain degree of suffering, for instance, in the initiation rites of passage of indigenous cultures. These rites were regarded as savage and horrible by many of the explorers and missionaries who encountered ancient tribes in the early history of Western exploration, and most indigenous tribes were encouraged to abandon such practices. But the tribes seemed to know more than we do about the suffering that is necessary if the sacred is to penetrate our lives.

The natural state overcomes itself

The movement of an individual into the life of the spirit is highly ritualised in tribal initiations. There are many kinds of initiations and the life cycle is seen as a series of rites of passage from a natural to a higher or spiritual state. Tribal societies hold no illusion that the spirit is always a friend or helper, but understand that spirit belongs to a different order, even as it attempts to reach into and transform this one. Initiations are ordeals and trials, involving scarring, mutilation and physical and mental hardship. In symbolic and physical ways, the natural state is impeded to make way for a different kind of reality, which cuts across the natural condition. (I speak of 'cutting across' advisedly, to highlight the image of cutting or scarification in tribal contexts. This anticipates my discussion of the psychology of self-harm in Chapter 7.)

The movement into maturity in indigenous societies is to some extent a work against nature, even a violation of this state, and to want to stay the same and resist transformation is not unusual. In tribal societies, youths often set foot reluctantly upon the initiation fields, as they do not welcome the ordeals that are to follow.[1] Rumours abound of how difficult it will be, often intensified by the secrecy that surrounds the rites. Despite human squeamishness, however, tradition dictates that such ordeals are to be endured. If young people try to avoid the hardships, they are put through the trials again in the next round of the initiations.

Central to this idea of initiation is the notion that we are not complete beings at the time of birth. As Mircea Eliade explores in his classic work *The Sacred and the Profane*, we need to be born again to grow into a different sense of ourselves and gain intimacy with our creator:

> Initiation rites express a particular conception of human existence: when brought to birth, man is not yet completed; he must be born a second time, spiritually; he becomes complete man by passing from an imperfect, embryonic state to a perfect, adult state. In a word, it may be said that human existence attains completion through a series of 'passage rites', in short, by successive initiations.[2]

In the experience of tribal life, the word 'natural' seems to have two meanings. It is 'natural' to be egocentric and contracted, blind to the life of the spirit. But it is 'natural' to be woken up from this sleep and stirred to new life in a way that demands reorientation. Spirit is seen as a part of nature, but it is a part that is deep, profound and often hidden. It is natural to hide from spirit and it is natural that spirit should seek us out.

The danger of Western attempts to describe indigenous religions is that we tend to see spirit as a force operating outside or above the natural order, as 'supernatural', rather than as a transforming agent from within. The dualism between natural and spiritual is a Western invention which we often impose upon tribal societies, but it is not found in them. Nor do recent accounts of indigenous spirituality support this dualism.[3] While tribal societies understand the conflict between spirit and matter, this conflict is felt to be contained in the one world. Spirit for tribal humanity is that aspect of nature that seeks its own transformation, whether we want it or not.

Metaphors of death and rebirth

In ancient systems of knowledge, the spiritual transformation operates under the insignia of death. Eliade says 'death is the preliminary condition for any mystical regeneration'.[4] Initiation is in fact a descent into the condition of death, followed by the hoped-for rebirth and regeneration:

> The novice dies to his infantile, profane, nonregenerate life to be reborn to a new, sanctified existence, he is also reborn to a mode of being that makes learning, knowledge possible. The newborn is not only one newborn or resuscitated; he is a man who knows, who has learned the mysteries, who has had revelations that are metaphysical in nature.

> During his training in the bush he learns the sacred secrets: the myths that tell of the gods and the origin of the world, the true names of the gods.[5]

Indeed, the initiate learns the names of the gods and the secrets of the tribe, but Eliade does not go far enough. In many initiations, and especially Aboriginal Australian initiations, the novice is transformed by realising that he is a reincarnation of an ancestor spirit.[6] His ego personality is eclipsed or overcome in the ceremony, and a new centre of identity is put in its place. The symbolism of initiation involves dying to the present form and being reborn to a new life in the likeness of an ancestor spirit. The point of the initiation is to make the initiate realise that he is not bound by time or space, he is more than temporal, and at the centre of his life he participates in the ancestral or transpersonal life of the tribe. Once he is initiated into this deeper understanding, he acts and behaves differently.

Spiritual initiation in the context of Jungian thought

How might we understand this process? It is difficult for us to think of ancestor spirits as anything other than relics of a bygone age. I spent years failing to grasp this element of the initiations, as the idea of the reincarnation of spirits was too difficult to comprehend. But as I began to think more about depth psychology, I began to see this tribal law in a new way. The initiation process is designed to 'kill' the *ego-bound personality* and replace it with a different centre of authority. We must not believe that the ego itself is being terminated or killed off; no ceremony that I know of seeks to do this and if we think this way we are, again, imposing a Western fantasy upon indigenous cultures. What *is* being destroyed is the notion that we live entirely in and from the ego. It is our *identification* with the ego that is terminated, a concept that is highly sophisticated from a psychological point of view.

In Jungian terms, Aboriginal initiations put an end to egocentricity and herald the beginning of a life lived in relation to the higher Self. This change is helped along by the revelation of ancestral lineage, that is, by recognising in ceremony that the initiate is not merely an ego but an ancient life. The ego has been the illusion, disguising one's real nature. For us, 'ancestral spirit' might be hard to come to terms with and we seem to have no contemporary equivalent. However we might think in terms of Jung's theory of the archetype. Jung refers to archetypes as 'ancestral traces', and describes them as 'the accumulated deposits from the lives of our ancestors'.[7] He also said the collective unconscious 'corresponds to the mythic land of the dead, the land of the ancestors'.[8] What Aboriginal cultures call ancestral spirits are perhaps similar to what Jungians call archetypes. It is worth considering this parallel in the attempt to build bridges across ancient and modern cultures. In his essay on rebirth, Jung takes seriously the possibility that there are 'ancestral elements which under certain conditions may suddenly come to the fore', in which event 'the individual is precipitately thrust into an ancestral role'.[9]

The keynote of both tribal initiations and Jungian psychology is the displacement of the ego and the surrender of our profane or non-sacred identity. In both systems, the ego is not our true identity but a temporary mask. The mask is useful but it becomes a prison if we take it too seriously and forget our deeper nature. In Jungian psychology, Christianity and Aboriginal religions, the deeper nature is conceived in radically different ways. In the first it is the *Self*, in the second it is *Christ*, and in the third it is an *ancestral spirit* and/or totemic animal. In Aboriginal cultures, the animals *are* the ancestors, and many ceremonies, dances and rites of passage focus on the lives and movements of animals. 'We cannot be human without learning the lessons from the animals,' I was once told as a boy in central

Australia. The lesson to be learned is that human existence does not only serve human ends. There is a broader field of relations that the individual and society has to acknowledge, and this is why Deborah Bird Rose defined the Aboriginal Dreaming as a 'moral relationship of care'.[10]

On the surface, the differences between these symbolic systems might seem too vast to reconcile. However as I see it, the religious object at the heart of these systems is not the central point. The point is that the ego is made to bow down to a greater authority, and here I become something of a relativist, because the *object* of this transformation is less important than the *process* of transformation. There is no religious figure, idea or icon which is 'better' than others. They serve a common purpose, which is to act as symbols of transformation so the ego can surrender to the other. Without a vibrant relationship with the Self, the ego is unable to be transformed. For individuation to take place, that is, for the capacity of the whole personality to become realised, the ego must be ousted from its central position and a new authority installed at the heart of personality. The important point is that the object of this transformation cannot be mundane or ordinary. The new authority must possess numinous power and cosmic dimension, as that is the only way in which spirit can be activated. And so in our godless modern age, it is becoming increasingly difficult to provide the symbols for our transformations to occur.

Surrender is difficult for the ego to understand, unless it is aided by tribal wisdom, religious culture or attuned to the demands of the spirit. From what I have seen of Aboriginal cultures, it seems as if surrender is written into our constitution as human beings, or 'hardwired' into the psyche. Surrender may disclose for us the nature of reality. There is every possibility that the human spirit is not entirely human. It could be part of a larger, transpersonal or archetypal spirit. We cannot know the cosmic spirit directly and so we need to develop metaphors to express it, such as God, Rainbow Serpent or Self. But it appears that the human spirit desires to reconnect with a cosmic spirit, which could be its origin and perhaps also its destination. It is not as if we have much say on the matter. If our deeper nature is spirit, and spirit wants to reconnect with a greater reality, we have to yield to this imperative. To make the reconnection, the ego has to surrender, so that the greater force can have its way with us. If we do not bow down or displace ourselves, the transformative and healing force cannot appear.

In initiation ceremonies, the novice's identification with the ego is severed, often in alarmingly violent ways. The reason for this is that identification with the ego – the orientation of the personality around the conscious life only – is seen to lead to anxiety, disorientation and, ultimately, to a desire for death. The human being is not designed to live within the frame of the ego forever, and if we stay inside the ego something inside us will go crazy because it seeks outward expression. Aboriginal cultures have determined that the human identification with the ego is a false condition, and that is why they seek to terminate it as soon as the individual stands on the brink of adulthood. If ceremony does not end the childhood ego-state, the person may be assailed by suicidal impulses as a desperate response to the need to release the larger life. The connection between tribal initiations and suicidal urges will be explored in Chapter 7. Suffice it to say here that the tribal initiations bring about a transformation that can be understood in Jungian terms as a movement from the ego to the Self.

The function and character of the Self

The word 'Self' is perhaps an odd choice to designate a reality that is essentially *other* than the ego, given the fact that the ego is widely and colloquially known as the 'self'.[11] In the secondary

Jungian literature, the Self is capitalised to distinguish it from the everyday 'self' and to avoid confusion with the ego. In Jung's writings, however, the Self is not capitalised, and thus the opportunity for confusion is rife, especially for new or inexperienced readers. Some try to qualify Jung's term by referring to the 'true self', and perhaps this goes some way toward resolving the confusion. The Self is a specific term in Jung's psychology and it has no equivalent in the Freudian system. Jung admits that the Self 'is a God-image, or at least cannot be distinguished from one'.[12] Its closest counterpart appears to be the *Atman* (the real self or God within) of Hindu cosmology, as well as the *Tao* (the 'right way' or universal order) of Chinese philosophy.

Jung argued that the Self is the true driver and controller of the personality. It produces the ego from itself and is present when the ego is disrupted by the unconscious. The Self has the capacity to hold the personality together in times of disruption, even when the ego feels it is falling apart. There is something almost miraculous about the workings of the Self, which leads some people influenced by Jungian thought to become blasé about psychic disruption. They tend to believe that the Self will always rescue the ego in times of crisis and bail us out if we get into difficulty. But given the reality and prevalence of mental illness, and the propensity of the psyche to lose balance and become disturbed, the integrative function of the Self is not something we can take for granted.

The Self is not to be reified as a 'thing' or entity. Even though Jung isolated it as an archetype or psychic figure he did not want it to be seen as a discrete object in its own right. Rather than an entity, it might be characterised as a bias in the psyche, a general aptitude or direction of psychic energy. Having said that, it has to be conceded that dreams encourage us to personify it. Symbols of the Self as persons or gods appear spontaneously in dreams, fantasies and visions, thus inviting us to view it in these terms. But it clearly does not always act when we want it to as it is not at the call of the ego. It contains the potential to act, to take a derailed life and set it back on track, and this capacity has obviously led people in previous times to believe that God or the gods can intervene in our difficulties and bring us out of them. But in my view we cannot 'count' on it and, if it does act on our behalf, we are to give thanks and praise but we must not imagine that this can be repeated, or that a saviour is always waiting in the wings.

Jung admits that his idea of the Self is theoretical and he calls it a 'borderline concept'. Although he writes about it at length, and it is the central focus of his work, he believes we must not rely on the Self in a naïve way. He is not an advocate of passive submission to divine forces, and his work assumes that the ego always has to do the basic work in the process of psychological development which he called 'individuation'. For Jung, the ego is the centre of consciousness, the locus of our personal identity, whereas the Self is the centre of the entire psyche, conscious and unconscious, and the seat of our larger identity. It is clear that he sees God on a par with the collective unconscious; both are vast, oceanic, infinite and extensive. Jung's Self, however, appears to represent a differentiation of the collective unconscious, an intense force which changes in some way the nature of God. His Self corresponds with the figure of Christ in the West and Buddha in the East. It is an archetypal figure that connects the human with the divine, a bridge or link to ultimate reality.

The Self is a transcendental concept that cannot be known directly by the ego, but only indirectly through symbol, dream and myth. In imagining the Self, it is as if Jung is reinventing the concept of a redeemer for a psychological age. He sees our scientific era as having largely rejected religion, but he wants to reinvent religion in psychological terms, replacing the Christ figure with the archetype of the Self.

While religious people might wonder why Jung feels the need to reinvent the religious wheel, and protest at his arrogance in attempting to do so, in his defence Jung would say that religious terms have lost their meaning. He wants to provide a new terminology for the ideas that have been found in religious and cosmological systems. Whether this is successful or not is for each person to decide, but I have already pointed out that to some extent depth psychology is an exercise in re-naming the core concepts of religion.

Jung's schema is remarkably ambitious, and although I cannot see many people being persuaded by his alternative system, I suppose one could say it is effective if it gets us thinking in new and fresh ways about stale religious concepts. Jung's motivation is to revitalise and not destroy religious ideas, but I can understand that some traditions have seen him as someone who demolishes rather than redeems. A recent Vatican document, for instance, constructs Jung as a destroyer of the Christian faith.[13] There is perhaps a fine line between these roles, because in order to 'make new' the truths of the past one has to overturn the old concepts and terms to some extent. Jung is best read in the spirit of the poet A. D. Hope's lines about the need to breathe new life into the forms of the past:

> Yet the myths will not fit us ready made.
> It is the meaning of the poet's trade
> To re-create the fables and revive
> In men the energies by which they live.[14]

Jung would add that this is not just the 'poet's trade' but the psychologist's. The effective psychotherapist, counsellor and pastoral care worker have a responsibility to make the ancient ideas of the past come alive in the psychic lives of suffering individuals.

The human journey and the stages of life

With this exploration of theoretical terms and ideas, we can now turn to the topic of the stages of life. In the first stage, the ego must plant itself in reality and establish a foothold in the world. In theological terms, we might call this a process of incarnation, the movement in which spirit, in the appearance of a human person and carried by an ordinary ego, insinuates itself in time and space and enters the stream of events. There are many ways to describe this: the realm of Being enters the process of becoming, the Essence takes on existence, or God takes on human form and exists in the field of manifestation. All this occurs quite unconsciously and is unknown to the person in whom this incarnational process takes place. The ego, in fact, has no idea that it is a messenger of another world, that its task is ultimately metaphysical and not entirely biological.

The psyche (or unconscious) might appear narrow as we first encounter it, but it is potentially of infinite extent. Freud thought that the unconscious contained mainly personal impulses, memories and traumas. But as we move further into it, the psyche seems to encompass familial, social, cultural and ultimately ancestral and spiritual realities which have nothing to do with our personal existence. The psyche is narrow at the top, as we first look into it, but it opens out like a funnel at its base, until it becomes identical with the universe. The ego is faced not only with the task of knowing its personal history, recovering its memories, or facing its traumatic past. The ego is also engaged in a larger project, which is to become aware of the *transpersonal background*, or what Jung calls the archetypes. In Platonic language, the task of the human being is to 'remember' more than his or her personal experience. The larger task is to remember the lost wisdom or legacy of the human soul, and the origins of consciousness from its spiritual source. The ego's work is to reach into the mind of God, remembering the *eidos* (ideas) of its unconscious beginnings.

This notion finds wonderful expression in Wordsworth's 'Ode: Intimations of Immortality':

> Our birth is but a sleep and a forgetting:
> The Soul that rises with us, our life's Star,
> Hath elsewhere its setting,
>   And comes from afar:
> Not in entire forgetfulness,
> And not in utter nakedness,
> But trailing clouds of glory do we come
> From God, who is our home.[15]

Wordsworth's ideas can be traced to Plato, who believed that at our birth the soul detaches itself from eternity and traverses the plains of forgetfulness, losing much of its original glory. It enters the world of time and space and experiences a certain amnesia regarding its sublime background. However the forgetting of our origins is not total, and thus we come 'trailing clouds of glory'. As Jung would put it, the ego is vaguely aware of a cosmic background to its time-bound reality. It is this vague awareness of 'something missing' that often sets us off on our spiritual journeys. Young children frequently make statements that confound their parents and grandparents, and this lends some weight to the notion that they are not who we think they are, empty slates without an ancestral trace. Rather, they appear to be souls who have histories and long ancestral backgrounds. In Eastern cultures, the theory of reincarnation accounts for such phenomena, but we do not have such a theory in Western philosophies or religions.

However, we do have the Platonic and Neo-Platonic traditions. Plato, Wordsworth and Jung – who may be usefully grouped together – believed that we do not enter the world as a *tabula rasa* or empty slate, but traces of our cosmic origins are imprinted on the soul. As the ego matures, the numinosity or divine essence of its background becomes clearer and more evident. We might say that in time the origin or source rises above the threshold of awareness, and beckons to us as a treasure chest of riches from the depths of the unconscious. If the ego is sensitive to this background, which it can access through intuition and introverted feeling, it may be able to bring up the lost glory into consciousness and transform itself. By so doing, it may enter a translucent world and experience a 'thinning of the veils' between eternity and time. This is the Romantic and Platonic version of paradise regained, returning to the past of the human species and recovering a link with a lost reality. I believe in this possibility, though I am not sure if this recognition can be sustained over a period of time. It appears to be given to us, if at all, in fleeting moments of insight.

Once the ego becomes aware of this background, it recognises that the unconscious is more than a Freudian 'subconscious' but represents a link or bridge to the 'world soul', or *anima mundi*.[16] At the same time, the ego recognises that the psyche is not only 'psychological' but spiritual. At this moment, the psyche returns to its Greek origins and is renamed the soul, an ancient term that modernity hardly uses without embarrassment. As the cosmic dimension rises like a star above the horizon of consciousness, the humanistic conception of the psyche dissolves and gives rise to a more mystical understanding. This is what Jung explored, especially in his book *Modern Man in Search of a Soul*.[17] Soul, for Jung, is the vessel or container of spirit. It is in the soul that the universal mind becomes aware of itself.

The spiritual meaning of life

This appears to be the meaning of life, insofar as I have been able to discern it: we are the instruments through which the cosmic forces, as in Plato's 'ideas' or Jung's 'archetypes', enter the finite dimension and are transformed. The point of our lives is to become conscious of our ancestral deposits and traces, so that they can become more conscious of themselves. We serve them in their individuation, just as they serve us in ours. In other words, the gods need us to help them mature and develop, which contradicts the mainstream religious view that the gods are already perfect, without any need of us. This makes a lot of sense to me and tallies with the beliefs of Aboriginal peoples. In these ancient cultures, the 'ancestors' seek to know and renew themselves through the rising generations of men and women.[18] They are not merely dormant forces that remain in some kind of eternal dream state. They are living, engaged, vital forces which demand to be experienced anew in each generational cycle. We are servants of archetypes, the instruments of gods. They are immortal and we are ephemeral, and just as the ego emerges like a tiny island from the sea at birth, so it is taken back into the sea at the end of its life. It 'passes away', as we like to say, but the archetypes or gods live on, because they have not crossed the threshold into time and space. It is our task to serve this larger design as best we can.

We gain most satisfaction from life when we do not live for ourselves alone. This is a view found in all cosmologies and religions, and it is verified by depth psychology. If we live for the archetypes or gods, that is, with an awareness of their presence, there is satisfaction awarded to the personality and the individual feels a sense of accomplishment. When we live only for the ego, recognising only our temporal lives, we feel empty and hollow. Some of us assume that the way to reward ourselves is to indulge our personal wishes, to be selfish and wallow in narcissism. This is an illusion promoted by the secular world. But to live an ego-bound life is not rewarding, and society cannot teach us how to better fulfil ourselves because it can only teach us how to live in and through the ego. It teaches only the ego's art of 'getting on', not the spirit's art of 'linking back' (*religio*, to use the Latin). If we feel unhappy some of the time, it is because the life that we *could* live but are not living is not being expressed. Consumerism and materialism arise as symptoms of our unfulfilled life. We long to have *more*, but the 'more' that we want cannot be supplied by a worldly mentality.

Exile and homecoming

In Jung's language, the ego is 'born' by exiling itself from the Self. Jung appears to be following Plato's idea of the *Anthropos*, the original being from whom all individuals emerge, as if souls splinter from a world soul. The Self is unknown to the ego at first. Often it is experienced indirectly through our parents or through religious traditions and sacred communities. The ego is split off from the Self and forced to live a separate life, which is painful and isolating. The journey of the ego is the 'Way of the Cross' in Christianity, or the way of exile and longing in Judaism. Trials and sufferings befall it, because it is designed to go into a world which does not see the divine background of our lives. The 'clouds of glory' grow ever more distant to the worldly ego in exile.

All religions have creation stories dealing with the ego's condition of alienation, in which it falls from an original state of grace. The ego is a tiny element of spiritual life that is wrenched from its source, and that separation often feels unbearable. This is why some people cannot endure the condition of the ego and its material world, and prefer to drop out, intoxicate themselves or otherwise avoid the egoic condition in society. Of course, this is a fool's paradise that never works. The avoidance of egoic development ends in greater pain and tragedy, as studies of the psychology of addiction, substance abuse and alcoholism have shown.[19] The pressure of the original source or Self is so great that the ego cannot find in itself the impetus or confidence to walk alone in the world. Such people often seek fulfilment in relationships but are disappointed, plagued as they are by fears of abandonment and emotional catastrophe.

The task of consciousness of the ego is to *befriend* the contents of the Self, through symbols, myths, relationships, rituals and experiences. What the archetypal contents are *in themselves* we do not know. How they came into existence and how we are related to them are unanswerable questions. These are metaphysical issues which can only be guessed at by intuition. The secret of life involves something akin to what the poet John Keats called 'negative capability', the ability to live 'in uncertainties, mysteries, doubts, without any irritable reaching after fact and reason'.[20] Jung felt that the intellect could help the individuation process a great deal, so long as it submits to an overarching mystery in which it is involved. However if the intellect becomes cynical and reductive, it can subvert the individuation process and become the biggest obstacle to the coming-to-wholeness which is our goal. One reason why the intellect becomes cynical is because it cannot *see* the forms or archetypes that are basic to the spiritual view of the world. In not seeing, it declares them to be nonexistent and misses out on the true depths of what is real.

The journey of individuation is threefold. First, in a state of innocence we are embraced and contained by a great mystery. Second, as the ego struggles to make its way in the world it is painfully separated from its origin, and must battle on through life with only glimpses of the glory from which it arose. According to Jung, the ego is not meant to return to the original state of bliss, for its task is to bring a new sense of wholeness into this world, not regress to the bliss state and lose its ground. The Self as origin, Garden of Eden, or infantile bliss must be sacrificed in the interests of moving to a higher stage of consciousness. Jung argues that the Self undergoes a transformation in its character as we move through the stages of life. If the ego has the courage to let go of infantile objects and desires and accept the isolation of consciousness, the Self transforms from being utopian in origin to being utopian in destination. In religious language, it shifts from Alpha to Omega, from womb to mandala, from Eden to New Jerusalem.

This shift is important and rarely understood. My first book was an attempt to map the terrain of this shift from womb to mandala.[21] How this transformation takes place is still a mystery, but it seems that when the ego summons the courage to accept its exile from Eden, the nature of God undergoes a change. It no longer acts as a parental source who protects, nurtures and demands obedience. The dictatorial and powerful nature of the god image changes when the ego embarks on its journey. The god image is broken down and reduced by the ego's claiming of its own authority and power. But in breaking down the power of the god who stands above it, the ego enables the god to reveal itself in a new way. It no longer crushes the ego with its authority or oppresses it with dictates and laws. Rather, it draws the ego to a new experience of life which releases the ego into a vision of wholeness.

But the ego has to transgress the original law and become a bit faithless to its god. It must be disloyal to the past if it is to move ahead with its heroic journey. If it remains too 'good' and obedient, nothing will happen in its life, and it will remain caught up in the parental figures. It has to take a few risks, and listen to the serpent who offers it the apple, in order to move on from the original bliss. If the ego is too aware of the 'clouds of glory' behind it and can see no similar or matching splendour in the journey ahead, the spiritual impulse to stay near to the Self conspires against life and development of the ego is subverted. It has to be encouraged to believe that a greater realisation of life's meaning can be achieved as an adult with consciousness, and not only as a child in its attachment to unconscious bliss. There has to be a life-affirming spirituality for adults, and not merely a pathological spirituality for those 'eternal youth' who want to crawl back into the womb of Eden.

The third stage of individuation is the conscious realisation of the state of wholeness. This is the age-old theme found in all great art, religion and literature. It is the theme of 'paradise regained' and is often signalled by the motif of a 'second childhood'. Seeing the divine vision is extremely difficult for the socially adjusted adult, and thus the breakthrough to an adult spirituality is often occasioned by the breakdown of the persona and the appearance of the child motif in dreams as a symbol of inspiration and hope. This motif is an ambivalent image at midlife, because it can be interpreted by the adult as a call to regression and infantilism. However if the symbol of the child can be integrated into the conscious life and not 'acted out' in a pathological way, there is a real chance of spiritual renewal. It is to the psychology of the midlife transition that I will now turn.

CHAPTER 3

The Midlife Crisis as Spiritual Interruption

The midlife crisis in changed conditions
The spiritual element which exists at the core of our personalities is to be found at every stage of life, but it stands out strongly at the so-called midlife crisis. The term 'midlife crisis' was coined by Canadian psychoanalyst Elliott Jaques in 1965,[1] and he meant it to refer to the realisation that, during the middle years of life, we must prepare for death and the acceptance of our mortality. While accepting that the youthful and idealistic dreams of childhood and early adulthood may not be achieved, we must also accept the limitations imposed on our dreams in the time we have left. While Jaques coined the term, it is often attributed to Jung, who worked on the same topic in the 1930s calling it 'midlife transition'. Jaques, a Freudian psychoanalyst, did not, however, give the midlife crisis the spiritual character that Jung has given it.

In 'The Stages of Life', Jung suggests that the first half of life is primarily concerned with our adaptation to the external world, society, family, children and employment. We are forced to make these adaptations due to the biological and physical demands of life. In the first half, the aim psychologically is to develop and stabilise the ego or consciousness, so that it can become a safe container and controller of the human journey. At least, the ego believes it is in control, and this attitude seems to be important for developing its confidence and skills. Jung believed that about thirty-five years were needed for the ego to organise itself and fulfil its duties. When the material obligations of life have been discharged, the non-material and spiritual impulses come to the fore and demand attention. Then the ego is ousted from its central position and becomes aware of a different source of authority in the personality.

This is the classical theory of the stages of life as it was developed by Jung in the 1930s. However in my view, this theory has dated and reflects a time in which society was more stable than it is today. The ego nowadays is not given the luxury of developing itself for thirty-five years, unimpeded by interior or exterior disruptions. As a university teacher who spends a great deal of my time with young adults, it is easy to see that the personalities of young adults are no longer – if they ever were – based on the direction and guidance of the ego. A great many young people have had the leadership of the ego disrupted by traumatic events in the personality, such as depression, anxiety or various kinds of phobias and addictions. They have often been subjected to traumatic events in their families, such as the early death of a parent, the collapse of the parental marriage, loss of connection with a parent or siblings, moving to different schools and communities, and loss of friendship circles. These events take their toll on the personality, and often prevent it from developing in ways that Jung would have considered 'normal'. Marriages, families, social institutions and habits are more rocky today than they were in the 1930s when Jung developed his theories.

I often notice in my students a process that Jung did not discern, in which young adults need to attend to contradictory movements in the psyche. Like young people everywhere, they need to consolidate the ego and develop it for life, and, at the same time, they need to deal with the displacement of their ego and the subsequent search for a deeper centre of personality. It is as if the psychological dynamics of Jung's first and second halves of life are occurring roughly together, as parallel and simultaneous movements. They are intertwined with each other, like the twin spiralic structure of DNA. This makes for a more complicated and crisscrossed experience of personal development, in which young adults are 'wise before their time' due to the disruption of their ego and the need to find a spiritual basis for their lives at an early stage. The process that Jung confined to the second half of life is in evidence in young adults, who are forced to search for a deeper meaning ahead of schedule, as it were.

Further work needs to be done in this area, and it may be that the proliferation of mental health disorders at ever-younger ages is directly related to the difficulty young people have in dealing with both stages at the same time. How can their therapists offer help if they are working with outdated images of psychological development? True, Jung's model represents the ideal situation, in terms of positive outcomes of personality development. However, society is more complex today and spirit can no longer be safely contained in the second half of life. I must add that not all young people experience difficulty or mental instability as they juggle these demands. In my view, some manage this double act well, especially those who contradict society's materialism and attempt a personal connection to a life-sustaining spirituality. This situation can give rise to a new and engaging individual, in whom the ego is both leading and being led at the same time.

When one becomes two

Returning to the classical theory of life's stages, we can see why the midlife period is an opportunity for development that is unparalleled at any other time. At midlife the personality is thrown into a new kind of chaos. The needs and wants of the ego may have been uppermost during the first half, but by the time we enter the second there is the 'non-ego' to consider. As Nietzsche famously put it, 'one becomes two' and the person is now a problem to himself. At midlife, the non-ego demands our attention with a new kind of insistence. It is 'also' us, a part of our psychic economy, and at this time we may begin to have dreams of persons who have been excluded from our lives, who demand to be received, loved and nurtured. But by the time we reach forty, we are often so used to having our ego needs met, and identifying ourselves with them, that the realisation that there are other parts of the self comes as a shock. This is as big a revolution as the onset of puberty, but because our society does not understand the life of the spirit, this later crisis is poorly understood, despite becoming a cliché of modern times – the cliché, of course, is merely a defence against the power of this crisis and its ability to profoundly disturb our lives.

Jung outlines the typical dilemma that greets us at midlife:

> The nearer we approach to the middle of life, and the better we have succeeded in entrenching ourselves in our personal attitudes and social positions, the more it appears as if we had discovered the right course and the right ideals and principles of behaviour. For this reason we suppose them to be eternally valid, and make a virtue of unchangeably clinging to them. We overlook the essential fact that the social goal is attained only at the cost of a diminution of personality.[2]

The ego is not keen to volunteer itself for individuation, or to put itself through the daunting encounter with the unconscious. It wants to remain connected to the outside world and tied in with the social structures that surround it. The ego that has not glimpsed a deeper meaning wants more power than before; it wants to conquer greater heights and achieve more goals. Typically at midlife, it looks for greater challenges into which it can channel its energy and anxiety. It has become a joke these days to label people reaching midlife as grasping for extra excitement and diversions to avoid looking at themselves. They know their time is up as mere egos but they cannot face it, and so they throw themselves into anything and everything to channel their dissatisfaction with their lives.

Transformation without cultural support

Secular or non-religious society has not prepared us for a wider and broader vision. Although Jung recognised the importance of secularism in the history of the West, he bemoaned the spiritual impoverishment that it has delivered. What spiritual resources does the modern ego possess, and how can it relate to powerful symbols of the Self when it is by definition secular? Without a lively and vibrant relationship with the Self and its 'symbolic life', the ego is unable to be transformed. Nevertheless, with or without religion, the ego must be transformed. If there is no spiritual system operating in society, the inner life is forced to teach us a new way of being. The inner world teaches us a lesson, and this can steal upon us in fits and starts, as Jung explains:

> At first it is not a conscious and striking change; it is rather a matter of indirect signs of a change which seems to take its rise in the unconscious. Often it is something like a slow change in a person's character; in another case certain traits may come to light which had disappeared since childhood; or again, one's previous inclinations and interests begin to weaken and others take their place.[3]

This is a stressful and difficult time, with not many guideposts to help us through. It often seems that, just as we have begun to figure out how life works, and how to succeed in the game of life, the goalposts have moved and we are made aware of a new set of rules, a different game. We are not just playing a game of the ego, with its goal of adjustment to social norms, but a game of the soul, with its goal of adjustment to the spirit. This can create dismay and disorientation in many lives. We have just begun to stand up when life rips the carpet from beneath our feet. We thought we knew who we were when suddenly life dictates another set of terms.

If we were a spiritually intelligent society, we would learn to welcome the self-division that comes at this time, because it means that we are being 'saved' from the egotistical life, and from a life enshrouded in illusion and despair. We are being introduced to an entirely new way of being and knowing. This is a process of intuition (or 'inner tuition') in which we are being taught about who we are, and what we are becoming or could become. But there is nothing enjoyable about the experience of self-division, and it is little wonder that most of us try to outsmart it by directing our attention to outward pleasures and diversions.

The second self that may emerge during this self-division confronts the normal ego like an alien intruder, a foreign body, an unfamiliar partner. Our task is to befriend the non-ego (second self), become familiar with it, realise that our life is also its life. Jung writes that 'the individual is faced with the necessity of recognizing and accepting what is different and strange as a part of his own life, as a kind of "also-I"'.[4] This is a lot to ask of both sexes, but particularly of men, who are not always gifted with intuition and who tend to live their lives in an external and extraverted manner. First they have to get over the prejudice that the inner life is more than a nuisance or source of trouble, an enemy to the forward impulse of the masculine ego. Then they must learn humility before a mystery they cannot comprehend. They have to allow themselves to be 'led' by the unconscious and shown a new realm of experience. This is a tall order for most of us, and the complexity of these demands makes psychological development a rarity in society.

Disruptions in gender identity

For men, the true inner self is often personified as a woman, the anima, who appears in dreams, fantasies and projections. She is the psychic figure who compensates and sometimes opposes the one-sidedly masculine direction of the ego. Men have a great deal of trouble with the anima, and in some ways it is easier for them to chase projected anima figures in the outer world than it is to come to terms with the feminine in themselves. To do this would involve toning down the masculinity, displacing the egotism and hard drive, and allowing oneself to be more receptive to the mysteries and wonders of the world. The problem is that as soon as a person heads in this direction, there are internal and external voices that say they are not being a 'real' man. This crisis is so real and present in society that many have learned to defend against it by turning it into a subject of farce and ridicule. The ego will invent any device to outwit that which opposes or displaces it. If a man wants to develop his inner life, he is often said to be wasting his time, going soft, or avoiding the material or financial opportunities in society. There is a great deal of social pressure not to listen to the voices within that would urge a man to rethink his life.

The soul or anima is not interested in more masculine conquests, and she finds this repeated activity to be boring and limiting. She has a different set of priorities. Her task, ultimately, is to urge a man to embrace that which is *not* of the ego within himself and, by way of sexual desire, persuasion and creativity, to build a bridge between himself and the spirit. She has a different concept of time and value, and she believes that continuing with the socially conformist track is wasteful. For her, the material things of this world lack lustre and excitement, and she can scorn a man who continues to seek diversions that fill him with self-loathing and despair. If the ego does not turn with love and affection towards the soul and its goals, the soul can become negative, haggard and worn in its unexpressed or buried life. This results in bitchy, sullen, moody or violent behaviour if the man does not attend to his inner world. He sometimes acts in ways that do not accord with his normal personality or best interests, and as such he sometimes wonders what has 'come over him', or why he is 'beside himself'. Unless he turns to the anima with compassion and love, it will grow against him and, in some cases, destroy his life.

I have seen this happen to friends and acquaintances, and yet there is almost nothing that one can do to help such people, who appear more prepared to fall to purgatory than to change their ways. It is easy to say that such men must 'attend to their animas', but this is a hollow and empty platitude unless one voluntarily submits oneself to self-examination and seeks transformation. The astonishing fact, to me, is that this pattern is so frequent and typical, and yet society as a whole remains oblivious to this spiritual aspect of the crisis. One would have thought that a pragmatic desire to protect the species from unhappiness and despair would have encouraged more general awareness about this crisis. But the ego is so dominant that it tends to edit out the despair and propagate the deception that 'things are great' as they are.

Women have a similar but different kind of challenge at midlife. They are required to develop the masculine spirit, which is often called the animus and is personified in dreams and fantasies as a male figure or a group of men. The task of the animus is to lead a woman deeply into herself, to inspire and direct her to creative activity, accomplishments and tasks that her ego might shy away from or see as beyond her normal capabilities. The animus is a formidable opponent to the woman's personality if she does not give way to its needs and allow its development. She can become what Jung calls 'animus possessed', that is, strident, assertive, pushy, critical of others and judgmental. It is always easier to see the failings and shortcomings of others than it is to explore one's own weakness and vulnerability. If such a woman would stop expecting others to be perfect and instead see that it is her own animus that needs to be developed, life would be smoother and complications in relationships would be reduced. As with men, women at midlife must realise that their direction has to change and they ought to turn towards life and its challenges in a new way.

Disruptions in sexual identity

We cannot go through the trials of midlife without encountering the 'contrasexual' element – the opposite sexual principle – in ourselves because our unconscious is calling us to a wholeness that is often expressed as a union of the masculine and feminine principles. Jung argued that the Self is a complex of opposites, and it frequently expresses itself as an androgynous or hermaphroditic figure. The call to wholeness is a call to Plato's primordial person, or *anthropos*, an amalgam of masculine and feminine characteristics. At this point, sexual imagery takes on a new meaning and intensity, because we are no longer exclusively male or female but androgynous. Sex is no longer a purely biological drive, and the time for procreating and having children is over. Sex is often appropriated by the spirit at this stage of life, and union with the Self can be imaged in dreams as the sexual coupling of mythic figures, animals or gods. Dreams at midlife are often rich in sexual imagery which can no longer be interpreted in a Freudian or reductive way, but must be read in terms of the spiritual reintegration of the self.

Homosexual imagery often arises at this stage too, which can be confronting for those who fear they are losing their heterosexuality and being challenged to a new mode of life. As Jung noted, the Self is frequently imaged in dreams and fantasies as a same-sex partner or lover, and the union of ego with Self is often a union of similar types or genders. I have written on this issue in a number of places, and it is an area that requires more research.[5] For similar reasons, incest can arise as a motif at midlife, because the union of ego with the *other* which is 'also-I' can be spontaneously imagined by the psyche as a union of brother and sister, for instance, or parent and child.[6] These images arise automatically, and it is not our doing that they so arise. On the contrary, we are often repelled by the suggestions of incest, but the psyche seems to love this particular metaphor.[7] If enacted literally, this can result in tragic, pathological and criminally deranged behaviour. However, if we understand that these potent images point to psychic and not literal unions, we can be admitted into a sacred communion with the Self.

Resistance to transformation

A typical counter-response at midlife is to stiffen and reject the approach of the Self. The ego often goes into a state of alarm, and begins to erect barriers against whatever wants to break into consciousness. This is especially the case if homophobic people are approached by the Self in homosexual guise or in homoerotic imagery and desires.[8] Then the Self can be shunned with enormous force and gusto, such that it hardly has a chance to communicate with the ego. Dreams at midlife can dramatise the internal conflict in other ways: a civil war breaks out between rival groups, and each side accuses the other of atrocities and evils. Or people are outside the house, wanting to come in, but we erect shutters and boards to keep them out, and install all kinds of security devices to keep away the unwanted parties. The ego does not give up its power and control without a fight, or some kind of elaborate resistance, as Jung explains:

> Conversely – and this happens very frequently – one's cherished convictions and principles, especially the moral ones, begin to harden and to grow increasingly rigid until, somewhere around the age of fifty, a period of intolerance and fanaticism is reached. It is as if the existence of these principles were endangered and it were therefore necessary to emphasize them all the more.[9]

We resist the approach of the Self because we are familiar with seeing ourselves as one person and not two. Our resistance is based on the illusion that the ego is the master of the house and has the right to eject others from the premises. However the 'second ego', as Jung sometimes calls it, has an equal 'energy value' to the ego, and when activated and angered it can sometimes snatch leadership from the ego. In other words, the Self can find itself with greater power than the ego, and continued resistance can lead to psychological catastrophe. Hence the second ego must eventually be accommodated if wellbeing and peace is to be restored. Resistance must ultimately be 'shattered', says Jung, so that we can 'build up a state of wider and higher consciousness'.[10]

Society without spiritual pathways

In the midlife crisis we encounter a crisis not only for the individual but also for culture and society as a whole. The midlife crisis and its negotiation and resolution is made more difficult and protracted by the fact that we are living in a society that does not make any real adjustment to the life of the spirit. Therefore our conversion to the 'second ego', the Self, and our breaking away from the ego and the world of surface appearances is not helped by society but hindered by its attitudes. It is as if society does not want us to grow up – or, at least, not in the fullest sense of the word. We remain caught in a social context that pretends that the first half of life lasts forever and the goals of youth and ego are somehow unchangeable. This is the colossal failure of society, which caters to the natural person but leaves the spiritual person bereft and unattended.

The cost of living in such a nonreligious society is that we construct a world based on ego values and forget to ask one important question: 'What's it all for?' By the time the ego reaches midlife, there are hardly any signs in the secular landscape that remind it of its true role. What greater reality? What higher authority? The ego sees little evidence of these because it has forgotten the past and does not have any intimation of the 'clouds of glory'.

The spiritual aim of a religious society, Jung explains, is 'to transform the human being into the new, future man, and to allow the old to die away'.[11] In traditional cultures the wisdom of this symbolic death and rebirth is held by the elders of tribes. Jung asks, 'Where is the wisdom of our old people, where are their precious secrets and their visions?'[12] Who can teach us how to die to our natural self and be reborn to our spiritual self? What has become of this sacred knowledge in secular times? How can we mature if our society and civilisation is structurally immature, that is, resistant to the life of the second self? Jung surmised that: 'Something in us wishes to remain a child, to be unconscious or, at most, conscious only of the ego.'[13] As a society, we do not want to know about the second self as we cannot see the point of it. The ego brings us material treasures, and sexuality serves our erotic goals and personal needs. What goal or need does the second self serve?

This is the weakness of secular society. It no longer understands the 'usefulness' of spiritual vision. It does not grasp the fact that the second self serves the needs of the second half of life. The task of religion and cosmology is to offer our consciousness goals to strive for and myths to live by.[14] This is especially true in the second half of life, where the purpose and direction of life is more obscure than in the days of youth. When the ego governs our lives, the goals and directions of life are obvious. But as soon as the ego is eclipsed the notion of what constitutes a meaningful life changes. It becomes important to have a spiritual and not merely a biological goal. 'Could by any chance culture be the meaning and purpose of the second half of life?' Jung asks.[15]

The goal of the second half is not to propagate the species but to give birth to the soul, the most difficult birth of all. If we do not live in a mature culture with spiritual goals and pathways, we will not know how to live properly or how to grow old with grace and wisdom. Instead of becoming elders, dignified by and valued for our wisdom, we simply become old people, and a burden on a society that prefers youth and achievement. When spiritual goals are absent, old age is a tragic and negative process, a loss of vitality and a relentless pining after the golden days of the past. Without a spiritual goal to lead us forward, we fall more readily into nostalgia and depression.

Spirituality at the end of life

Finally, there is reason to believe that a spiritual attitude plays an important role in the last days of life. The art of 'dying well' has been widely discussed in such areas as gerontology, palliative care, and care of the terminally ill and elderly. These fields have concluded that a 'good death' is often linked with a spiritual outlook that sees death as part of the broader life of the spirit. Although the spiritual question poses a challenge to medical science, and although reason does not understand the longings of the soul, these difficult and obscure elements in our lives have enormous impact and serve a therapeutic purpose. At the end of his 'Stages of Life' essay, Jung writes:

> As a doctor I am convinced that it is hygienic – if I may use the word – to discover in death a goal towards which one can strive, and that shrinking away from it is something unhealthy and abnormal which robs life of its purpose. I therefore consider that all religions with a supramundane [or transcendent] goal are eminently reasonable from the point of view of psychic hygiene ... From the standpoint of psychotherapy it would be desirable to think of death as only a transition, as part of a life process whose extent and duration are beyond our knowledge.[16]

The fact that we do not understand this process, nor how spirituality works, nor why it makes a difference, is no reason to discount its significance to the ageing process. The question of 'life after death' has become a silent, even taboo, topic in today's world, but there is therapeutic value in the idea that the soul or spirit lives on after the death of the body. Jung again:

> It is particularly fatal for old people to look back, for a prospect and a goal in the future are absolutely necessary. That is why all great religions hold out the promise of a life beyond, of a supramundane goal which makes it possible for mortal man to live the second half of life with as much purpose and aim as the first.[17]

Jung admits that to have a belief in life after death is problematic for modern educated people, who find this question embarrassing and difficult to deal with. We cannot know about life after death with our reason or intellectual capacity, which necessarily falls short of such a mystery. Perhaps it is because our official culture finds the idea impossible to deal with that the popular spirituality movement has picked up 'reincarnation' as one of its favourite themes.[18] Jung does not denigrate reason and education, but their legacy is often spiritual impoverishment and loss of hope if we are unable to imagine anything more than extinction at the point of death.

Jung argues that the idea of an afterlife is a primordial or essential idea, which may require of us a different kind of thinking. Throughout the ages, humanity has affirmed the reality of an afterlife, and this idea, although rendered nonsensical by our scientific education, may have more importance than we have hitherto believed:

> By far the greater portion of mankind has from time immemorial felt the need of believing in a continuance of life. The demands of therapy, therefore, do not lead us into any bypaths but down the middle of the highway trodden by humanity. For this reason we are thinking correctly, and in harmony with life, even though we do not understand what we think.[19]

But to not understand what we think is not to the liking of modernity. It has become obsessed or even *possessed* by the workings of the intellect, and if the mind cannot verify any aspect of our experience, we tend to jettison it. Therefore, any belief in the continuance of life is dealt with as a form of error, and the soul finds no consolation. Instead, we adopt a stoical attitude, thinking that this is mature and adult. We even pride ourselves on having the courage to face the existential 'certainty' of no life beyond the ego.

Primordial thinking

But what if there is a deeper and more authentic kind of thinking than our modern form? At various stages in his work, Jung reverses our normal expectations about rationality. At vital moments in his theorising, he abandons the modern point of view and takes the side of the most ancient and traditional kind of thinking, which modernity has regarded as useless:

> Besides [rational thinking] there is a thinking in primordial images, in symbols which are older than the historical man, which are inborn in him from the earliest times, and, eternally living, outlasting all generations, still make up the groundwork of the human psyche. It is only possible to live the fullest life when we are in harmony with these symbols; wisdom is a return to them. It is a question neither of belief nor of knowledge, but of agreement of our thinking with the primordial images of the unconscious. One of these primordial thoughts is the idea of life after death.[20]

In such moments, Jung seems to abandon science or to admit to the limits of its reason. He is more interested in wisdom than knowledge, in 'primordial thinking' than rational thinking, at least where the care of the soul is concerned. Thus he seems to tip the scales of his thought in favour of life after death, virtually on a mixture of therapeutic and primordial grounds. It is simply that things go better in the psyche – that combination of ego and unconscious – when we follow the laws of the ancient past. Jung tries to be a man of science, but he distrusts science and feels that it lands us in a wasteland. There is no scientific evidence for life after death, but he is prepared to go with his intuition and put forward a case for the continuance of the spiritual life.

One reason why the afterlife has fallen into disrepute is because our popular images of the afterlife are maudlin, improbable and sentimental. The notion of graves opening up and people walking into the light as 'glorified' bodies or recognisable personalities hardly inspires confidence in the notion of an afterlife. But just because our popular images of life after death are so improbable is no reason to abandon the notion entirely. There is every possibility that the immortal part of the psyche, which we call spirit or, from the Greek, *pneuma*, returns to its source at the end of life.

My own belief is that our egoic existence ends with this life, but we have an archetypal core or essence which lives on, perhaps in a developing or potential form. This, if you will, is our ancestral life, and just as we do not enter life as empty slates but as persons who carry immortal features into the world, so we exit life with these same immortal features intact. The spirit lives on and it is not for us to decide how this might happen or formulate a definite view of the afterlife. But 'something' happens at death which is more than death, just as something happens in life which is more than life. My intuition tells me that death is not the end. We should not look to death with a morbid fascination, but we do need to welcome death when it arrives with an attitude that is receptive to its possibilities and mysteries. To adopt this attitude is to die well, and to honour the life force that carries us through this and possibly other incarnations.

Returning to the source

If the idea of the continuance of life is so important for the soul, and the mind is unable to affirm any such life, we end up in a stalemate which is a source of neurosis in modern times. But if religious or spiritual solutions are out of reach of our realm of belief, we may be able to find solace in the philosophical tradition. In this regard, our key source is Plotinus, the founder of Neo-Platonism. He said that life begins and ends in a mysterious unity which surpasses our normal understanding:

> What, then, is it? The power which generates all existence, without which the sum of things would not exist, nor would intellect be the first and universal life. What transcends life is the cause of life; for what activity of life which is the sum of

things is not primal, but itself pours forth as if from a spring
... It is a wonder how life in its multiplicity came from what
is not multiple; and the multiplicity would not have existed
unless before multiplicity there had been a simple principle.
The source is not fragmented into the universe; for its
fragmentation would destroy the whole, which could no longer
come to be if there did not remain by itself, distinct from it, its
source. Universally, therefore, things go back to a Unity.[21]

For Plotinus, each person's soul is a part of the original unity before their birth, and it returns to that original unity after death.[22] It is the task of each person's life, according to Plotinus, to develop a relationship with this unfathomable source so that we might befriend our 'eternal' life before it befalls us in death. His last words were, reportedly, 'Strive to lead back the god within you to the Divine in the universe.'[23] In Jungian terms, the divine element in the human is the Self, and this has to be educated or 'led out' in the course of our development. The Self might be imagined as a wave of numinosity that surrounds us, its glow extending right across the stages of life, from birth and childhood, through the isolated ego stage and its experience of the world, to spiritual rebirth, and to death and beyond. To connect with this primordial reality grants us a vision of eternal life, which is not the continued life of the transitory ego, but the infinite life of the source from whence we came.

CHAPTER 4

Cancer Phobia as a Doorway to Soul

> In cancer, non-intelligent cells are multiplying, and you are being replaced by the nonyou. Immunologists class the body's cancer cells as 'nonself'.
>
> Susan Sontag[1]

Back door to soul

A neurosis is a nervous disorder that reduces our mental wellbeing and restricts our adaptation to the world. It shows that we are divided against ourselves and are unable to function as a whole personality. If we are able to work with it and tolerate the humiliation it entails, neurosis can be a back door to the soul, and it is no less valuable for being a 'tradesman's entrance'. It would be preferable to have a more dignified entry point, but in our world these are disappearing as the world becomes more preoccupied with the needs of the ego. A front entrance might involve a socially sanctioned rite of passage or initiation ceremony that allows us to walk into the house of the soul, away from the busy and profane world of the street. Our culture is in danger of forgetting that there is a world of soul, where we can renew ourselves in the depths of our being. Our culture compels us to remain in the world of *doing*, preventing us from finding the secret doorway lest we stop producing and consuming goods. But despite what our culture demands, the soul has its own set of claims which often run counter to the dictates of society.

Cancer as growth gone wrong

This back entrance to the soul will remain a common one for us today and in the future because, even if society is against our discovery of it, the psyche will push us into the silent room of the soul, since entering this dimension is part of our necessary spiritual growth. If this growth does not occur then something 'grows against' us, and in Jung's view this is what cancer represents. As he wrote to his cousin Rudolf Jung:

> Your views on the origin of a carcinoma seem to me largely correct. I have in fact seen cases where the carcinoma broke out under the conditions you envisage, when a person comes to a halt at some essential point in his individuation or cannot get over an obstacle. Unhappily nobody can do it for him, and it cannot be forced. An inner process of growth must begin, and if this spontaneous creative activity is not performed by nature herself, the outcome can only be fatal.[2]

Jung's suggestion in this letter, which he did not seem to develop in his scientific papers, is that cancer might occur when a much-needed growth fails to take place. If growth is necessitated by the psyche but is blocked or inhibited, then growth occurs anyway, but in a fatal form. This suggestive remark is elaborated by Jungian analyst Russell Lockhart in a remarkable but little known essay on the archetypal approach to cancer. Lockhart writes:

> There are moments and seasons in one's life when genuine sacrifice of the most valued thing is essential for further

growth. If this sacrifice is not made willingly, that is, consciously and with the full conscious suffering of the loss, the sacrifice will occur unconsciously. One then will not sacrifice to growth but be sacrificed to growth gone wrong.[3]

The kind of growth he points to here is not typical or normal growth, where something is 'added' to what already exists. Spiritual development is growth by subtraction. We diminish the world of ego so the soul can find room to flourish. This is what I take as the meaning of the scriptural adage 'the first shall be last'. Growth by subtraction is sacrifice in religious language, and that is why Lockhart refers to sacrifice. Although our world is no longer religious, the language of the soul remains essentially religious. As Lockhart says, if we do not sacrifice for the sake of growth, we may be sacrificed to 'growth gone wrong'. If growth is archetypal it cannot be suppressed, but it can shift from a positive to a negative register. I would like to say a bit more about neurosis before discussing a case of cancer phobia.

Neurosis as arrested development

Jung greeted the appearance of a neurosis in a welcoming fashion and he considered that his patients were 'fortunate' to have one. Its appearance meant that there was something inside them which wanted a larger life and sought to free them from the ego. He saw the illness as an opportunity for growth and yet he appreciated the suffering and humiliation it caused at the same time. The personality is constantly getting stuck in narrow limits and unable to move forward. When growth is arrested, it is menaced by an emotional or mental disorder which represents the unlived life that has accumulated in the unconscious. This can manifest in a variety of ways, including intrusive or obsessional thoughts, hysteria, anxiety and depression.

The task of therapy is not to get rid of neurosis, which is what conventional medicine seeks to achieve. Rather, psychotherapy asks the neurosis what it wants. It seeks to transform the neurosis by understanding why it arose in the first place and what it wants to accomplish. The unlived life must be given a chance to express itself and it can only do this if the ego is displaced, as Jung writes:

> A neurosis is truly removed only when it has removed the false attitude of the ego. We do not cure it – it cures us. A man is ill, but the illness is nature's attempt to heal him, and what the neurotic flings away as absolutely worthless contains the true gold we should never have found elsewhere.[4]

As repellent as it seems, we have to learn to embrace the neurosis, which is 'nature's attempt to heal'. Or as Jung writes elsewhere: 'There is no illness that is not at the same time an unsuccessful attempt at a cure'.[5]

Fairytales often represent the *other* in the psyche in negative or ugly ways. The protagonist has to find the courage to embrace the negative form and connect with it: the princess has to kiss the ugly frog before her prince can be released from the spell. This happens not only in fairytales but in ordinary life. The neurotic symptom is secretly the 'true gold', as Jung says above. A patient seeks therapy because something unpleasant has arisen in his or her life, and the patient's first thought is how to get rid of the symptom and assume a normal life. However the therapist's role is to ascertain the purpose of the symptom, which the patient is at present unable to comprehend. To them the symptom is the enemy, and they require that it be exterminated. The ego's reason is limited and it thinks only of self-preservation. Those who are besieged by a mental illness often say they want to beat it, overcome it, or use willpower to break through.

The therapist must appreciate the desire to overcome adversity, but the role of therapy is to locate the *purpose* of the neurosis and bring it to the patient's awareness. This is a balancing act of some delicacy: to support the patient in his or her suffering, but to counter their desire to terminate the suffering so things can return to normal. A neurosis is a developmental crisis and there is no going back. A person has a neurosis because the ego's values are wrong or its attitude is defective. The old ego has to be shattered in the therapeutic situation, and the therapist has to protect the patient's humanity while bringing the bad news that the former self is no longer viable. The ego which finds itself saddled with a neurosis is part of the problem, and the self-preserving nature of the ego is a menace in disguise and a block to healing.[6]

The unlived life accumulates in the unconscious and this situation is tolerated for a time, until the psyche can stand it no more. The appearance of a neurosis is a sign that the psyche is on the side of life. If a neurosis does not occur, we know that life is being lived to the optimum degree, or, on the contrary, the psyche has lost energy to such an extent that its compensatory function no longer operates. Psychic energy can become so depleted that neurosis does not occur and the person has no way of knowing that a fatal accident or devastating situation is just around the corner. In such cases, the failure to generate a neurosis can lead to schizophrenia, a more serious splitting of the mind in which healing is difficult because the psyche has regressed to an archaic level. But even if a psychosis did erupt, Jung would insist that healing could still take place so long as the patient could be made to understand the situation. Taking the psyche seriously and acknowledging its reality 'pays the unconscious a tribute that more or less guarantees its cooperation'.[7]

Cancer phobia and the diseased soul

Let's now consider an example from Jung's essay 'Psychology and Religion'.[8] This is the case of a scientist who suffers from the belief that he is dying of cancer – he is *not* dying of cancer, but the intrusive thought has overpowered him and he cannot shake it off. Jung intuits that an unlived life has festered in the scientist's unconscious and turned against him. The life of the soul has been neglected and produces a toxic poison that seeps through his body-mind. He is overwhelmed by the thought of cancer to such an extent that his will is paralysed and he is unable to continue with normal life, seeking therapy to free himself from the menace.

The patient thinks he is living the whole of life and has no intimation that the 'cancer phobia' could be an expression of an undeveloped part of himself. Jung has to be careful to introduce this possibility with subtlety. If he told the patient outright that his soul had turned against him, the patient would most likely reject this suggestion as preposterous. As Jung explains, to his scientist patient 'the word "soul" was nothing but an intellectual obscenity, not fit to be touched with a barge pole'.[9] Jung had to tread softly and not upset the patient's worldview, at least, not in the early stages of therapy when resistance is acute. Resistances are present when it comes to facing a neurosis, since 'every neurosis is connected with man's most intimate life'.[10] Resistances are based on the desire not to disclose any inward facts or information that might make the patient feel abnormal or out of step with the values of the day. After all, the neurosis has already humiliated him and he seeks assurance from the therapist that he is a worthy person.

The so-called 'normal' person in a scientific world has lived life as it has been presented to him by his culture, profession and social milieu. How could he have gone wrong if he has done the right thing by all the social influences in his life? Resistances arise to protect the ego from the revelations of an inner life. The patient 'will be reluctant or even afraid to admit certain things to himself, as if it were dangerous to become conscious of himself'.[11] Jung says, 'One is usually afraid of things that seem to be overpowering.' He then asks, 'Is there anything in man that is stronger than himself?'[12] The answer is yes, there is something stronger than the ego, and to awaken to this fact is humbling and even humiliating if we think we are in charge of our own lives, but then discover that the 'executive ego' is merely a kind of working fiction.

In some ways it is difficult to follow this case study, since Jung's essay is more concerned with broader questions of meaning and neurosis, and the case gets buried in the larger issues. Jung seems impatient with the case study format, as if the details of the case are incidental and not worth bothering with. But he prefaces this case with a few helpful remarks:

> If a man is neurotic, he has lost confidence in himself. A neurosis is a humiliating defeat ... and one is defeated by something 'unreal'. Doctors may have assured the patient, long ago, that there is nothing the matter with him, that he does not suffer from a real heart-disease or from a real cancer. His symptoms are quite imaginary. The more he believes that he is a *malade imaginaire*, the more a feeling of inferiority permeates his whole personality. 'If my symptoms are imaginary', he will say, 'where have I picked up this confounded imagination and why should I put up with such a perfect nuisance?'[13]

Jung never gives this patient a name, a biography or a background. We know nothing about him other than he is a scientist. Jung is not interested in the clinical minutiae and gives little information about how he handled the case or what methods or techniques he used. His essay was based on a lecture for large audiences at Yale University, and he does not want to bore his audience with clinical matters. We are not told at what stage in the treatment Jung became alert to the fact that the rejected aspects of this man's life had 'grown against' him like a cancer. Perhaps Jung had this intuition from the start, but one can imagine the difficulties he faced.

To speak of soul

To begin to speak the language of soul and spirit to a scientist such as this patient, who would most likely have dismissed these ideas in his early youth (if he had ever held them), is to risk being dismissed as a mystic. This is part of the problem of the soul in our time. It carries with it a sense of fairytale and lack of worth, and those who speak up for soul are likely to also be branded as somehow inferior. There is the additional problem of explaining to the scientist how 'soul', which would normally be seen as something that enhances life, has grown malign and destructive. This is a lot for a scientist to accept and it would strain his credulity. Not only does the soul exist, but it exists in a dynamic way such that when it is neglected it can turn into a negative force and rise up against the person.

Jung summarises his own predicament in this colourful way:

> What, then, shall we say to our patient with the imaginary cancer? I would tell him: 'Yes, my friend, you are really suffering from a cancer-like thing, you really do harbour in yourself a deadly evil. However, it will not kill your body, because it is imaginary. But it will eventually kill your soul. It has already spoilt and even poisoned your human relations and your personal happiness and it will go on growing until it has swallowed your whole psychic existence. So that in the end you will not be a human being any more, but an evil destructive tumour.'[14]

This is what Jung would like to say but does not say. It would sound ridiculous, and the patient might suspect him of madness. The great difficulty in treating cases such as this is finding the right approach to the truth. It is a matter of finding the right language and adjusting the conscious mind to the reality of what is taking place. The struggle with neurosis is in part a linguistic problem, finding the right words to say what the patient does not want to hear, and indeed saying what the world does not want to know.

It is easy to speak in terms of complexes and phobias, but what do these terms mean to the patient? With his scientific voice, Jung speaks of a 'complex' which is 'capable of interfering with the intentions of the ego'.[15] But anyone with a lay knowledge of psychoanalysis would know this already. Knowing this as mere information has no healing or transformative effect. What is needed is a correction of the whole person, a reorientation of being. Jung does not define what the complex is, or how it fits into the larger picture of this patient's psychic life. He merely says:

> Despite his culture and intelligence, he was a helpless victim
> of something that obsessed and possessed him. He was
> unable to help himself in any way against the demonic power
> of his morbid idea. It proliferated in him like a carcinoma.
> One day the idea appeared and from then on it remained
> unshakeable; there were only short intervals when he was
> free from it.[16]

Jung explains that the patient was too fearful of the unconscious to give it any recognition. He discusses at length the 'perils of the soul' that give rise to our fear of the psyche. Jung's most compelling point in this case study is his view that neurosis has a purpose and is not merely malign. Despite the horror of the cancer phobia, it is an expression of the psyche's reality in the only way that the psyche can communicate with a rational person: by threatening his life with a nonrational fact. Jung writes that the unconscious 'only needs a neurosis to conjure up a force that cannot be dealt with by rational means'.[17] He admits that 'it is indeed pathetic to have an intelligent man almost imploringly assure you that he is suffering from an intestinal cancer and declare at the same time in a despondent voice that of course he knows his cancer is a purely imaginary affair'.[18]

Breaking the stranglehold of reason

The monopoly of reason can only be broken by an assault on the conscious attitude, and this is what the neurosis represents – and why Jung appreciates the appearance of a neurosis, because it shows that the psyche cares enough about our wellbeing to scare the hell out of us when we are not living correctly. As a therapist, Jung has to maintain an empathic connection with the patient while at the same time acting as spokesperson for the neurosis, since the neurosis represents an attempt by the psyche to reorient the personality to the fullness of its being. The neurosis is a positive contribution to this larger life, and Jung treats it as a kind of treasure: 'He had the great advantage of being neurotic and so, whenever he tried to be disloyal to his experience or deny the voice, the neurotic condition instantly came back.'[19] At this point Jung explains his clinical strategy:

> Our cancer case shows clearly how impotent man's reason and intellect are against the most palpable nonsense. I always advise my patients to take such obvious but invincible nonsense as the manifestation of a power and a meaning they have not yet understood.[20]

It is hard to respect something as disturbing as a neurotic symptom when it appears at first to be 'the most palpable nonsense'. How do we respect something that is so horrible? We must view the neurosis as something we have not yet understood, with more to it than we had originally seen. There is something behind the symptom, and it is trying to tell us of our own wider personality of which we are still unconscious. The neurosis is a message about what we do not yet know about ourselves. The problem is, nothing has prepared us for this crisis. No one has told us that there is a larger personality that we are not living and that when we fail to live this self it turns against us like a demon. Our materialistic society is incapable of preparing us for such dramatic truth.

It is important not to think that this force is imaginary or invented by ourselves. We must learn to respect the objectivity of the psyche and its ability to speak to us in its own language and on its own terms. There is no point in telling the patient that he or she is personally responsible for the crisis:

> Our patient is confronted with a power of will and suggestion more than equal to anything his consciousness can put against it. In this precarious situation it would be bad strategy to convince him that in some incomprehensible way he is at the back of his own symptom, secretly inventing and supporting it. Such a suggestion would instantly paralyse his fighting spirit, and he would get demoralized. It is far better for him to understand that his complex is an autonomous power directed against his conscious personality. Moreover, such an explanation fits the actual facts much better than a reduction to personal motives.[21]

This is where art therapy and creativity become useful, because by drawing or painting our 'contrary will' we might be able to gain an understanding of what is holding us hostage. Dreams are also important at this point, because they mythologise the unconscious situation and represent the split-off parts of ourselves as characters in a play. The psyche's capacity to dramatise the internal strife is astounding and it is a vital source of self-knowledge and healing.

Jung explores a series of dreams of this patient, which I will not go into here. Suffice it to say that the dreams demonstrate that there are figures of the psyche, especially feminine or anima (inner self) figures, which are not happy with his conscious attitude and demand some kind of readjustment. Jung points out that even the testimony of dreams is often not enough to effect change in the personality, since those of us who are intellectual by nature tend to dismiss dreams as more of the 'nonsense' which the psyche is throwing at us. As he writes with sarcastic humour: 'How could an intelligent man be so superstitious as to take dreams seriously!'[22] Jung's focus on dreams is strategic as well as revelatory. He not only looks to the dreams to provide the missing information about the psyche but he also uses dreams to provide the statements that might be less than convincing if they came from outside, from the therapist's worldview or pool of information. 'I never preach my belief,' he insists,[23] and he arrives at his interpretation indirectly. He relies on the dreams to provide the necessary corrective, to come up with the wisdom that can alter the patient's consciousness and turn their life around.

Jung brings this study to a rapid end, telling us that the neurotic was able to become a scientist again, but only after he had made certain radical readjustments in his values and attitudes. We are not given much information about the resolution of the case, because Jung moves off into other areas. But we are left to presume that the neurosis disappeared or was reduced when the patient learned to take his feminine soul seriously. The missing bits of his personality had to be gathered into his care and range of attention. As that was done, the hostility of the second ego was diminished, and it began to cooperate with the personality as a whole. As Jung writes in 'The Stages of Life', 'the individual is faced with the necessity of recognizing and accepting what is different and strange as a part of his own life, as a kind of "also-I"'.[24]

Against the tide

Our culture does not take the soul seriously, and the psychic forces that previous ages called 'gods' are seen as phantasmal and ridiculous. How can we learn to respect the forces if our culture tells us that they are illusory and invented by ourselves? How can we engage in objectifying the forces if we live in an age that is involved in demythologising and debunking? It is extremely difficult for us to develop spiritual lives unless the individual has enough courage to move against the tide and claim for him or herself a symbolic life. Today the individual has to withstand the criticism that by even recognising the forces he or she is crazy.

What is it worth to do this? Is it worth the stigmatisation, is it worth running contrary to the wisdom of the day and to convention? Is it worth these things to win the soul and gain freedom from the intrusive idea? Our answer has to be a resounding yes. To gain the soul one must indeed renounce the worldliness of the world and its literal thinking. The spiritual life has a certain eccentric or radical aspect, especially in times of intense rationality such as now. But to a person who is gripped by a neurosis, and who experiences relief when the psyche is listened to, this eccentricity is a small price to pay when one regains possession of one's life.

CHAPTER 5

Sexuality and the Sacred

> But where we had thought to find an abomination, we will find a god.
>
> Joseph Campbell[1]

Desire is a powerful and complex force, and our tendency to reduce desire to sexual instinct misrepresents the nature of human longing. As innately religious beings, we long for the source from which we came, and this places sexuality in an entirely different light. Sexuality and spirituality are intimately connected, since both describe our erotic longing for the *other* and thus form part of an 'axis of eros'. If we take the complexity of desire into account, this can radically alter our interpretation of sexual disorders and our appreciation of divine factors in human diseases.

Part 1: The father/daughter entanglement

It is sometimes said that spirituality is removed from clinical realities and philosophical issues should be put to one side as the clinician considers the practicalities of a case. But the cosmic dimension of our lives has a real impact on our physical and mental health, and the separation between cosmos and clinic is artificial and often forced. Jung worked to undermine the dividing line between spiritual and clinical realities:

> I can hardly draw a veil over the fact that we psychotherapists ought really to be philosophers or philosophic doctors – or rather that we already are so, though we are unwilling to admit it because of the glaring contrast between our work and what passes for philosophy in the universities. We could also call it religion *in statu nascendi* [in its original form], for in the vast confusion that reigns at the roots of life there is no line of division between philosophy and religion.[2]

When we turn to the 'roots of life' there is no division between therapy, philosophy and religion. These are day-world distinctions that are irrelevant to the sources of life. In the world of consciousness, we like to make divisions between various aspects of our experience, but in the psyche there are no such compartments. If we want to care for the soul, we have to be prepared to trespass on areas that we are not always 'qualified' to deal with. None of us can be an expert in several fields at the same time, but as we engage the soul we have to be ready to do away with rational divisions.

This is very much the case in human sexuality and its role in the formation of neurotic problems. We often think that we know all we need to know about sexuality, but we may not understand this impulse at all. If we have kept sexuality and religion apart, we may not be able to discern the metaphysical objects towards which sexual desire points. I am referring to our 'love of God', which has been repressed in our time. Our failure to think across borders and boundaries might prevent us from understanding the full range of factors at work in the formation of neuroses.

The archetypal core of a complex

Jung's patient is an unnamed woman who presented with an hysterical neurosis. After several clinical sessions he surmised that the woman's neurosis 'had its principal cause in a father-complex' and her 'peculiar relationship to her father stood in her way'.[3] The patient's father, now dead, was the source of her deepest, fondest and most passionate feelings. Thoughts and memories associated with him and their earlier lives had 'become overvalued and preyed on the conscious mind', luring her back into the landscape of childhood dependency. She had tried various activities, including the study of philosophy, to overcome her fixation on the father. The intellect of the daughter, says Jung, is sometimes employed to form a 'bridge to the world', to escape from the infantile psychic situation. She might have 'extricated herself from the emotional entanglement with her father' if she could 'form an emotional tie with a suitable man, equivalent to the former tie'.[4] However, 'in this particular case, the transition refused to take place, because the patient's feelings remained suspended, oscillating between her father and a man who was not altogether suitable ... The progress of her life was thus held up, and that inner disunity so characteristic of neurosis promptly made its appearance'.[5]

As a result of this disunity, her energy seemed to 'flow off in every conceivable direction, apparently quite uselessly'. Jung says she was unable to find a focus in her life, and could not develop a commitment or dedication to anything because her libido was tied to a primal and infantile object. Her psychic energy, unable to find a normal outlet, became somatised – absorbed back into the body – as physical problems and nervous disorders, including 'nervous disorders of the stomach and intestines' and a hyper-activation of 'the vagus and the heart'.[6] It was as if the psyche's energy, denied a positive channel, flowed back to its source and ended up contaminating her body with symptoms. Her energy became negatively charged through the body and nervous system, producing an hysterical neurosis with numerous complications.

A Freudian reading of her condition would recognise a stock-standard incestuous connection between daughter and father. To this reading, the bond with the father would be erotic and sexual, and the task of the analysis would be to bring these unacceptable erotic tendencies into the field of awareness. When the patient was ready and able to integrate the incestuous fantasies, the Freudian assumption would be that these would stop blocking her forward movement into life. The neurosis would be arrested at its source and she would overcome her difficulties and assume a normal existence. This might take a considerable amount of time, and the transference with the analyst would serve as the container during the period of accepting her 'unacceptable' incestuous longings. Until these desires were made conscious, she would likely remain a victim of infantile wishes and her energy would be unable to reach out towards the world. Meanwhile, she is only able to lead a 'provisional' life, aware that her interest is not directed toward life in a committed way.

The Jungian reading would respond: yes, but there could be more to it than this. What if her erotic energy is not for the *personal* father but for the *archetypal* father, of which the personal figure was a merely transitional carrier? What if the sexual bind could be seen in a different light, as a libidinal interest in an archetype or god? The father figure is found in all cultures, religions and cosmologies, but how we experience this archetype will depend on our childhood experience of the personal father and on other father figures in our lives. We think we understand 'father' from our limited point of view, and we take this everyday figure for granted, assuming we know what it means. We have humanised this figure to such an extent that it no longer seems a mystery to us, but straightforward, conventional and mundane. Father is just plain old dad, as ordinary as cornflakes and milk.

But behind our experience of the father stands the archetype of God the Father. I am not simply referring to the Judeo-Christian deity but to all cultures and contexts, including pagan and non-Christian ones, in which gods are seen as father figures. The archetype of the father may come from the primordial mind, the mind of God, or the cosmos itself. There are many theories about the origin of archetypal forces, but all we can know is that our recognition of their existence matters to us, and apparently it matters to them. The forces like to be acknowledged, which suggests that they play a role in the creation of our consciousness. Perhaps we have been created as mortal beings primarily so that the archetypal forces can reach an awareness of themselves through us. Metaphysical speculation such as this is impossible to resolve in a definitive sense – all we can know is that there are forces beyond our conscious range which require attention and respect, and giving them that respect can be synonymous with our achievement of mental health and wellbeing.

Neurosis as distorted religious interest

In this archetypal context, the attachment to the personal father is a misinterpretation on the part of the patient. She actually wants to bond with a god, but has no way of knowing this. She has to extricate herself from the personal attachment to pay attention to the true object of interest. This is easier said than done, for the underlying object is no *object* as such but a focus of psychic attention, a strange attractor. Jung approaches this case study from this point of view and asks this question:

> Could the longing for a god be a passion welling up from our darkest, instinctual nature, a passion unswayed by any outside influences, deeper and stronger perhaps than the love for a human person?[7]

He broadens the issue to one of passion in the general sense, rather than to sexual fixation. If this is true, then not only has the patient misunderstood the nature of her desire but Freud and his circle have misunderstood it as well, reducing the passion for a god to a sexual attraction for a parent. If passion has no outlet in agape, the love of God, it gets re-channelled as eros, the love of a human. Perhaps we all suffer from this at various times of our lives. Perhaps we look to partners and possible companions, as well as to 'impossible' partners such as parental figures, with the longing that is meant for gods. But since we do not believe in gods, we have no option than to turn this libido back to the human. If energy cannot go to the gods, it can only go to a person upon whom we are 'hooked'. Our lives burn with passions which are meant for gods, but they cannot reach their destination since our imaginations do not extend far enough to allow our eros to be fulfilled.

Jung saw the libido as a spectrum of energy and compared it to the colour band of a wave of light. One part of it is 'the psychic infra-red' or 'the biological instinctual pole of the psyche'; the other pole is what he called 'the psychic ultra-violet', which 'exhibits none of the peculiarities of the physiological' and ultimately fuses with pure 'spirit'.[8] In terms of sexual libido, we could say that the red pole seeks the biological goal of coitus, the release of physical and emotional tension, and pregnancy, but the ultraviolet pole seeks union with what we are unable to grasp with our senses. Our age understands the *red* level of desire and goes crazy over it, but we remain pitifully unaware of the ultraviolet or spiritual aspect.

In earlier times, this spiritual aspect of desire was known to religious and spiritual communities. Even in our time, Pope Benedict has referred to the vital link between sexual desire and religious passion in his encyclical *Deus Caritas Est*.[9] The transformation of desire from *eros* to *agape* is at the basis of the monastic traditions, and is the spiritual knowledge found in ancient cosmologies, rituals and devotions. When we think, for instance, of the divine ecstasy of St Teresa of Avila captured in Bernini's sculpture, we see a figure almost dying of pleasure in her relationship with her God. In this sculpture we catch a glimpse of a time-honoured form of ecstasy about which our age draws a blank. We have cast ourselves over to the infra-red level, and for this we have lost even the language and understanding that makes the realisation of divine love possible. It looks crazy to us, or at most a kind of sublimated or repressed form of the 'real' thing, which we see as the physical expression of sexuality.

But what if this is not the real thing? It is the other side of desire that has long intrigued me, and I think our age has lost something crucial about human love. Jung holds that the libido strives to connect with higher symbols and recognising this is important for psychic health.[10] But if our age does not encourage higher symbols, how do we find them? Jung's answer is that we find them in the unconscious, and especially in dreams and in the contents of fantasies. These unconscious symbols need to be treated with care and respect. If we subject them to the familiar Freudian reading, the sacred potential of the symbols will be obliterated, and we reduce everything to sexual acts and human genitalia. In dealing with the 'numinous dimension', Jung says we must strive against our natural tendency to be ironic or sceptical in the face of mystery. He says our 'conscious criticism ... always seeks to reduce things to human proportions'.[11] The modern prejudice, of which Freud is the ultimate example, is that mystery is a raft of nonsense and to pander to mystery is little more than what Marx called 'mystification'.

The creative role of transference

The formation of the transference to an analyst may be one way in which the libido is withdrawn from the parental attachment.

'A new motive is needed to put an end to the morbid suspension,' Jung writes. 'Nature paves the way, unconsciously and indirectly, through the phenomenon of the transference'.[12] On this point Freud would agree, but he would disagree with Jung's notion that the libido seeks a transcendent or spiritual goal. For Jung, the transference provides only a short-term solution, in that it gives some visibility to the nature and scope of the problem:

> In the course of treatment the patient transferred the father-imago to the doctor, thus making him, in a sense, the father, and in the sense that he is not the father, also making him a substitute for the man she cannot reach. The doctor therefore becomes both a father and a kind of lover. In him the opposites are united, and for this reason he stands for a quasi-ideal solution to the conflict. Without in the least wishing it, he draws upon himself an over-valuation that is almost incredible to the outsider, for to the patient he seems like a saviour or a god.[13]

Jung admits this sounds bizarre. He tries to win a degree of support from his readers by saying, 'This way of speaking is not altogether so laughable as it sounds.' He argues that in our romantic fantasies and aspirations we are constantly projecting inappropriate psychic contents to the beloved. We load human relationships with divine or sacred projections, and then we wonder why our relationships are unable to bear these expectations and why we are often disappointed in our erotic lives.

Jung appeals to our sense of ironic disproportion when he says:

> It is indeed a bit much to be a father and lover at once.
> Nobody could possibly stand up to it in the long run,

precisely because it is too much of a good thing. One would
have to be a demigod at least to sustain such a role without a
break, for all the time one would have to be the giver.[14]

He draws attention to the impossible burden that the client places on the analyst in the transference. By emphasising irony and disproportion, he hopes to build up in the reader's mind an appreciation that the attachment seeking to be transferred to the analyst is something beyond the human. 'She knows that I appear to her as a semi-divine father-lover, and she can, at least intellectually, distinguish this from my factual reality.'[15] Everyone is familiar with the problem of having high expectations in our romantic lives and how these are foiled by reality; Jung seeks to emphasise this to mount his case for the archetypal method. His method is to appeal to something 'higher' to explain the hysterical neurosis. It is the reverse of Freud's method, where something 'lower' is used to expose the neurosis: the sickness is explained by seeking to bring to consciousness an incestuous desire for the actual (or personal) father, or his living substitute.

Jung confesses that his patient tends to collude with the Freudian reading, since it activates her romantic fantasies and gives a certain charge to her sexual instinct, which is pleasurable. The Freudian reading is a mixture of the rational approach underpinned by an attachment to a libidinal object. Rationality and genitality conspire against the spiritual approach, which tries to push the drama to a higher level. Jung's patient seems happy with the transference, but its solution can only be temporary: 'To the patient in the state of transference, this provisional solution naturally seems ideal, but only at first; in the end she comes to a standstill that is just as bad as the neurotic conflict was'.[16] Jung concedes that the transference proves ineffective in this and every case. Its benefit is that it 'holds out the possibility of a cure', but it is 'far from being the cure itself'.[17] The transference points beyond itself to the real transformation that is required of the personality.

The intensity of the romantic fixation, or what he calls the 'obstinacy' of the attachment, is what provides the clue for analyst and patient. Jung surmises that the transference must have a true purpose, and that 'the energy of the transference is so strong that it gives one the impression of a vital instinct'.[18] The analyst, who is 'gigantic, primordial, huger than the father, like the wind that sweeps over the earth', is a temporary container for spiritual energies that overspill the human domain. Jung destroys this over-valuation of himself created by the transference by pointing to the mythic figure behind the psychological drama. He tells how he began to grope in the dark toward a 'transpersonal' figure, an intuitive process that some might see as unscientific. Yet his intuition told him that this was the way to proceed.

He shows courage at this point, and risks his scientific reputation by allowing his intuitive process to reach its conclusion. The libido is afflicted by a striving for something non-human, which is 'misunderstood' because we do not belong to a wisdom culture which values such things. Our consciousness is not aware of a world of divine forces, gods or spirits. To our minds, these are fairytale figures, stories in books or forms of entertainment. We are not initiated into a cosmology, but that does not mean the cosmological dimension does not continue to exist and affect our lives. It is not that cosmic reality is invented as a field of fantasy. Rather, it could be that *we* are invented by cosmic forces, and are made to enact dramas that have their origin in a reality that consciousness can barely comprehend: as Shakespeare tells us, 'We are such stuff as dreams are made on, and our little life is rounded with a sleep.'[19]

Religion for the non-religious

There were a great many dreams considered in this analysis, but towards the end of the treatment the patient had this dream:

> Her father (who in reality was of small stature) was standing with her on a hill that was covered with wheat-fields. She was quite tiny beside him, and he seemed to her like a giant. He lifted her up from the ground and held her in his arms like a little child. The wind swept over the wheat-fields, and as the wheat swayed in the wind, he rocked her in his arms.[20]

This dream might be read as an infantile regression to the father who is 'disfigured' by the dream into a gigantic figure. Such a reading would insist that the incestuous desires have merely been veiled by a 'dream censor', and that anyone can see that sexual union with the father is the true meaning of this dream. But Jung argues that the dream is in fact an expression of the patient's desire to be held by a divine cosmic Father, revealing 'an archaic god-image that is infinitely far from her conscious idea of God'. In religious matters, the patient 'had a critical and agnostic attitude, and her idea of a possible deity had long since passed into the realm of the inconceivable'. Notwithstanding her agnosticism or atheism, her unconscious had fashioned an image of God that aligned with ancient notions of wind and spirituality: 'an invisible breath-spirit'.[21]

What we could say is that her consciousness is atheistic, but her unconscious is religious in a sense that she can barely imagine. It is not the case that her unconscious is religious in the conventional sense, because it seeks a God who is 'infinitely far from her conscious idea of God'. So we are not talking about the return of a childhood image of a Christian or Jewish God, but about something new emerging from her depths. Healing in this case consists in helping her come to terms with the shock of her innate religiousness, a strange reversal of the Freudian need to help her come to terms with her lustful desires. In today's world, the shock of being religious may be more horrific than the shock of harbouring incestuous fantasies. Religion is the great repressed of the secular age.[22]

Jung makes philosophical statements and then he withdraws from them for a moment, to catch his breath and allow readers to catch up. He wants us to entertain our natural suspicions, doubts and questions, especially since he is raising a thesis that might seem preposterous. His next move is to admit a critical reflection: 'The question now is, can we regard the possibilities set forth above as a valid hypothesis?'[23] He admits that the interpretation of an hysterical neurosis as an unconscious striving for a god seems barely credible. 'No one will doubt the reality of a passionate longing for a human person,' but to long for the embrace of a God would be seen as 'an historical anachronism' and 'a medieval curiosity'.[24] Anticipating being accused of primitive thinking or witchcraft, Jung offers these thoughts before they can be thrown at him. He concedes that the fact that a longing for God 'should come to light as an immediate living reality in the middle of the consulting-room, and be expressed in the prosaic figure of the doctor, seems almost too fantastic to be taken seriously'.[25]

This is part of Jung's argumentative style: he puts the opposite case in a bid to disarm his potential accusers. The reader is allowed to return to the rational world of scepticism. Jung casts off his spiritual mantle and returns to science and empirical observation. He makes an intuitive leap into the realm of the gods, and his scientific training forces him to pause, reflect and ponder. In this method, Jung reveals himself to be modern after all, and not a throwback to medieval times. He shares the contemporary suspicion of the archetypal method, even as he puts it forward and acts as its advocate. He wants to be among the ranks of his readers and critics, and to appear as baffled as they are by the notion that our little lives and dramas are shot through with non-human longings.

He points out that 'this new hypothesis was not entirely plausible to my very critical patient'.[26] She was unimpressed by his interpretation. After all, the dream reflected the unconscious object of her longing, and her consciousness was not yet reconciled to what was happening in her depths. Jung had to back off at this point, and not insist on his interpretation. With a mixture of humour and seriousness, he says, 'the earlier view that I was the father-lover … presented an ideal solution of the conflict [and] was incomparably more attractive to her way of feeling'.[27] Yet the dream 'produced a living effect – an effect which might well give the psychologist of religion food for reflection'.[28]

Although not much was said about God or spirituality, the dream – and this was only one in a long series of dreams – seemed to work a transformative effect on the patient. She did not become overtly spiritual but there is an 'implicit' spirituality at the end of the analysis.[29] She became more sure of herself, less dependent on the analyst, and Jung noted 'a subterranean undermining of the transference'.[30] Her romantic relations with a male friend deepened perceptibly, and gradually she found herself in a sustaining love relationship. Jung believes that what he calls a 'transpersonal control-point' was reached in her development: the dreams expressed symbols that were significant for her life and these provided a channel, so that her libido could flow into the world. Her libido moves into the inner life based on an archaic symbol of God (the wind dream), and into the outer world via her choice of a partner. A spell is lifted from her psyche and creative relations are established with both archetypal and human worlds.

We do not come out of this case thinking that the patient has made some kind of dramatic conversion to religious faith.

The point is that 'she' is not religious; her soul is religious, or something in her is religious. In this regard, I am reminded of a remark made by Victor Frankl in *Man's Search for Ultimate Meaning*: 'Something within me is religious, but it is not I who is then religious; something within me drives me to God, but it is not I who makes the choice and takes the responsibility'.[31] Jung comments finally that the patient has not become a convert to a church or creed and she did not develop an explicit philosophy of life. But something happened at a silent, inward level. There was a recognition of life in the depths, and this had helped her 'grow out of the pointless personal tie'.[32] She had won for herself an inner life and an implicit spiritual attitude, namely, a sense of reverence for the mystery of life. This is what heals her from the neurosis.

Part 2: Freud, Jung and the sacred

Human desire is a complex field, and the notion that the sacred is an element of that desire seems worthy of great exploration. In *Memories, Dreams, Reflections*, Jung argues that Freud sought to discover the core principle of life, but on discovering it he understood only its sexual aspect. What Freud had found in the unconscious was the principle of *eros*, and eros is not only a biological urge. Eros impels us not merely to sexual intercourse and acts of procreation but to 'erotic' union with gods, God and the transcendent. To mistake eros for genital sexuality is a kind of optical illusion, but easy to do if we are looking at eros through a mechanistic lens.

The repression of spirit

For Freud, sex was sex, pure and simple a biological and material drive. There was nothing divine about it and in fact he suspected it was closer to the demonic, which is why society sought to suppress it. For Jung, it was a god-principle, but the godly aspect did not appear on the Freudian horizon and was strongly, even violently, curtailed. Freud saw Jung's emphasis on the mystical aspect of desire as empty mumbo jumbo, and he became suspicious of what he called Jung's 'fairytale forest feeling'.[33] To Freud, Jung's mysticism was a defence against the facts of sexuality and an attempt to avoid the less savoury aspects of psychoanalysis by shifting the focus 'upwards' into religious fantasy. He charged Jung: 'You hide behind your religious-libidinal cloud.'[34] Freud ignored the religious aspect of eros, but nevertheless attempted to make a pseudo-religious *dogma* of sexuality. His sexual theory was virtually 'religious' in its certainty, absolutism and repetition. Freud developed unconscious religious aspects, but the conscious direction of religion, the attempt to 'link back' to cosmic forces, was repressed in his psychoanalytic model.

Jung argues that Freud could not cope with the spiritual aspect of desire and attempted to foist this element on his rival in the hope of removing it from himself. The numinosity of the sexual drive was projected on Jung and this accounted for Freud's construction of Jung as a despised prophetic figure. With the convenience of this projection, Freud could banish Jung from the psychoanalytic fold and thus expunge the religious element from his theory. Jung said that at their first meeting he had had a 'strong intuition that for [Freud] sexuality was a sort of *numinosum*'.[35]

> I had observed in Freud the eruption of unconscious religious factors. Evidently he wanted my aid in erecting a barrier against these threatening unconscious contents ... Sexuality evidently meant more to Freud than to other people. For him it was something to be religiously observed.[36]

Jung was not the first to note that the devotion of the scientist to his or her work borders on religious devotion. In his *Pragmatism* William James had argued that whereas the content of scientific discovery was secular, the 'scientific temper is devout'.[37] However Jung is arguing something slightly different. He is claiming that there is religiousness in not only Freud's style but in his content. In their professional meetings, Jung noted that 'the emotionality with which [Freud] spoke of [sexuality] revealed the deeper elements reverberating within him'.[38] 'When he spoke of [his sexual theory], his tone became urgent, almost anxious, and all signs of his normally critical and sceptical manner vanished.'[39] Jung is intuiting a depth dimension which the originator of psychoanalysis was unable to see, because he did not want to see. He could not accept that in his explorations of the unconscious he had touched on the sacred.

Jung's argument is that 'science' can be read as a kind of smokescreen which blocks out the numinous dimension of what so fascinates the scientist. In 'Psychology and Religion' he writes that the 'so-called "scientific" creed, holding that the contents of a neurosis are nothing but repressed infantile sexuality or will to power' is often little more than a 'shield' which protects against the 'living fire' of the numinous.[40] He says 'a scientific theory that simplifies matters is a very good means of defence because of the tremendous faith modern man has in anything which bears the label "scientific". Such a label sets your mind at rest immediately'.[41] Jung delivers a kind of backhanded compliment to the rigidly held sexual theory:

> If, therefore, a patient is convinced of the exclusively sexual origin of his neurosis, I would not disturb him in his opinion because I know that such a conviction, particularly if it is deeply rooted, is an excellent defence against an onslaught of immediate experience with its terrifying ambiguity. So long as such a defence works I shall not break it down, since I know that there must be cogent reasons why the patient has to think in such a narrow circle.[42]

Although Freud sees the mystical as a defence against the facts of sexuality, Jung sees the sexual theory as a defence against the numinous. It is satisfying to the intellect in that it has seemed to do justice to the unconscious, but it has not done justice to it. Such a theory has pleased the intellect and reason, but betrayed the soul. The soul's longing for the numinous has been subverted and sold out to the intellect's desire for a 'sensible' theory about what is going on.

Jung's sense that Freud is a reluctant prophet of a new God-image, who tries to turn the idea of eros into a dogma, is memorably portrayed in this passage:

> I can still recall how Freud said to me, 'My dear Jung, promise me never to abandon the sexual theory. That is the most essential thing of all. You see, we must make a dogma of it, an unshakable bulwark.' He said that to me with great emotion, in the tone of a father saying, 'And promise me this one thing, my dear son: that you will go to church every Sunday'. In some astonishment I asked him, 'A bulwark – against what?' To which he replied, 'Against the black tide of mud' – and here he hesitated for a moment, then added – 'of occultism'.[43]

Freud may have feared that he had dredged up a fish from the deep unconscious that was too big for the container in which it had been placed. The principle of eros was larger than his theory could allow, and it exerted some kind of secret pressure on his scientific framework. He feared a 'black tide of mud of occultism' would rise up in the wake of his description of the eros principle. He sought to repress this religiousness as much as possible, to bury it beneath his science. Jung adds that 'what Freud seemed to mean by "occultism" was virtually everything that philosophy and religion, including the rising contemporary science of parapsychology, had learned about the psyche'.[44]

He sums up Freud's position in a memorable passage:

> One thing was clear: Freud, who had always made much of his irreligiosity, had now constructed a dogma; or rather in the place of a jealous God whom he had lost, he had substituted another compelling imago, that of sexuality. It was no less insistent, exacting, domineering, threatening, and morally ambivalent than the original one. Just as the psychically stronger agency is given 'divine' or 'daemonic' attributes, so the 'sexual libido' took over the role of a *deus absconditus*, a hidden or concealed god. The advantage of this transformation for Freud was, apparently, that he was able to regard the new numinous principle as scientifically irreproachable and free from all religious taint. At bottom, however, the numinosity ... remained the same.[45]

A substitute god-principle had been established to replace the old God, but the hidden numinosity of the new concept is clearly apparent. Jung notes cryptically: 'The lost god had now to be sought below, not above.'[46] The old transcendence had collapsed and the new God-principle was to be sought in the darkness of the unconscious and the realm of sexuality.

The claims of the sacred

In Jung's view, the God-principle demands to be recognised as a god, no matter whether it is discovered above or below. If it is discovered below, in our unconscious, we have to exercise our imaginations more fully since our civilisation has taught us only to look for the holy in what is above. In this sense, Freud demonstrates a typically Western prejudice in failing to recognise the divinity of what is found below. But in Jung's view, Freud's refusal to accept the divinity of what he saw cost him his health and peace of mind. Jung claims that the 'one characteristic of [Freud's] that preoccupied me above all [was] his bitterness':

> He gave the impression that at bottom he was working against his own goal and against himself; and there is, after all, no harsher bitterness than that of a person who is his own worst enemy. In his own words, he felt himself menaced by a 'black tide of mud' – he who more than anyone else had tried to let down his buckets into those black depths.[47]

Something came up from the unconscious that Freud could not accept. For Jung, the 'monotony of interpretation' which was characteristic of Freud's method, in which all dreams were treated as sexual images, 'expressed a flight from himself, or from that other side of him which might perhaps be called mystical'.[48] Freud was the real mystic, and he tried to deal with this fate by projecting it upon Jung. Freud had considered 'only half of the whole, with the result that a counter-effect arises out of the unconscious'.[49] That counter-effect was a movement towards the religiousness of his sexual principle, which he defended against. The suspension of his 'normally critical manner' whenever he spoke of the sexual theory, and his desire to make a dogma of the theory, betray a displaced religious urge. In these and other ways, the repressed religious impulse 'returns' to make its claim.

Freud's addictive interest in collecting figurines and sculptures from ancient mythologies and cosmologies was one expression of his repressed religious impulse. Most of his figurines were religious and iconographic, and many were ancient symbols of fertility, phallic potency and sexual arousal. In *The Gods of Freud*, Janine Burke suggests that a suppressed and somewhat obsessive religious urge showed itself in Freud's fascination for these figures.[50] The black goddess Isis, symbol of fecundity and the womb, loomed large in Freud's collection, as did the phallic gods Priapus and Dionysus, ancient religious images of the procreative urge. According to Janine Burke, Freud collected so many of these religious icons that at times he was unable to find space on his desk to write, since they had claimed so much attention in his mental world.

Freud would have rejected this interpretation as nonsensical. He would have claimed a merely aesthetic interest in the figurines and sculptures, and a scientific interest in protecting his theory of sexuality from detractors and opponents. The Freudian universe is not large enough to encompass the presence of religious factors, since these are ruled out at the start as an illusion.[51] Jung's resistance to Freud's theories was seen by Freud as a sign of Jung's Oedipal attack on fatherly authority, and not as a legitimate criticism which saw more than Freud could see. In his essay 'On the History of the Psycho-Analytic Movement', Freud dismisses Jung as an egomaniac who was incapable of accepting Freud's authority: 'The choice [of Jung as my heir] was a most unfortunate one, in that I had lighted upon a person who was incapable of tolerating the authority of another ... and whose energies were relentlessly devoted to the furtherance of his own interests.'[52] There was no value or credibility given to Jung's objection that Freud was trying to expunge the religious element from psychoanalysis.

Eros, or human love, is a spectrum or axis, of which one end is instinctual and biological, and the other godlike and archetypal. Freud saw one end only, and rejected the idea that there might be another. He divided matter from spirit in the typically Cartesian manner that was widespread in the natural sciences of the nineteenth century. But the power of eros could not be removed from the 'love of God' and the 'power of the Holy Spirit' of which the religions speak. When an archetype is prevented from being expressed, this creates a tension which stops a person from experiencing happiness and wholeness. In Jung's view, Freud's bitterness, his habitual sense of resentment and lack of joy, the monotony of his interpretations, and his lack of a goal to which the psyche pointed were due to his refusal to accept the total nature of the force that he had discovered.

Splitting the force

Jung was an intuitive explorer of the mind who saw more than the scientific paradigm would allow. In 1913 he was punished by Freud with excommunication from the hallowed circle of psychoanalysis. Jung seemed to believe that the work left undone by Freud and his followers had to be completed by himself. He therefore rejects the widely popular view that sees his work as entirely cosmic and spiritual: 'It is a widespread error to imagine that I do not see the value of sexuality.'[53] If we look closely at Jung's works on alchemy and medieval mysticism, they are 'Freudian' to the extent that they focus on sexuality, libido, the 'sacred conjunction' of king and queen, Sol and Luna, brother–sister incest and the religious iconography of erotic desire. His essay 'The Psychology of the Transference' and his opus, *Mysterium Coniunctionis*, are extended meditations on the sacred aspect of sexual imagery. The notion that Jung is somehow opposed to sexuality is a complete error. He was simply 'dreaming onward' the sexual theory to its logical and further stages of erotic union with the divine.

In this sense, the rift between Freud and Jung, and between Freudians and Jungians, is a completely unnecessary split that continues in our time the gaping divide between matter and spirit. The polarities of eros belong together, and while we keep splitting them apart we distort the nature of human reality and our search for meaning/soul. Both pioneers of psychoanalysis were excavating the same unconscious life, the same new-old god and daimonic force. They were both summoned to bear witness to the intensification of the sexual instinct in our time. Freud reported what he saw, and what he saw was focused by his rational lens. Jung's famous redefinition of Freud's concept of libido, which precipitated their split in 1913, tried to reunite the scientific eros with its religious background and history. Jung was not introducing anything new, but was trying to awaken the scientific paradigm to the religious memory which it was trying to expunge. Freud saw the might and fascination of sexuality, and he viewed it as the 'devil' in the unconscious. Jung saw the greatness and mystery of eros, and he saw it as a god with sacred potential. Together they make up the daemonic–divine paradox of which the contemporary experience of the numinosum – God experienced as a source of power – is composed. Having looked at the splitting of human desire into spiritual and instinctual drives, it is now time to look more specifically at the topic of incest.

CHAPTER 6

Incest, Child Abuse and Alcoholism

Part 1: Incest as a spiritual pathology

The incest taboo is synonymous with culture, and when this taboo breaks down it means we no longer have culture or religion to direct our energies towards spiritual goals. The breakdown of the taboo indicates that the symbolic thinking needed for spiritual transformation is absent or, if present, is no longer functioning in an effective way, or no longer understood by the people.

The symbolic core of incest is rebirth. We are first born to our fleshly existence and our lives in the ego, but myth and psyche compel us to search for a second birth, by which we become 'born again' of the spirit. This desire for rebirth is natural, but nature does not supply us with the means by which we can be reborn. To find rebirth, we need imagination and culture. If we merely follow the path of instinct, it might suggest we achieve rebirth through sexual means, by returning to the bodily source from whence we came. As Nicodemus asks Jesus: 'How can a grown man be born? Can he go back into his mother's womb, and be born again?'[1]

The notion of returning to the womb of the mother – or to the womb of sister, cousin, daughter – is connected in a man's mind with the notion of rebirth. Admittedly, it is the unconscious mind of man, or perhaps his reptilian brain, that makes the association of womb with rebirth. It is not an association that is conscious – in fact, the conscious mind of an incest perpetrator might find the idea of sexual relations with a family member abhorrent. But darker impulses of the unconscious and the disordered instincts can be activated, especially under the influence of alcohol or drugs. Under such conditions the incest taboo is weakened to such an extent that the suggestion that incest = personal rebirth inspires criminal action.

Freud, Jung and incest

In most 'normal' cases, the impulse to commit incest is confined to dreams and fantasies, and that is why the incest motif played such an important role in the early days of psychoanalysis. In their pioneering explorations of the unconscious, Freud and Jung found the incest motif in the fantasies and dreams of their patients. They quarrelled about the meaning of this motif, since Freud had interpreted it literally as the desire of the patient for sexual relations with the parent figure or substitute. He thought this was so significant that he used the Greek myth of incest, Oedipus and Jocasta, as the basis for his theory of personality and sexual desire.[2] Jung disagreed with Freud's reading of the incest motif, as can be found in his work *Symbols of Transformation*, which formally announced his theoretical departure from Freud.[3]

Jung was astonished by Freud's naiveté when it came to his interpretation of fantasies and dreams. Although Freud claimed to understand symbols, and to be working with the symbolic contents of the unconscious, he did not view the motif of incest in a symbolical way, but saw it as a mere 'sign' of the patient's desire to cohabit with a parental figure. Jung maintained that the incest motif had a spiritual significance, but Freud could barely wipe the smile off his face as Jung expounded on the 'deeper meaning' of incest. To Freud, this was an attempt to hide the unpleasant fact that we seek sexual relations with parental figures, and that parents harbour desires to have sexual relations with their children. To Freud, our darker impulses were as plain as day, and Jung was avoiding the unpleasant facts by attempting to erect a charade of mysticism. Freud and Jung were so contrary in their views that the astonishing thing is not that they were forced to part company, but that they ever got together in the first place.

To Jung, the incest motif arises whenever we need to find a relation to higher meaning. It arises whenever we are exhausted, depleted, lost or empty. At such times, dreams and fantasies spontaneously throw up images of incest, as pointers to rebirth. Jung felt that it is important to conduct this process of rebirth in symbolic terms, and that to enact it in literal terms is a misreading or 'category error'. What needs to be enacted symbolically, in the psyche or spirit, becomes a moral and ethical disaster if enacted in the flesh. This is why the incest taboo is so strongly defended and supported by all human cultures, because the 'suggestibility' factor might sway a person to literally enact this fantasy, especially if one feels broken, hurt or wounded. The ethical part of the mind can be suspended or displaced if the impulse to seek rebirth is strong and yet no outlet or expression can be found. Incestuous motifs are, not surprisingly, found in all rituals of rebirth and spiritual renewal, and they are especially found in the artistic works of alchemy and gnostic religions. But these motifs or images arise spontaneously in modern dreams and fantasies, especially in times of spiritual desolation.

The community view is that the incest taboo operates to protect us from improper sexual relations with, and exploitation of, young children who are vulnerable and need to be protected from predatorial behaviour. There is as well the biological view that the species has to avoid incestuous couplings because of the possibility of giving birth to children who would be deformed or otherwise handicapped due to the genetic confusion of like uniting with like. In other words, the bias in the community has to do with both moral and medical reasons for the existence of an incest taboo. This is to be expected in our times, when the spiritual dimension of experience has been eclipsed, lost or forgotten. But Jung and others have argued that the incest taboo serves not only biological, moral or ethical functions, but that its primary function is spiritual. The way to incest is forbidden precisely because we must search for the spiritual pathway to rebirth. The libido invested in incestuous coupling has to be converted into the energy that drives us to union with our god or archetypal source. Hence religions and myths are 'symbols of transformation', in which the libido is prevented from a taboo carnal expression so that the spirit can be born.

In many religious traditions, this reasoning is applied to sexuality more generally, not only within the family but also outside it, in which case priestly celibacy has become a religious ideal because it allows a full-bodied, erotic union with the divine to take place. We see this reasoning in Christian, Buddhist, Hindu and other traditions, and in every case the notion at the basis of celibacy is that the libido has to be dammed up and sublimated into higher activity or striving. The base instincts of sexuality have to be transformed into *eros*, *philia* (fellowship), and eventually *agape* (love of God), so that the religious life of humanity can be furthered and spiritual union with the Beloved can be realised. For Jung, the religions draw incestuous libido towards them, allowing it to be transformed into numinous experience. The unconscious imagines the return-to-origins as a return to the mother and sometimes to the father. The child may dream or fantasise about a return to the parental source, either as a sexual or presexual return to the body of the parent.

For the adult, the psyche's desire for reconnection or *religio* can attach itself not to the parent as such, but to the child, youth, or sibling, in which case the child carries the image of rebirth for the adult in the form of a renewed Self.

Freud: incest as criminal act or hysterical fantasy?

When Freud started hearing reports of childhood sexual abuse from his patients in the 1890s, he regarded these as memories of historical events. This was, in itself, a revolutionary act of defiance against his medical profession. We must remember that the neurologists and psychiatrists who had heard these stories before Freud had typically dismissed them as the hysterical lies of insane patients. In taking the stories seriously as firsthand accounts of vicious sexual assaults, Freud was taking a professional risk and running counter to prevailing views. In April 1896 he delivered a landmark paper to the Society for Psychiatry and Neurology in Vienna. According to Jeffrey Masson, Freud's scientific peers were horrified by the paper and its social and political consequences, and they urged Freud not to publish it.[4] However, in the face of a storm of protest, Freud published his so-called 'seduction theory' in 'The Aetiology of Hysteria'.[5]

Later Freud reversed this view, contending that the stories were 'memories' of emotionally laden infantile fantasies so powerful and psychically entrenched that, when the adult female patient dug them up during the course of her analysis, they were regarded as traumatic experiences of the past. But these were not memories of real events, according to Freud's second and final stage of thinking, but memories of incestuous fantasies that were unacceptable to the adult mind. For him, the real 'trauma' was connected with the shocking recognition that the patient had previously entertained such possibilities in her sexual life and she continued to harbour such fantasies in the murky regions of the unconscious. In Masson's view (which, however, is by no means a dispassionate one) 'Freud's abandonment of the seduction hypothesis [represents] a failure of courage.'[6] The argument of Masson and others is that Freud caved in to social and political pressures, and that the incest epidemic in polite society was too great a burden for him to champion. The apparent 'evidence' revealed by Masson to support his case has been sensationalised as the 'Watergate of the psyche' by the *New York Times*, which, in turn, has a long history of debunking psychoanalysis. I am inclined to agree with Paul Kugler that Masson and others have distorted Freud's revised views to create controversy and diminish Freud's contemporary credibility.[7]

Nevertheless, fierce debates continue to rage in society and in our law courts about whether some of these incest attacks occur in reality, or whether they are invented by mentally compromised patients. The debate has polarised the community and the professions, giving rise to a cohort of outraged activists who argue that the incest epidemic is real and being covered up by conservative social forces.[8] On the other hand, a tradition of medical opinion has given rise to the view that a 'false memory syndrome' is in operation, and we should not incriminate fathers accused of these crimes based on evidence supplied by those who are mentally unstable. Like Freud himself, many scientific witnesses testify to the existence of unconscious and unacceptable wishes that cannot be digested by the conscious mind, and hence are projected onto the parental figures as perpetrators of sexual attacks. In this view, victims of incest are themselves victims of their overactive or hysterical imaginations. However from my consideration of legal findings and court documents, it seems that scientific commentators today admit to the possibility that allegations of incest may be based on fact and not all memories of these attacks are spurious.[9] It seems that each case is based on its individual merits, as it should be, and there is no single ideological lens which is applied to all cases.

Freud has been severely criticised for his part in the supposed 'cover-up' of the scandal of incest, and the voices of protest include Masson, Alice Miller, Milton Klein and others.[10] Most damaging is the allegation that Freud suppressed a number of important documents that dealt with the reality of incest in the 1890s, but I am not convinced that these allegations have any basis in truth. Be that as it may, the critics of Freud are right to the extent that they saw Freud turning a blind eye to brutal facts, perhaps to protect the senior patriarchs of Vienna from moral criticism, as feminists have argued, or to turn the victims of incest into irresponsible fantasists, as social workers and activists have claimed. Freud went wrong in trying to place all blame about incest attacks onto the victims, failing to see that this was also a moral and criminal problem of society.

But what the criticism fails to realise is that Freud had a different agenda to those of social activists and human rights groups. His main interest was not to put men behind bars but to focus on the reality of the psyche and the centrality of the motif of incest within it. Admittedly, he went too far in this quest by denying the literal event in favour of the 'fantasy' of incest. But Freud was trying to show that there was something psychological in the motif of incest, and he was right to support this against those who were unable to see his point. For it would not be an exaggeration to say that psychoanalysis was born at the moment that Freud recognised the unconscious nature of the incest complex. By isolating the fantasy aspect of incest (as opposed to the taboo literal act), Freud had pinned down the importance of the unconscious as a determining influence on behaviour. The unconscious was so powerful that it could 'create' reality for us, and its dynamic effects could have lifelong effect on the sexual identity and personality structures of individuals. Even if his 'evidence' was based on sick patients in the first instance, Freud extrapolated from this evidence that similar mechanisms are at work in so-called normal or sane individuals. In other words, we are all influenced by the tendency of the libido to flow towards incestuous union with parental figures. Or in Freud's language, we are all Oedipal by nature.

As argued in the previous chapter, Freud was spellbound by the numinous power of sexuality in general. He was right to identify incest as a central aspect of our psychic structure and dynamism, but he did not go far enough. He knew he had touched something primal in our nature, but he did not realise that he had landed on something holy. This 'fantasy' was not representing a desire to have genital contact with parental figures but a desire to connect with the archetypal fundaments of our being. Incest was more important psychologically than even Freud had surmised. If it is an image which brings together our carnal and spiritual desires in one potent symbol, it has ramifications beyond those Freud imagined. The key to our spiritual rebirth, as Jesus explained to Nicodemus, lies in our ability to be able to comprehend the mystical potency of the incest motif.

Unlike Freud, we do not need to downplay the reality of incest to emphasise its psychological dimension. All we need do is adopt the view that incestuous fantasies are vital to psychic development and that incest is a sad and tragic fact of social life. There is no need for an either/or in this regard and no need to privilege fantasy above reality. From the papers I have read in this field, I take the view that incest attacks are real, and that, if anything, they are likely to be massively under-reported. Incest is revealing of the nature of the psyche as fantasy and as fact. In this regard, we can move on from Vienna in the 1890s, when incest seemed either to have to be constructed as a heinous crime or as an hysterical lie.

Symbolic images in child sexual abuse

One of the tasks of an archetypal analysis of child sexual abuse is to draw out the *symbolic* content of the act and to urge this upon the conscious mind. The perpetrator of the crime has to be made to see that he is seeking his own renewal or rebirth in this act. We must also realise that it is not only the daughter whom such men molest; sometimes it is also, or only, the young son. A same-sex object choice is often made, for instance, in the case of sexually abusing 'celibate' priests, who seem to target boys rather than girls. In a perverse way, these men are seeking revitalisation by way of sexual connection with their projected new or renewed youthful self. They are mesmerised by the prospect of achieving rebirth by sexually penetrating an image of what Jung calls the Self. The Self can be imagined as a 'divine child' of the same sex, as much as it can be seen as a figure of the opposite sex through the projection of the anima. This archetypal perspective is in no way meant to explain or excuse pathological activity. Psychologising does not validate rapists, sadists or child abusers but points to the symbolic image, or impulse, at the core of this activity.

Often our first response to the act of sexual abuse is to ask: Why are they attacking the child? Why do they want to harm the child? The literature indicates that many men are not aware that they are abusing children. Blinded by the image of the youthful Self, the abusers do not perceive the child's distinct, separate reality and are completely insensitive to the child's individual needs. Some men believe that their children enjoy incestuous sexuality and that it is not harmful to them. Studies of abusive parents reveal that the majority were abused themselves as children. This indicates that awareness of the actual child has been eclipsed for generations by the unreal image of the child as erotic-regenerative plaything, to be exploited by the adult.

Robert Stein argues that the more identified the male parent is with the father archetype, or *senex,* the more narrowly rational, dry and rigid he becomes. When men feel burnt out in this way, Stein writes, 'the more desperate is the need of the *senex* to unite with those qualities of innocent wonder, openness, vulnerability and virginal freshness which the child carries'.[11] The compulsive need for sexual intimacy in abusing fathers as well as paedophiles may not be motivated by hate or aggression, as it appears to outsiders, but rather by a desire to unite with the child as carrier of the Self in the form of the child archetype.

We are reminded of this in the outbreak of incest and child sexual abuse among the indigenous people of central and northern Australia. In recent years, reports of incest in Aboriginal communities have soared, and in 2007 this prompted the Federal government to declare a state of emergency in remote communities in the Northern Territory. This moral crisis has gone hand in hand with a decline of indigenous culture and tribal dignity, as a consequence of colonisation, modernisation and detribalisation. The June 2007 report into this crisis was called *Little Children are Sacred*, and the epigraph of the report is a statement from the Yolngu people: 'In our Law children are very sacred because they carry the two spring wells of water from our country within them.'[12] Tragically it might be the case that because the little children are sacred they are now the targets of sexual assault. Precisely because nothing else is sacred, the children become targets of perverse adult fantasies. The adult self seeks union with the sacred, but what can it do if no living symbols are to be found? If spiritual water can no longer be found in ritual, art and ceremony, in prayers, petitions or symbols, the thirst for this water might lead some to seek it in previously unthinkable places.

It is at this point that we begin to understand the hugely important role of culture and religion in regulating the sexual urges and keeping us within an ethical frame. In the Bible, we read: 'Where there is no vision, the people cast off restraint.'[13]

This is relevant when we see how the decline of Aboriginal culture and religion is directly related to the soaring incidence of incest in these once proud and safe communities. The urge for renewal and rebirth becomes demonic when it no longer operates within any cultural or spiritual context. Because the urge can no longer be satisfied in cultural ways, and yet must be satisfied in some way, the scene is set for child sexual abuse in a culture that once hardly knew this form of social violence. It reminds us of the words of novelist Christopher Koch: 'The spirit does not die, of course, it turns into a monster.'[14]

What prompts the incest image to cross over into a literal act is the degree to which the personality is held in thrall by it. The power of the unconscious is enormous and if the ego is unable to reflect upon the psyche's promptings, the image will be acted out. So it is vital that the image of incest be distinguished from its literal enactment. The image must be respected, no matter how much we abhor the literal act, for the incest image is sacred and may be our healing doorway into the archetypal realm. In my experience it has been difficult to convince community welfare workers and health professionals of the value inherent in the image of incest, because the social reality of incest is so terrible that all related images are dismissed as abominations. This is a great loss, because by confusing the psychic imagery with the literal enactment we lose the rich symbolism of the unconscious. Robert Stein is again helpful on this point: 'Healing does not lie in attempting to overcome these "perverse" desires, but in being able to experience fully the incestuous desires emotionally and imaginally.'[15]

Such a view seems opposed to the commonsensical, community health and welfare approach to solving the problem. Common sense would prefer us to banish the ugly imagery of incest, as well as its horrific enactment, altogether. The therapeutic approach, however, is to stay with the imagery.

Discuss the incest images with those haunted by them in a therapeutic setting, intensify the imagery through amplification, dream work and association, and see if a breakthrough beyond the literal expression can occur. These monstrous fathers may actually find their way to a caring connection with their own inner child, thus releasing the monster – the unconscious impulse to rebirth – and transforming their lives. But no real cure true to psyche and society can arise from simply admitting wrongdoing, enforcing punishment and indulging in moralistic condemnation. The symbolic core of the problem must be addressed, and if it is not, no resolution can take place. When symbolic integration occurs, however, 'the sexual drive is gradually transformed, and the child (inner and outer) can be loved, honored and respected as a unique being'.[16]

The story of Nicodemus

I would like to return to the dialogue between Jesus and Nicodemus that I mentioned at the start of the chapter as this famous scene in the Gospel of John tells us a great deal about spiritual rebirth. In this story, the Pharisee Nicodemus comes to Jesus in the night, to learn from him the mystery of rebirth. Presumably he comes in the night because Jesus is viewed as a radical who disturbs the established religion, and the rabbi does not want to be chastised by his peers for consulting a reprehensible figure. Some scholars believe the story reflects John's anti-Semitism at the time of writing the gospel. Nicodemus is described as a 'leading Jew' and it is seems that John is scoring points at his expense and making Christianity appear superior to Judaism in that it has possession of the secret of rebirth. John portrays the Pharisee as a fool for not understanding the basic elements of religious life. Nicodemus opens the dialogue by approaching Jesus: 'Rabbi, we know you are a teacher who comes from God,' and the structural irony suggests that Nicodemus's authority comes not from God but from man and Jewish institutions.

Jesus responds to Nicodemus's call for wisdom by saying: 'I tell you most solemnly, unless a man is born from above, he cannot see the kingdom of God.'[17] Nicodemus replies, sounding like an undergraduate who is overawed by a master's wisdom: 'How can a grown man be born? Can he go back into his mother's womb, and be born again?'[18] Jesus responds, echoing his previous words:

> I tell you most solemnly, unless a man is born through water
> and the spirit, he cannot enter the kingdom of God: what is
> born of the flesh is flesh; what is born of the Spirit is spirit.[19]

Jesus is saying: as a man is, so he thinks. If we remain earthbound, and confined to our fleshly nature, we think literally about these things and get nowhere. If we want to aspire to the spirit, we have to break with earthbound, literal thinking and begin to think metaphorically. Literal thinking is a travesty of the spiritual life. If we think literally about rebirth, we end up confusing it with the act of incest. Such thinking is a perversity of the right approach. Metaphorical thinking comes from the spirit – it is 'born of the Spirit' – and hence generates a new approach to reality. For us today, the 'kingdom of God', which is so divorced from our secular understanding, might be reconceived as the 'realm of the spirit', access to which is achieved through acts of intuition and insight.

But Jesus does not let Nicodemus off lightly. He admonishes the priest for his literal-mindedness:

> Do not be surprised when I say: You must be born from
> above. The wind blows wherever it pleases; you hear its
> sound, but you cannot tell where it comes from or where it is
> going. That is how it is with all who are born of the Spirit.[20]

This is a beautiful and haunting passage. It is a testimony to the mystery, wonder and awe of the spirit. The spirit is a transcendent reality and we ought not attempt to pin it down with our thinking, because it 'blows wherever it pleases', or 'bloweth where it listeth', in the memorable King James Version. The reply of Jesus achieves the status of pure poetry. It represents the reply of wisdom to the conventional yet stupid logic of Nicodemus. It shows that Jesus is a poet and by virtue of that status he knows the truth.

Nicodemus, however, cannot make the shift from logic to wisdom. He turns to Jesus after hearing his poetry and asks, 'How can that be possible?'[21] Jesus is forced to admonish the rabbi: 'You, a teacher in Israel, and you do not know these things!'; or in the King James Version: 'Art thou a master of Israel, and knowest not these things?'[22] Once more there is the suggestion that the priests of Judaism are divorced from the experience of spirit. They seem to know the letter of the law but not the spirit of the law. The spirit is known not by rote or intellectual learning, not by logic or reason, but only by imagination and poetry. It is poetry and metaphor that allows us to see the kingdom of God. Only metaphor and symbol can carry us over from normal thinking to spiritual thinking.

Criminality and spirituality

Like many readers, Jung found the Nicodemus story moving. He commented on the passage as follows:

> Jesus' challenge to Nicodemus [is this]: Do not think carnally, or you will be flesh, but think symbolically, and then you will be spirit. It is evident that this compulsion towards the symbolical is a great educative force, for Nicodemus would remain stuck in banalities if he did not succeed in raising himself above his concretism ... The reason why

Jesus' words have such suggestive power is that they express the symbolical truths which are rooted in the very structure of the human psyche. The empirical truth never frees a man from his bondage to the senses; it only shows him that he was always so and cannot be otherwise. The symbolical truth, on the other hand, which puts water in place of the mother and spirit or fire in place of the father, frees the libido from the channel of the incest tendency, offers it a new gradient, and canalises it into a spiritual form.[23]

Today there is no Christ-figure to instruct the literal-minded Nicodemus in all of us. Culturally, we possess no wisdom by which the incest tendency can be 'canalised into a spiritual form', as Jung puts it. Psychologists, therapists and community workers can warn perpetrators of the crime to stop doing it or risk severe punishment and social reprimand. But they cannot suggest how the offending act can be transformed into a profound symbolic experience or spiritual revelation. Health professionals as well as offenders often have little or no access to the symbolical dimension, which alone can bring a cure to this worldwide epidemic. All of us – the incest-taboo enforcers and the incest-taboo breakers – need to be educated about the realities of the inner world and its transformative and symbolic capacities. Today we remain caught at the physical, sexual, pre-symbolic level. When the incest image arises in the psyche, it is expressing a real need for transformation, but if there is no response, it is perversely acted out in a literal way.

We need to consider that spirituality alone can free us from the tyranny of this kind of criminality. Our punishing, moralistic, humanistic society cannot solve the incest epidemic but merely suppresses or denies it. Modern society is paying a high price for abandoning what Jung called the 'symbolic life'.[24] We believe we have outgrown the need for symbol, ritual and liturgy, in which we enact ancient rites of renewal and rebirth. The typically modern person links such activities with the 'superstitious' peoples of the past, who liked to conceive of other worlds or different realities. Our pragmatic era is governed by technology and the scientific perspective, and we see no 'relevance' to these rituals and customs. For many of us, there is no 'other world', no 'kingdom of God', which seems so remote from our understanding of reality. But whether we *believe* in the kingdom of God or not is beside the point. The fact is that this 'kingdom' is a spiritual reality and not merely an object of belief. We have to adjust ourselves to spiritual reality, and if we fail to make this adjustment, the soul will go mad or we will be driven to criminal behaviours.

Whether we believe in a religion or not, the psyche is still very much present and real. If we make no room for it, its images and forces act on us negatively, compelling us to irrational, senseless, dehumanising behaviour. The force that could bring transformation brings only violence and degeneration. Our rational society, ostensibly governed by science, is torn apart from within by savage forces. In this context, Jung wrote:

> It is as necessary today as it ever was to lead the libido away from the cult of rationalism and realism – not, indeed, because these things have gained the upper hand (quite the contrary), but because the guardians and custodians of symbolical truth, namely the religions, have been robbed of their efficacy by science. Even intelligent people no longer understand the value and purpose of symbolical truth, and the spokesmen of religion have failed to deliver an apologetic suited to the spirit of the age.[25]

The psyche seeks rebirth and transformation, with or without the aid of clergy, priests, or 'the guardians and custodians of symbolical truth'. But without any cultural or religious outlet, the psyche will resort to pathologies to express its interior life and impulses. When the gods become diseases, we can only heal the diseases by returning to the gods. This is apparent in the contemporary incest epidemic: the only cure for this epidemic is an increase in symbolic awareness, so the desire for rebirth can be enacted in culturally transformative and life-affirming ways.

No matter how much society has trained us to think of incest as an ugly abomination of moral conduct, the sacred image of incest as a symbol of spiritual renewal has to be rescued from it. In the abomination is a god, a transcendent force, a gift, that must be won back from the literal domain. The motif of incest will not go away, because the psyche fastens onto it as a powerful expression of the desire to be born again. Since that desire is archetypal and probably biological as well, it is not going to disappear. The less we know about this image, the more likely are certain members of society bound to act it out, because it is an act of compulsive unconsciousness. The perpetrators of incest do not know what they are doing, nor what impact it has on others. All they are aware of is the force of a libidinal impulse which has caught them and won't let go.

Part 2: Alcoholism: Under the influence

A great deal of sexual molestation and child abuse is fuelled by alcohol and drugs, frequently occurring when men are 'under the influence'. I find that phrase suggestive: under the influence of what? Of alcoholic spirits, of course, but also of a spiritual force gone wrong. Under the influence of a wild and savage god, which we might identify as Bacchus, a degenerate form of Dionysus, god of wine and revelry. Alcoholism and binge drinking exist in epidemic proportions in the world, and increasingly we see these problems affecting young people as well as adults. I read alcoholism as a pathology of the spirit, and it shows how spirit manifests in a culture that is in denial of the spiritual life. We have an innate desire to transcend normal boundaries and break through to the other side. If we cannot do this in cultural ways, we will find pathological ways of smashing through barriers and becoming addicted to ersatz (or artificial) transcendence. In Australia, we see the problem of alcoholism in all cultures and communities, but it is particularly marked in Aboriginal communities.

Alcohol as a substitute for transcendence

Aboriginal people have been affected by the traumatic and sudden disappearance or eclipse of spirit in their lives through contact with the modern world in colonisation and materialism. In traditional life, spirit was expressed in rituals, ceremonies, corroborees, initiation rites and spiritual attitudes to the physical world. There was no such thing as a purely physical world for tribal cultures, because the landscape was animated with ancestor spirits, totemic animals and sacred sites. Indigenous people did not walk through a physical world, but through a spiritual or animated cosmos.

Jung estimated that tribalised Aboriginals spend over half their waking lives in a spiritual state of being, through various kinds of symbolic action:

> There is a peculiar value in the symbolic life. It is a fact that the primitive Australians sacrifice to it two-thirds of their available time – of their lifetime in which they are conscious.[26]

Although I object to his language about 'primitive Australians', I take his point. The idea that tribal Aboriginals devote two-thirds of their time to symbolic life came to Jung from the anthropology of Spencer and Gillen.[27] To shift from a symbolically saturated reality to one in which little or nothing is sacred was too great a shock for Aboriginal people. It is, naturally, a shock for any human community, but more so for a people who had been steeped in sacred consciousness for millennia. European culture had been weaned off the sacred in the course of centuries, at least since the time of the age of reason and the rise of science. But for Aboriginal culture, which was ushered into modernity overnight and forced to live in a desacralised universe, the impact has been devastating. It is true that the impact of colonisation has been lethal, but the typical political analysis of the Aboriginal crisis fails to take into account the existential impact of the loss of the sacred. Micrea Eliade puts it well when he writes:

> The man of traditional societies ... can live only in a sacred world, because it is only in such a world that he participates in being, that he has a real existence. For him, profane space represents absolute nonbeing. If, by some evil chance, he strays into it, he feels emptied of his ontic substance, as if he were dissolving in chaos, and he finally dies.[28]

This religious dimension of the Aboriginal crisis is not understood by mainstream secular culture, and not even by some of those good-natured and well-intentioned people who try to attend to the problems in Aboriginal communities. In addition to the external problems wrought by colonisation and dispossession of land, the spiritual problem of the loss of sacred space and straying into a world devoid of 'ontic substance', that is, the substance of Being, is the hidden dimension of the crisis. It is clear that alcohol furthers the process by which some Aboriginal people are dissolving in chaos, but at the same time alcohol gives the false hope or illusion that one might almost reach into the sacred dimension once more.

The effect that alcohol has on consciousness, and its intended aim of loosening the ties of the ego and exposing us to other dimensions, has been seductively attractive to all Australians, whether Aboriginal or not. Australian social attitudes tend to be constricted, overly rational, at times cynical and often pessimistic. It is little wonder that alcohol has become such a huge attraction in this country, because alcohol has the effect of loosening our ties to rationality and opening us to dimensions of the psyche that say *yes* instead of *no*. It was William James who first identified this thirst for alcohol as a religious problem:

> The sway of alcohol over mankind is unquestionable due to its power to stimulate the mystical faculties of human nature, usually crushed to earth by the cold facts and dry criticisms of the sober hour. Sobriety diminishes, discriminates, and says no; drunkenness expands, unites, and says yes. It is in fact the great exciter of the Yes function in man. It brings its votary from the chill periphery of things to the radiant core. It makes him for the moment one with truth.[29]

The fact is that we cannot tolerate our orderly, rational lives all the time. There are times when we must break out, and release through alcohol and drugs has become a kind of ceremonial release for many of us who are caught in rationality during the week. We are not just searching for alcohol and the poisoning that it inflicts on the body and nervous system. We are searching for altered mental states, and for what James calls 'potential forms of consciousness entirely different from our own'.[30] In a secular culture we do not know how to transcend the normal state of consciousness, except through eating, drinking and various kinds of substance abuse. This is where the loss of religious awareness takes its toll, because we stand dumb and mute before the innate human need to transcend our profane state and achieve the condition of *homo religiosus*, to use Mircea Eliade's phrase for the true nature of humanity as 'religious man'.

Adopting the language of Greek mythology to explain our modern dilemma, analyst Robert Johnson claims that our secular culture has a poor relation to Dionysus, the god who teaches us how to transcend the rational.[31] By day and during the week, we carefully erect an Apollonic structure around ourselves that by night and on weekends we feel compelled to tear down. But we are so far removed from Dionysus, his rituals, ceremonies and arts, that we do not know how to conduct this transcendence in a positive way. Instead we turn to the lesser rituals of the drunken Bacchus, or to what Johnson calls 'low-grade Dionysus',[32] and attempt to drink or consume our way to a breakthrough. Recent statistics show that alcohol-related ambulance attendances have tripled and the number of drunks presenting to emergency departments has doubled in Australia over the past decade.[33] Alcohol-fuelled violence is a part of this same pattern. Violence is not only a deliberate form of antisocial behaviour but a symbolic attempt to break out of the mental prison of the ego by fighting other people and smashing things. A report suggests that alcohol is the 'primary cause' of Aboriginal violence, and that indigenous people are up to twenty times more likely than the rest of the population to commit violent crime induced by alcohol.[34]

The loss of spiritual ecstasy in all cultures, ancient and modern, indigenous and transplanted, has been replaced by the spurious, artificial ecstasy of alcohol and drugs. The word 'ecstasy' comes from the Greek *ekstasis*, to stand outside the self. If we do not cultivate a symbolic reality or find life outside the ego, inferior ecstasy will invade the body and psyche, destroying both in a disorderly spectacle. The destructiveness of alcoholism in Aboriginal cultures could symbolise, at a bodily level, the disorienting effect of 'low-grade Dionysus' on a people who have traditionally been in a positive relationship with the sacred.

Dionysus was referred to in ancient times as 'the loosener', as one who weakens our grasping to ego and rationality, and Aboriginal people lived in this 'loosened' condition until recently. But with the collapse of their Dreaming, and spirit, soul and meaning shattered by colonisation, detribalisation and loss of ancestral lands, the enticement to negative forms of transcendence is accentuated. The temptations of alcohol and binge drinking in this context can be placed alongside those of petrol sniffing, glue sniffing and 'chroming' (paint sniffing). The spirit must have transcendence, either positively in spiritual forms, or negatively in substance abuse and self-destruction. The negative 'spirit' of alcohol destroys the ego rather than 'transcends' it, and it can destroy the body and its organs as well as society itself.

Alcoholics Anonymous

Jung was indirectly involved in the founding of Alcoholics Anonymous, and he realised that to combat the negative power of alcohol an addict would need to discover a spiritual life. Jung wrote to William Wilson, the famous 'Bill W' who was co-founder of the New York-based Alcoholics Anonymous:

> I am strongly convinced that the evil principle prevailing in this world leads the unrecognized spiritual need into perdition, if it is not counteracted either by a real religious insight or by the protective wall of human community.
> An ordinary man, not protected by an action of grace and isolated in society, cannot resist the power of evil ... You see, alcohol in Latin is spiritus and you use the same word for the highest religious experience as well as for the most depraving poison. The helpful formula therefore is: spiritus contra spiritum.[35]

By this cryptic Latin phrase he means that only an experience of spirit can contradict the effects of an addiction to the 'spirit' of alcohol. Like cures like, or more precisely, like takes away the symptoms of like, and this is the philosophical basis of homeopathic medicine. One needs to employ a higher or more distilled form of the substance to combat the poison.

In the case of Aboriginal alcoholism, only the reintegration of traditional spirit can calm the chaos wrought by the invasion of intoxicating fluids. Alcohol is a perfect symbol of an alien, non-indigenous spirit, since this intoxicant was unknown until imported by Europeans. While living in Alice Springs I was impressed by the fact that the Aboriginal people who had best learned to overcome alcoholism were those who had made a personal conversion to a religious faith. Although some claim that religion is the 'opium of the masses', its capacity to provide a creative channel for the chaotic spirit cannot be underestimated.

The Alcoholics Anonymous movement is one of the most successful recovery programs in recent history. There has been a great deal of scientific research conducted on this movement and why it seems to work for so many alcoholics. The first three of the Twelve Steps are related to spiritual conversion:

1. We admitted we were powerless over alcohol – that our lives had become unmanageable.
2. We came to believe that a Power greater than ourselves could restore us to sanity.
3. We made a decision to turn our will and our lives over to the care of God as we understood Him.[36]

The central component of this program is the belief that the addict has no personal control over the addiction. Addicts admit to a lack of control and balance and hand their lives over to a higher power. Although this operates in a Christian framework, my sense is that it could work just as well in other religious and cultural contexts. The main element is to renounce the leadership of the ego and to induct oneself into a larger worldview. I appreciate the wording of the third step: we turn our lives over to God *as we understood him*. I take this to mean that one does not have to subscribe to an institutionally sanctioned image of God but simply to sense a power greater than oneself. Some may not choose to call this archetypal power 'God' but spirit, life, guardian angel, Goddess, energy, Chi or whatever. As the Buddhist monk Thich Nhat Hanh wrote: 'But the Holy Spirit is not just for Jesus alone; it is for all of us.'[37] The notion that only one group can receive these gifts is quite preposterous. The gifts of healing and renewal come from life itself, and we are all benefactors. The important point is to surrender to a greater force and believe in the existence of the force as if one's life depended on it – because it does.

Once this surrender is made and the ego renounces control, the healing powers come into operation. The AA steps are not unlike the structure of the Catholic Mass, in which the faithful are invited to say, while kneeling: 'Lord, I am not worthy to receive you, but only say the word and I shall be healed.'[38] The Mass is a healing ritual, where celebrants come to the divine and ask for healing. The AA Twelve Steps understand the importance of humility: 'We humbly asked Him to remove our shortcomings.' The AA language is patriarchal, and this may not suit our taste today where we are more likely to be critical of a religious system that adopts an outdated style. But again, the point is that we have to lower ourselves before a transpersonal *other*, otherwise the healing grace cannot be experienced.

Unfortunately, the critical mind often interprets surrender as subordination or humiliation, and thus no healing can take place. If the ego cannot displace itself, or be lowered, the spirit cannot find a place to enter. As is said in Buddhist religion:

'Only the empty glass can be filled; a glass already full can receive nothing new from the higher realms.'[39] The modern ego, determined to take charge of our lives, experiences the sacred as a source of oppression rather than of healing. This is where things can go wrong for us today if the meddling intellect interferes too much in the process of recovery.

CHAPTER 7

Depression, Self-Harm and Suicide

> We are led to a mystery that is embedded in all initiations and in every rite of passage: the end of a previous form of existence is felt as a real death.
>
> Thomas Moore[1]

Two factors have prompted me to turn to the subject of suicide and depression. Suicidal depression has claimed the lives of some of my students, colleagues and friends, and I remember them as I explore this topic. Hardly a year goes by without suicide causing devastation in one of my circles of personal or professional life. It often seems that suicide has reached epidemic proportions and the research in this area confirms this impression.[2] A second factor that has inspired my interest is that I have been invited to speak on the subject by chaplains, psychiatrists, hospitals, schools and an umbrella organisation called Suicide Prevention Australia. It has to be admitted that it is not a happy subject, but it needs to be addressed, and it seems that there are many people who want to discuss it, especially in terms of depth psychology and spirituality.

Depression as a struggle with an alien will

The conventional views on depression and suicide are humanistic and based on the ego's standpoint, but what do these problems look like from the perspective of the soul? Depression is a painful experience with its roots in the autonomy of the psyche. One is living one's life as best one can and according to one's lights, but an *other will* interferes and calls us away from the world. It is best, as explained in Chapter 1, to personify the emotions that attack us from within, as this gives us a chance to dialogue with them. Some call this alien will which prevents us from continuing with normal life the 'black dog'. Energy is withdrawn from normal activities and is no longer at our disposal. The black dog, the mythic companion of Hades, god of the underworld, has recalled us to the depths and prevents us from moving forward. Our first response is: What have we done to deserve this? Why has this situation befallen us? We would like to get back to normal, but are unable to do so. We are made up of many pieces, but just one part of us forces us to stop in our tracks.

Depression is a forced opportunity for reflection. It does not come with a user's manual or a how-to guide. We don't even know the black dog's name. But the psyche withdraws its support for our lives as we have been living them. The psyche provides no apology, excuses or directives, it simply cuts off our energy and we have to learn to 'manage' our depression as best we can, using self-care, medication, therapy or whatever means we choose. Because we do not live in a wisdom society but in an information age, we are not told by medical practitioners that our depression has been caused by the psyche and we had better get in touch with it and understand its demands. We tend to look outside, not inside, for causes. It is as if our society has no ability to approach the interior world. Our depression, we tell ourselves, has been caused by this or that external factor, prompted by a sudden loss, a disappointment in a relationship, a change of conditions or foiled expectation. There is no doubt that these can trigger depression, but it is not these factors that sustain it. We rarely stop to ask the black dog what it wants. We are caught by it, and try to shake it off, but we do not sit with the depression or ask what meaning we might find in it.

The dying of immature innocence

If we apply a model based on initiation, we might begin to reconceive depression as a meaningful act on the part of the psyche, rather than an unfortunate condition visited upon us from outside. What if the condition has something to say and we need to read it like a symbol or image of the inner life? Then we have to realise that our life is not ours alone – there is another who makes its claims upon us. There is an inner self and it has 'pulled the plug' on our lives because it is not happy with what we are doing. The inner self has a different idea about things: it wants us to act differently in the world, to be truer to our thoughts and feelings, which have been suppressed for too long in order to fit in with social norms. It may want us to think less about conforming to the expectations of others, workmates, institutions and social conventions, and to pay more attention to our needs and desires. It may want us to live closer to the heart and core of who we are. And so, unceremoniously, it cuts us off from our energy and we are forced to go back to the source to restore the connection.

But the current of life will not be restored because we ask for it. There are things we have to do and adjustments to be made. A former age might have said that we have to please a defiled spirit or maligned god before the energy can be returned. Since we no longer believe in gods, we have to use a new language about an inner or true self, and talk about making peace with it. We have to personify and objectify the alien will as a black dog or dejected self. We have to journey within to find out how and why we are not living according to our true self and where the breakdown has occurred. When the ego is able to go humbly to the true self and ask it how to live, then the lights can come back on and the depressive darkness can be lifted.

But how do we find these answers? Looking for what went wrong in terms of our regular 'day world' logic will rarely, if ever, divulge a reasonable explanation. Normal reasoning about what we have done to 'deserve' this or what others may have done to get us into such a jam lead nowhere. Rather, we have to understand that the depression is a calling for a new way of life, a terrible and dark initiation into an inner life that we have not experienced before. It is as if Hades, god of the underworld, has grabbed us by the heels and, in the same way that he abducted Persephone as she innocently picked flowers in the Eleusinian fields, he is saying to us: 'You are not getting away from me this time; you are coming with me.' After this moment, our lives are no longer fully ours, and we are responsible to a different centre of authority. This is a terrible experience for an ego that tries to remain innocent of the claims of this other force.

Becoming aware of another claim

In his autobiography, Jung admits that he suffered from depression in his adolescence. He felt, in retrospect, that his depression was caused by his failure to live his inner life at this time. In adolescence he was primarily concerned with fitting in with others and meeting the expectations of parents and teachers. Jung writes:

> This period of my life was filled with conflicting thoughts. Schopenhauer and Christianity would not square with one another, for one thing; and for another, No. 1 wanted to free himself from the pressure or melancholy of No. 2. It was not

No. 2 who was depressed, but No. 1 when he remembered No. 2.[3]

At this point in his autobiography, Jung referred to himself in the plural, as two persons. No. 1 was his conscious personality, which was concerned with the world and social adaptation, and No. 2 was his darker, more secret, inner life. The inner life was held down during the period of social adjustment, and it is significant that he says the second personality was not depressed or caught in melancholia. It was No. 1 who was depressed when he remembered No. 2, when the conscious personality was made aware that it was not living to its full capacity, that it had split off a part of the psyche and was not allowing it to flourish. This is a useful insight because it shows that the pathology does not come from the inner life per se but from the dissociated condition itself. We are sick because we are not connected. We cannot blame that on the greater force even though it may appear to be overshadowing us with malicious intent.

Depression is paradoxical: it may be trying to lead us to the light, but we have to travel via the darkness to get there. It is hard for us today to trust this dark passage because we are not taught about this experience. Not being part of the common fund of knowledge, we are less likely to trust it or to look forward to a new experience of the world. If we try to shake off the darkness we are less likely to get to the light because, as Jung reminds us, 'One does not become enlightened by imagining figures of light, but by making the darkness conscious. [This] procedure, however, is disagreeable and therefore not popular.'[4]

Cognitive Behavioural Therapy (CBT) asks depressed people to gain a more realistic view of themselves and the world by examining their negative distortions and automatic reactions. After several sessions with a psychologist, victims of depression are expected to be able to tune into 'thinking errors' by using such objective methods. This is all very well as a remedial measure, but in my view it does not get to the heart of the problem. This method attempts to reprogram us to cope with our situation, but it does not ask the symptom what it wants. In other words, it does not take the unconscious into account, or view the depression as an initiation into meaning. No therapy is truly effective if it treats the depression as a pure enemy; we only view it correctly if we see depression as a potential teacher. The black dog must become our guide, and we ought not ask it to heel.

Self-esteem as a gift from the soul

Depression and suicide are invariably connected to the problem of self-esteem. In his essay 'Mourning and Melancholia', Freud wrote that the difference between everyday 'low' moods and full-blown depression or melancholia has to do with self-esteem.[5] Freud argued that low self-esteem or insecurity seems to be a trigger for clinical depression. Most forms of therapy discuss the importance of self-esteem but, as with other aspects of depression, we rarely get beyond a superficial grasp of the topic. We know it is vital, but what is it?

Today we are bedevilled by the problem of self-esteem because, I would contend, it is not the ego but the soul that supplies our sense of worth. In a world governed by the ego, which so often seems oblivious to soul and its values, it is little wonder that we cannot get to the heart of self-esteem. A great many of us talk about self-esteem, but beyond the learned chatter there is a mysterious dimension which is not being seen. Our ego-based society cannot understand it, because something other than the ego gives us our deep and secure sense of worth.

I have been helped in my thinking in this regard by some encounters with Aboriginal people. I once asked an Aboriginal elder in Perth why so many indigenous youths are harming themselves, or engaging in glue or petrol sniffing, or attempting suicide. His response was simple and yet profound: 'They don't know who they are.' At first he was reluctant to say more, as he was thinking about sacred matters and the sacred is protected by secrecy in Aboriginal culture. But when I enquired further, he did say that the 'natural' self is unable to understand its true identity or worth. 'The task of culture,' he said, 'is to tell the person who he or she really is.' When Aboriginal people use the word *culture* they are referring to what we in the West call religion. They don't mean culture in the secular sense, which is non-existent for them, they mean culture as spiritual wisdom. When people know who they are, they no longer want to harm themselves, for they have received, as a gift from their culture, their true dignity and worth.

This gave me the clue I needed. The impulse to terminate our lives is an expression of what Jung calls 'loss of soul'. Loss of soul can undermine our lives in an instant, causing us to be disturbed, anxious and confused. When the soul is lost, the sense of meaning goes out of us and the lifeblood drains away. There may be a crippling emptiness which indicates that something is missing, and this can express itself as despair, chronic anxiety, or deep uncertainty, as well as in addictions or suicidal feelings. This emptiness can assail us, no matter how well adjusted we seem on the surface, and despite the existence of a caring, concerned family, school community or friendship network. Our true worth can only be gifted by a spiritual source, and in traditional cultures this gifting is bestowed in initiations.

Ordeals and trials in ancient and modern contexts

Suicide, in this understanding, can be read as a rite of passage (in psychological terms) which has taken a tragic turn. The suicidal impulse is deep and non-rational. We find it hard to fathom, until we have been there ourselves and experienced its persuasive power, but examining traditional initiation rites can offer some enlightenment.

In some Aboriginal rituals, the initiate is painted white and placed in a shallow grave to signify the death of the old self. Sometimes an eye-tooth is knocked out, scars are made across the chest, and the ritual of circumcision is performed on boys, to signify the death of the natural man.[6] In this weakened state, the elders introduce the initiate to the sacred stories and mysteries of the community, and these are offered as a source of strength. Often the initiate is given a new name to symbolise the emergence of a new identity, as we find in the Bible story of Jacob, who becomes Israel after his ordeal. The initiate is re-introduced to the community as a different person at the end of the initiation trials.

These trials are painful and the early anthropologists and Christian missionaries were often horrified by the Aboriginal rituals.[7] However, Aboriginal elders warned that if the trials of initiation were stopped an even greater suffering would be unleashed upon uninitiated persons, because the spiritual life would still have to invade the human world and without ceremony this might be more painful, prolonged and life-threatening. There could be no guarantee that the vengeance of the spirit wouldn't kill people without the formal constraints of ritual, which are designed not only to subject young people to spiritual law but also to restrain the ancestral spirit from destroying the mortal who stands before it.

Thus initiations serve a double function: to induct the human into the spiritual and to 'humanise' the spirit so it does not destroy the human. If Jacob had not told the angel his name and asked for a blessing, the implication is that the angel would have killed him. After all, the angel had already dislodged his hip from its socket, and henceforth Jacob walked with a limp.

Spiritual processes are matters of life and death, and that is why the sacred is so often secret and taboo, protected from the criticism of the profane or secular eye.

In our modern world we have dispensed with the initiation practices of old and feel ourselves to be liberated as a result. We experience freedom from the rites of passage that can be viewed as indoctrinations and impositions on our individuality. However, what we lose by our modern condition is at least as great as what we have gained. We have lost the sense of community based on sacred values and a shared language that might enable us to understand and describe our transformations from ego to Self. We have lost a ritual which makes possible the displacement of our egocentricity. Without this ritual we are at a loss to know how to conduct our passage to the other side. Moreover, without the relatively 'safe' ritualised attack on the ego, we might fall prey to more dangerous assaults on our personal life by a violent and repressed 'transpersonal' spirit. Without cultural regulation, the psychological dynamic within us can become a monster of destruction, forcing us to attack ourselves in a way which is alarmingly sado-masochistic.

The spirit can turn against the ego in a violent rage and compel it to self-injury, risk-taking and even suicide. It is crucial to realise that death is part of the symbolism of rebirth. We can be reborn only if we 'die' to our former selves. If rebirth is not possible because of an absence of ritual and symbolism, the individual can become obsessed with thoughts of death and self-harm, which are called 'suicidal ideation' in medical language. There are suffering people who cannot get the idea of harming or killing themselves out of their heads, and mostly they are treated by medication in our society. But if we look more deeply at the problem it could be a desire for rebirth that has got stuck at what I would call the 'death phase' of the process.

Self-harm and abuse

There are many ways to engage in violence against the self today: chroming, binge drinking, overeating, undereating, antisocial behaviour, violating the body by cutting or piercing the arms or legs, which seems to attract more girls than boys. There are various kinds of risk-taking behaviours or extreme sports which, in turn, are more attractive to boys. There are overdoses of tablets, substance abuse and an almost limitless number of ways to engage in self-harm. All of these forms of pathology could be reframed as attempts on the part of the spirit to terminate the old self, which has to be violated and overcome. There is something symbolically apt in what seems to be our instinctive desire to harm the self because this is the basis of all rituals, found in every religion and tribal culture throughout the world. However, to perform this in sacred ritual is healthy but to perform it in ordinary life is a form of sickness. Aboriginal people would say that these pathological forms are demonstrations that the person is detribalised, that is, has no culture or religion. If you have culture or religion, you have the language which releases you from 'demonic' behaviours and pathologies.

In tribal initiations in many parts of the world there are numerous methods used to enact the death of the natural self. Hallucinogenic and mind-altering drugs are used to create an altered state of mind and, with it, the conviction that a change is taking place. This casts the problem of teenage drug addiction in a new light. There may be forces at work in the teenage use of drugs that our secular authorities know nothing about.[8] This is not to condone drug taking but to indicate that dangerous habits in today's youth may be following ancient patterns, and we would do well to study this problem in a broader context.

Intoxicants have long been used in African and New Guinean initiations, and the mescaline-rich peyote is used in Mexican and

Native American rituals. In some cultures the initiate is led on a 'vision quest', often accompanied by deprivations and trials. A common feature of initiation is to half-starve the initiate, or to frighten him or her with unearthly sounds and tribal dances. There is a 'rushing of forms', sometimes referred to as 'hazing' and often associated with totemic animals.[9] Popular youth culture, rock videos, rave parties, trance dancing and film clips are fast, dizzying and disorienting. Perhaps some of the fascination for these technical forms derives from a desire to collapse normal perception and turn the mind around.

The transition from personal ego to transpersonal Self is a painful journey, and in this regard we have a lot to learn from indigenous cultures. It may be better to ritualise the pain and share it with the community rather than experience it in a solitary way. Organised rituals have the effect of containing the pain, which otherwise might go on without closure. Today, without rituals, self-harming behaviours may be indulged indefinitely, way beyond the dangerous years of the teenage period. As a result of this lack of regulation of life's transitions, adolescence is starting earlier and lasting longer. In tribal cultures, which could not afford the luxury of a long adolescence with its rebelliousness, awkwardness and alienation, the teenage period was terminated by the event of initiation. Nomadic tribes could not allow members to act irresponsibly and antisocially, lest the fragile social ecology be ruptured. As an Aboriginal elder once told me: 'For us, adolescence lasts five days – the length of the initiation. Before initiation he is a child, after initiation, he is an adult.'

In our culture, adolescence is threatening to last forever. It is expanding as time goes by and as our culture fails to teach us to grow up, that is, to transfer our identity from personal ego to transpersonal Self. The cost of not finishing this journey is enormous for society and the individual alike, since both end up caught in narcissism and pleasure-seeking. Perpetual adolescents become more extreme and violent in their behaviour because they know that the 'world' in which they exist should be exploded. In Africa there is a saying: 'If the youth are not initiated, they will burn down the village.' As adolescent violence and antisocial behaviour escalates in the West, the only solution is to facilitate a spiritual transition into a meaningful adulthood.

Cutting, piercing, tattooing

In many tribal rituals, minor wounds or violations are inflicted upon the body. Young adults may emerge from the initiation grounds with scarring across the chest, back and body, with cuts and abrasions to the arms and legs, missing teeth and circumcised genitals. According to Eliade, such violations are outward signs that the mortal body has been 'marked' by spirit and interrupted by another reality.[10] We have been touched by eternity, scarred by the divine.

Such rituals provide the archetypal background to a variety of modern practices found in youth culture. Many schools and colleges are reporting that teenagers are practising self-mutilation. Young adults, especially women, are cutting themselves using blades or knives to wound their hands, fingers, abdomen and thighs. Less pathological, but within the same range of activities, are the popular habits of body piercing and tattooing. There is a desire to mark the body, to announce that it has been touched by something decisive and is no longer normal, no longer free of markings or imprints. The body is a 'text' and cultural messages have been inscribed upon it; the innocent body has been sacrificed to an unnatural law.

Today we also find rings, studs and pins in nostrils, ears, tongues, eyebrows, navels and sundry other locations, including labia and genitalia. In his study of youth culture and its 'irreverent' styles of spirituality, Tom Beaudoin writes:

> Like its related trend, tattooing, the permanent cut of body piercing is more than just teen folly. To pierce one's body is to leave a permanent mark of intense physical experience, whether pleasurable or painful. The mark of indelible experience is ... proof that something *marked me, something happened*. Contemporary youth are willing to have experience, to be profoundly marked, even cut, when religious institutions have not given them those opportunities.[11]

Beaudoin points out that 'safety' pins are used in body piercings: 'A pin named safety – an artefact meant to avoid harming babies – becomes a social statement about harm and danger.' Young people sense that the world is not safe; we have not constructed the 'safe haven' that is supposed to protect us from the intrusions of the sacred. Something unsafe bears down on us and it is not just the threat of terrorism or violence; we are not protected from the incursions of the spirit. Contemporary fashions such as piercing and tattooing are acknowledging that something unnatural and unsafe makes its presence in our lives. We cannot remain innocent, but something else is at work, leaving its signature, its cut on our bodies.

Beaudoin believes that youth perform these rituals as deliberate attempts at religious experience. I am not so sure. My reading is that they are spontaneous acts and the religious element is mostly unconscious. They perform these acts because they feel impelled by an inner impulse. The fact that these acts such as cutting, binge drinking and drug taking are pathological and harmful is itself a sign that they are unconscious. When religious acts are performed consciously they are never demeaning or pathological. We need more than a response of disapproval or moral outrage to these practices. We can say that the cutting is bizarre and it should stop, or the tattooing is in poor taste and should stop. But youths are trying to mark the body because there is an innate need to mark their passage from one state to another. A youth is driven to 'unnatural' acts because something 'unnatural' needs to happen. If this does not happen in the spirit, the body is used as an outlet for its expression. The less successful we are in changing the spirit, the more likely we are to inflict pain on the body.

The expectation of transformation

In this regard the timing of the Aboriginal initiations is important. The tribal initiations take place at the moment that early adulthood expresses itself in bodily and sexual changes. Nomadic tribes cannot afford unwanted pregnancies or irresponsible experimentation with sexual acts. For us today, the teenager is often the one who is beset by negative thoughts, self-harming desires or suicidal urges. We say we have no way of understanding these destructive impulses when young adults appear to have a world of opportunities before them. Often in the prime of their lives, with a bright future ahead, young adults can become sullen and withdrawn, prone to depression and suicidal thoughts. Indigenous cultures provide a new window into this problem by showing that teenagers may be more interested in winning the soul than in gaining the world at this stage in their lives.

The education theorist Joseph Chilton Pearce understands the importance of the role of spirit in the life of the young adult. He argues that young people seem to know, instinctively, that there is more to life than what secular society presents. They eagerly await for something big to happen:

> A poignant and passionate idealism arises in early puberty, followed by an equally passionate expectation in the mid-teens that 'something tremendous is supposed to happen' and

finally by the teenager's boundless, exuberant belief in 'the hidden greatness within me'.[12]

A transformation should take place but often it does not. The young person can be overwhelmed by negativity if the change does not happen. Who or what am I? What is my place in the world? I need a cause to believe in, but what cause is big enough to contain my idealism? Why do people say I am too big for my boots? Am I expecting too much from society? Is there something wrong with me? Why don't I fit in?

The young adult is looking for rebirth to a higher order, an unseen order which is greater than society. If the spirit wants to be reborn, it will find its way to cultural symbols of rebirth if these are present in a person's life. For us, this is the time when we might feel sudden religious urges, whereas before we were happily identified with secular culture. The religious urge is a desire for rebirth and that is why evangelical religions are doing so well in today's climate, because many of us feel these urges from time to time. The churches that offer rebirth and speak this language are generally the Pentecostal or evangelical traditions, where the spirit can become 'activated'. The more traditional churches, which are more wordy and doctrinal, are less appealing to the youthful spirit that is seeking rebirth.

Suicidal impulses in young adults

But what if the symbolism of rebirth is not available to us when we need it most? Then, I would suggest, thoughts of suicide easily insinuate themselves into our consciousness, intruding like unwanted mail into the mind. Here it is apposite to refer to some alarming statistics gathered by epidemiologist Richard Eckersley, according to whom the numbers of young adults who think about suicide is astronomical:

> A study of Australian university undergraduates ... found
> that almost two-thirds of the students, with an average
> age of 22, admitted to some degree of suicidal ideation or
> behaviour – broadly defined – in the previous twelve months.
> 21 per cent revealed minimum ideation, saying they had felt
> that 'life just isn't worth living', or that 'life is so bad I feel
> like giving up'; another 19 per cent revealed high suicidal
> ideation, agreeing they had wished 'my life would end', or
> that they had been 'thinking of ways to kill myself'; a further
> 15 per cent showed suicide-related behaviour, saying they
> had 'told someone I want to kill myself', or had 'come close
> to taking my own life'; and 7 per cent said they had 'made
> attempts to kill myself'. Another study found 27 per cent of
> a sample of university students indicated suicidal ideation in
> the 'past few weeks'.[13]

Psychiatry often interprets this critical situation in terms of the self-punishing responses of students to the pressures of higher education. The menacing force driving them to suicide is said to be their perfectionism and performance anxiety.[14] But this is too limited. The deeper force driving them is not environmental but internal, not rational but archetypal. That force is the desire to live authentic lives, not to be fake, phoney or worthless. Young adults cannot stand a life that is not authentic. Psychiatry should look beyond its current horizon and begin to address the larger existential issues.

If two-thirds of university students think about suicide, what does this tell us? I put this question to an audience in Brisbane and one woman in the audience answered, 'Don't send your children to university, because they only become morbid and suicidal.' I don't think that is quite the point! The point is that the impulse to change the personality, to find a spiritual core, to seek rebirth, to move from ego to spirit, is archetypal and could be biologically programmed into our lives.[15] There are tragic consequences if we do not begin to think along the lines of rites of passage, that is, of life as a spiritual journey which requires initiation events and radical transformations.

In this regard, Mircea Eliade is again helpful and suggestive:

> In modern nonreligious societies initiation no longer exists as a religious act. But the *patterns* of initiation still survive, although markedly desacralized, in the modern world.[16]

Our life-transitions are no longer sacred but profane or pathological.[17] We no longer have painful initiations supervised by elders but personal traumas, crises and meltdowns. We no longer have initiatory 'deaths', but are plagued by suicidal thoughts, bouts of depression, burnout and self-doubt. Although we are obsessed with the personal self, we do not have secure self-esteem because this is gifted to us by something now inaccessible to the ego. Society no longer initiates us into the mysteries but the soul still goes through its age-old patterns of change and growth and reaches towards new stages of development. But without the language of the spirit, the soul is unable to fulfil its desires.

Today we are burdened with a troublesome inner life and what society fails to accept as its responsibility falls to the individual. The buck stops with the individual, even if society no longer sees any sense in the ancient initiations. The individual has to initiate him or herself into the new life phase, but how can we do this without shared wisdom? Without supervised initiations, we still need to make the perilous transition from innocence to experience, egocentricity to responsibility. The spirit still pushes us from one state to another, and nothing can stand in its way, not even a materialist society that has no belief in the sacred. Our consciousness may be emptied of all content regarding the initiations, but there is an older, unconscious part of the mind that still thinks in this way, that continues to imagine life in terms of death and rebirth. Something in us knows that we have to die, be displaced or interrupted, so that a greater life can emerge. Our dreams still speak this language of death and rebirth, and our emotions and desires continue to be influenced by this ancient thinking.

Suicide as a collective problem

The Aboriginal elders whom I have met consider suicide to be a cultural rather than an individual problem. This appears to reverse the concern for suicide found in our Western medical system, where the emphasis is placed on the suicidal person and why they are unhappy. In a meeting with Charles Ilyatjari, a *ngankari* or spirit doctor of the Pitjantjatjara people, I asked about the high rate of suicide in his community, especially among adolescent boys, and what could be done to prevent suicide in his community.[18] His response shocked me:

> There's too much worry about preventing suicide, and not enough worry about showing these boys how to die in ceremony. If we show them how to die in ceremony, their living takes care of itself.[19]

This pointed again to the importance of ritual in organising the emotional and psychological life. Charles Ilyatjari was saying that if Aboriginal boys could die in ceremony, they might not want to die in life. He was not blaming the boys themselves, or treating this as a personal problem. He was saying it is the lack of tribalised culture that is the problem. It is the modern world that is defective because it fails to provide the necessary rituals to allow people to terminate the natural self and emerge as a new personality. If we show them how to die in ceremony, in symbol and spirit, then their living will 'take care of itself'. It is an absence in *society* – not in the individual – that brings us to moral insanity and self-mutilation, because the duty of care that was invested in our spiritual wellbeing has been abandoned by the modern attitude. This was the voice of tradition casting judgment on the modern world. For Ilyatjari, to live outside sacred law is a dangerous state because we have no way to regulate the alien will that wants us to move from ego to spirit.

A similar view was put by another Aboriginal lawman I met from the Kimberley region of the northwest country.[20] David Mowaljarlai expressed his concern about the young men in the Kimberley who had succumbed to petrol, glue or plaint sniffing. Mowaljarlai visited a hospital which had a whole ward full of young men who had damaged their brains from chroming. He explained the situation in this way: 'All these boys, you see, lack ceremony. They haven't died in initiation. If you take away the sacred law, you take away their lives.'[21]

The men of high degree view the problem of self-destruction from the inside. They recognise that the spiritual core of the human being has needs, and if these needs are not attended to the results can be tragic. They discern that we only want to harm ourselves, or engage in self-injury, if we have not broken through to the authentic part of ourselves. When we touch the authentic part, we find a secure base and have no further desire to harm ourselves, only to nurture and deepen ourselves. But for them the problem is invariably connected with the condition of culture. The individual crisis reflects a larger crisis about loss of tribal law, loss of respect for tradition and ignorance about the necessity of ritual.

Who or what wants to die?

Jungian psychology uses a similar language to that of Aboriginal culture. In his classic work *Suicide and the Soul*, James Hillman writes that when we are beset by suicidal ideation we have to ask a psychological question: What is it within me that wants to die?[22] That question not only yields insight but also shifts something in the psyche. The dark force is no longer against us, but it now works with us. Or rather, we are working with it to determine what changes need to occur. If we can ask this question, we are no longer possessed by the impulse in such a way that we have no alternative other than to kill ourselves. We regain control of our emotions if we objectify the impulse that wants to harm us. In the context of the suicide epidemic, the symbolic approach would put it this way: 'Don't be surprised if you feel called to die, for something within you needs to die so that something else can live.'

What we can learn from the ancient wisdom of Australia is that where there is symbolic understanding, the spiritual aspect of our impulses can be realised. Where there is no symbolic understanding, the impulses of the soul are misinterpreted, leading to ideas of suicide. The impulses that drive us to change are powerful and lethal if misinterpreted. There is nothing more practical, useful or pragmatic than a spiritual wisdom that makes sense of the impulses that overtake us from within.

An ancient reflection from the early Christian tradition gives a final insight; the passage that follows is from the Gospel of Thomas from around CE 140, a Gnostic text which was found in Egypt in 1945 among the papyruses of Nag Hammadi:

> If you bring forth that within yourselves,
> that which you have will save you.
> If you do not have that within yourselves,
> that which you do not have within you will kill you.[23]

In our present context, this makes a very clear and real point. I take what is 'within yourselves' to refer to the spirit that longs to break free of the ego. If we dare to bring this forth, it will change and thus 'save' us by linking our lives directly with spiritual reality. If we do not draw out what is within, it will turn against and destroy us.

This is a hard lesson to learn, especially for those with sentimental ideas about God or ultimate reality. The god element in us is entirely capable of destroying us if we do not befriend it; if, in the language of the Jacob story, we refuse to give our name and ask to be blessed. The theme can be restated as one of sacrifice. If we sacrifice our orientation to the ego for an orientation to spirit, we win our lives and gain a new direction. If we do not sacrifice to the spirit, we are sacrificed to spiritual reality gone wrong.

CHAPTER 8

The Storm Gods and the German Psychosis

Thundering come the gods
Friedrich Hölderlin[1]

An ancient god let loose

When Jung announced 'the gods have become diseases',[2] he argued they have the capacity to addle and disorder not only the individual but entire societies and nations. He explained the explosion of violence and aggression in Germany in the 1930s and 40s as an uprising of energy that could not be understood by a rational model of behaviour. This explosion was an outbreak of pure, unmitigated evil which had arisen from the depths of the unconscious. It had come from the psyche but its origins were not from consciousness but an archaic level below it which is both godlike and demonic. He argued that this explosion of evil called for a symbolic container, such as a religion or a mythology, which might be able to account for such terrifying forces. But in the absence of a 'god' who might hold this lethal energy for us, we are contaminating ourselves with it: 'Something of the abysmal darkness of the world has broken in on us, poisoning the very air we breathe and befouling the pure water with the stale, nauseating taste of blood.'[3] A god of lust and murder had been unleashed in the German soul and yet it was invisible to those who were caught in its grip.

How could an archaic god take possession of a modern nation? To many, this seemed mystical and far-fetched. It seemed that Jung was retreating into what Freud had called his 'fairytale forest feeling'.[4] And yet there was a persuasive element to this theory, even though it strained credulity at first hearing. There was a need to become conscious of what had possessed an advanced technological society, to let it be named, recognised, and given an identity. If such things could happen in our time, the naming of the offending party might stem the upwelling evil and arrest its forward movement. If the psychic content remained at an unconscious level, people were likely to remain at its mercy. So long as evil remained unacknowledged, it would be projected upon others and experienced as a content outside the self.

In the case of Nazi Germany, the internal evil was projected upon Jews, gypsies and homosexuals, who became scapegoats for the nation. By projecting their evil, the Nazis could feel exonerated in their stance. The dark god could do with them what he willed and they would not raise any objections because evil had found an outlet. This is how the psychology of projection works, and how it serves to defend a pathological condition and prevent criticism from interfering. If things are bad it is someone else's fault, and to fight the chosen opponent is to rid oneself of the suspicion that one might be guilty. Projection is one of the greatest obstacles to civilised morality.[5]

Watching the developments in Germany from his neighbouring Switzerland, Jung felt that the outbreak pointed to possession by an archetype which was long thought to be dead and buried. He identified the archetype as the Nordic god Wotan, referred to in Norse mythology as the god of storm, magic and war.[6] Wotan, or Odin, was a psychopomp, a leader of souls to the other world, who had a special affinity with death. In the *Prose Edda* of Germanic paganism, Wotan is an ambivalent god, and if he is so moved he has the capacity to lead a people to ecstatic self-destruction and ruin.[7] In his 1936 essay 'Wotan', Jung writes:

> An ancient god of storm and frenzy, the long quiescent Wotan, [has awoken] like an extinct volcano to new activity, in a civilized country that had long been supposed to have outgrown the Middle Ages. We have seen him come to life in the German Youth Movement, and right at the beginning the blood of several sheep was shed in honour of his resurrection. Armed with rucksack and lute, blond youths, and sometimes girls as well, were to be seen as restless wanderers on every road from the North Cape to Sicily, faithful votaries of the roving god.[8]

The essay continues:

> By 1933 they wandered no longer, but marched in their hundreds of thousands. The Hitler movement literally brought the whole of Germany to its feet, from five-year-olds to veterans, and produced the spectacle of a nation migrating from one place to another. Wotan the wanderer was on the move ... Wotan is a restless wanderer who creates unrest and stirs up strife, now here, now there, and works magic. He was soon changed by Christianity into the devil, and only lived on in fading local traditions as a ghostly hunter who was seen with his retinue, flickering like a will o' the wisp through the stormy night.[9]

This old 'devil' seemed to Jung to be on the march, stirred to activity by several factors. The German people were looking for renewal after the devastating experience of the First World War and the loss of national pride and territory in the Treaty of Versailles. These losses and blows in the early part of the twentieth century seemed to set the scene for the atavistic reactivation of the Germanic spirit. At the same time, the decline of Christianity and its spiritual and moral ineffectiveness had opened the way to the possibility of a pagan revival, so that when the Germanic spirit was summoned by the crazed figure of Hitler, the spirit would not breathe the air of Christianity but of unadorned, lethal paganism. Jung described Hitler as a figure who was 'possessed' by a spirit which had 'infected a whole nation to such an extent that everything is set in motion and has started rolling on its course towards perdition'.[10]

The blond beast awaits redemption

Germany, Jung said, is like the nervous system of Europe and it registers first the crisis of our times – namely, that modernity is singularly incapable of dealing with the gods and demons of our nature. He argued that ever since the Middle Ages Christianity worked its moral and spiritual message on only one 'half' of the German psyche, the 'brighter half' which was open to moral persuasion, education and ethical values. But it left the old Germanic barbarian, and its pantheon of brutal gods, out of the picture. In an eerily prophetic essay of 1918, Jung predicted that the lethal aspect of the Germanic god would rise again:

> Christianity split the Germanic barbarian into an upper and a lower half, and enabled him, by repressing the dark side, to domesticate the brighter half and fit it for civilization. But the lower, darker half still awaits redemption and a second spell of domestication. Until then, it will remain associated with the vestiges of the prehistoric age, with the collective unconscious, which is subject to a peculiar and

ever-increasing activation. As the Christian view of the world loses its authority, the more menacingly will the 'blond beast' be heard prowling about in its underground prison, ready at any moment to burst out with devastating consequences.[11]

The prescience of this statement is astonishing, given the spectre of the Nazi uprising – and its 'blond beast' – of the 1930s and 40s. Christianity had not acted as a civilising influence on the German psyche as a whole. It could not engage the dark god Wotan but merely declared it to be the devil, banished or nonexistent. This god, who was central to the Germanic tradition and cultural legacy, was repressed, making the nation all the more vulnerable to its return and lethal attack.

What happened in Nazi Germany was a psychosis at a national level. We witnessed the eruption of psychic contents that could not be contained by the consciousness of the day. It was extraordinary how little resistance the Nazis faced in Germany among the ruling elites, the educated classes, the learned professors and leading-edge scientists. Even Jung himself was drawn into this madness for a short time before he could discern the psychotic signs of what he had originally thought was a positive revival of national pride.[12] The lack of critical resistance among the German intelligentsia revealed that the archetypal world was erupting with lethal force and could not be contained by the norms and standards of human decency and ethical codes. The psychosis could not be halted, and it ran rampant through all the nations of Europe and the world, stirring Japan to a similar kind of psychotic upheaval on the opposite side of the globe.

Godlikeness, inflation and immorality

Germany revealed in spectacular fashion the inadequacy of conventional morality to contain the dark gods of our nature.

These gods have the power to destroy personalities, societies and civilisations. Although depth psychology calls these gods 'psychic forces', they have nothing to do with the conscious mind, 'fond as we are of playing with the idea that consciousness and psyche are identical'.[13] The human psyche is a gateway or threshold for forces that come to us from beyond the human domain, and beyond the morally developed and 'Christian' part of the psyche. Wotan, the god of storm and frenzy:

> disappeared when his oaks fell and appeared again when the Christian God proved too weak to save Christendom from fratricidal slaughter. When the Holy Father at Rome could only impotently lament before God the fate of the *grex segregatus* [the flock of the church], the one-eyed hunter, on the edge of the German forest, laughed and saddled Sleipnir [Wotan's eight-legged horse].[14]

Jung argued that the ruling archetype does not remain in a dominant position forever, and the time of the Christian God seemed to have reached its historical limit.

As in the narrative of the Apocalypse, the millennial 'reign' of Christ seems to have been eclipsed by the darker forces of the unconscious, referred to in the Bible's Book of Revelation and in Yeats's poem 'The Second Coming' as the 'Beast' or 'Anti-Christ'. But whether we name the ascending archetype Wotan or Odin, Dionysus, Beast, Devil or Anti-Christ, the effect is still the same. As Yeats writes: 'Things fall apart; the centre cannot hold;/Mere anarchy is loosed upon the world.'[15] The bringer of this anarchy, for Jung, is the Germanic Wotan who 'has attacked Christianity on a broad front'.[16] He goes on:

> Wotan is a fundamental attribute of the German psyche, an irrational psychic factor which acts on the high pressure of

civilization like a cyclone and blows it away... A god has taken possession of the Germans and their house is filled with a 'mighty rushing wind'. It was soon after Hitler seized power, if I am not mistaken, that a cartoon appeared in *Punch* of a raving berserker tearing himself free from his bonds. A hurricane has broken loose in Germany while we still believe it is fine weather.[17]

He ends this passage with a memorable description:

Germany is a land of spiritual catastrophes, where nature never makes more than a pretence of peace with world-ruling reason. The disturber of the peace is a wind that ... scatters the nations before it like dry leaves. It is an elemental Dionysus breaking into the Apollonian order.[18]

What happened in Germany, he implies, could happen anywhere. He says it only happened in Germany because it is, as he put it, 'the nervous system of Europe'. The eruption in Germany was, for Jung, a sign of a disruption in Western civilisation, as the savage gods gather force in a society that continues to deny the reality of those forces and to insist that our rational order is intact. 'We are living on the edge of a volcano,' Jung said in his pre-war Terry Lectures at Yale, 'and there is, as far as we know, no way of protecting ourselves from a possible outburst that will destroy everybody within reach.'[19]

Once human beings fall under the sway of an archetypal power such as Wotan or Dionysus, it is difficult to maintain moral balance and civilised virtue. This is because the archetypal power is seductive. People feel themselves to be elevated beyond human limits and to be above good and evil, as Nietzsche put it.[20] The savage god fills those caught by its influence with a sense of euphoria and inspiration and in this state all things become possible. 'Where there's a will, there's a way' was a favourite slogan of the Nazis. So as Wotan drives the *Deutsche Volk* to restlessness and wandering, thence to organised marches and parades, aggressive militarism, storm-trooping and the invasion of other countries, the moral savagery of this spectacle is not observed by the majority of people because they are possessed by a negative spirit and under its spell. As the frenzy builds, so do the crimes, including terrorist activities, conspiracy, totalitarianism, eugenics, ethnic cleansing and genocide. The manic desire to establish a white master race, the *Herrenvolk*, seems to justify all atrocities just as it indicates the presence of a 'more-than-human' impulse which urges the people to overcome human limits in their desire to become like gods. The moral barometer is suspended in the midst of this frenzy and all is permitted.

The crisis of the West: Failing to acknowledge the gods

After the war, Jung felt that the West had still not learned the lessons of the Nazi uprising, but had merely placed a lid on the seething mass of disruptive energies. In his postwar essay 'After the Catastrophe', Jung wrote:

> For the first time since the dawn of history we have succeeded in swallowing the whole of primitive animism into ourselves, and with it the spirit that animated nature ... No one will deny the important role which the powers of the human psyche, personified as 'gods', played in the past. The mere act of enlightenment may have destroyed the spirits of nature, but not the psychic factors that correspond to them. The demons have not really disappeared but have merely taken on another form: they have become unconscious psychic factors.[21]

Our concept of the human psyche is too narrow, and we have left too much out of the picture. What has been left out is capable of destroying the world we live in, both in terms of the wellbeing of the human psyche and the integrity of the physical world. This is why Jung spent so much time trying to understand religious systems, cosmologies and mythologies. He did not just have a spiritual, aesthetic or cultural interest in these systems, but he felt that they were keys to the mental health and wellbeing of humanity now and in the future. He was vitally concerned about what happens to these projected deities once they are integrated or 'swallowed' by the human personality.

In Jung's view, civilisation will remain precarious and teetering on the edge of chaos until we recognise the need to build a conscious and cultural relationship with the gods. This would be a tall order, he realised, since intellectuals today habitually see the 'gods' as man-made entities which are transparently created by projection. But while acknowledging the anthropomorphic element in all cosmological and religious systems, Jung observed that the gods of the past were in fact human *responses* to pre-existing spiritual realities and not merely products and projections of the human mind:

> Although our whole world of religious ideas consists of anthropomorphic images that could never stand up to rational criticism, we should never forget that they are based on numinous archetypes, that is, on an emotional foundation which is unassailable by reason. We are dealing with psychic facts which logic can overlook but not eliminate.[22]

We pay a high price for our dismissive and brazen approach to the gods. We miss the glimpses of eternity and the orientations to the cosmos which such gods afford. We denigrate the stories that could give us direction and spiritual wealth.

The gods need culture and religion to clothe them and give them contour and shape. When culture and religion stop carrying the gods, they become invisible and are then more difficult to detect. As Jung says, they fall into the unconscious, and in that psychic darkness we need great effort and focus to track them. Writing in the early 1800s, the German poet Hölderlin felt that religion was no longer an effective container of the gods as it had become too dogmatic, and so the gods had disappeared from view. Society had banished them as well, due to its newfound rationalism. However, it was, Hölderlin said, the task of poets and artists to follow the trace of the fugitive gods. In addition to the arts and poetry, we might say that depth psychology devotes itself to tracking the gods in a godless time. This is a thankless task, but a necessary one.

Based on the assumption that the gods are projections of the mind, rational science set about to withdraw these so-called projections. But, Jung says, it did not know what it was doing:

> To the man of enlightened intellect it seems like the correction of a fallacy when he recognizes that what he took to be spirits is simply the human spirit and ultimately his own spirit. All the superhuman things, whether good or bad, that former ages predicated of the *daimonia*, are reduced to 'reasonable' proportions as though they were pure exaggeration, and everything seems to be in the best possible order.[23]

We thought we were doing the right thing by integrating religious projections into ourselves, but we were in fact swallowing archetypal spirit, and this would in turn make us demonic and evil. In numerous essays and articles, Jung argues that we have swallowed the gods, not realising what this means. Most humanists and secularists see the gods as empty ghosts, and believe no harm could come from withdrawing these projections into ourselves. For Jung, it is as if we had swallowed live plutonium, and yet we look at each other and say we are doing well and nothing has changed. 'Things are great' seems to be the motto of modernity.

Nietzsche as the portent of an epoch

Jung was moved and chastened by the example of Friedrich Nietzsche. Nietzsche said 'God is dead', withdrew the so-called 'projection' of God into himself and tried to become superhuman.[24] Jung wrote about Nietzsche in numerous essays and articles, and he delivered a mammoth two-volume seminar on Nietzsche's philosophical novel *Thus Spoke Zarathustra* that extended over six years (1934–39).[25] For Jung, Nietzsche represented the very real danger of modernity: that God and gods 'die', only to be reborn in the human being to become the cause of our downfall. The gods blow us up to demonic proportions, and we explode like a balloon, unable to contain the forces we have unconsciously adopted. In *Zarathustra*, Nietzsche wrote:

> God is dead! I teach you the Superman. Man is something that should be overcome. What have you done to overcome him?[26] …
>
> The Superman is the meaning of the earth. Let your will say: The Superman shall be the meaning of the earth![27] …
> All gods are dead: now we want the Superman to live.[28]

Nietzsche became obsessed with the idea that the death of God was a great opportunity for modern man. He could take the god power into himself, overcome his mere humanity, and take on the likeness of a god. The tawdry human being would pass away, to be replaced by a deity with great power and will.

Nietzsche would apply the Christian prayer to the superman or *Übermensch*: 'Thine is the kingdom, and the power, and the glory, for ever and ever.'

Jung felt that Nietzsche's life and career represented a fateful parable or warning to modernity. In losing our divine symbols, we fall more readily into 'godlikeness', which can destroy both the personality and civilisation. Jung said that we are moving ineluctably toward 'anarchy and destruction because inflation and man's hubris between them have elected to make the ego, in all its ridiculous paltriness, lord of the universe. That was the case with Nietzsche, the uncomprehended portent of a whole epoch'.[29] After announcing the death of God and the gods, Nietzsche aspired to become divine, as is evident in his identification with the grotesquely inflated prophetic figure of Zarathustra. Nietzsche became so inflated with his self-worth and idealism that his psyche exploded, and he ended up in an insane asylum in a state of catatonic schizophrenia, from which he never emerged.

But those with a religious education should hear echoes from the past. In the myth of Eden, Satan promises Eve that if she eats of the forbidden tree she will not die, but her eyes will be opened and she and Adam will 'be as gods, knowing good and evil'.[30] They eat the fruit and suffering is unleashed. Then there is the temptation of Christ, when Satan leads Christ to the top of a mountain, where he promises: 'All these things I will give you, if you fall down and worship me.'[31] We also have the memorable story of Lucifer, the angel who was the most beloved in the company of heaven. Lucifer got bored serving a higher power and decided he would attempt to usurp the power of the Almighty. As the story has it, he was cast out of heaven, darkened in appearance, and forced to live forever in the hellfire of the underworld. The moral of these stories is that a divine spirit that is incorporated into the ego becomes a 'fallen spirit'.

The temptation to become a god is fatal. Jung felt this was the ever-present danger of modern humanity: if we do not objectify the spirit as a sacred force and treat it with respect, we fall to a lower level and become possessed by spirit gone wrong. The ego is too small to 'withdraw' the gods into itself. The best way to ensure that we do not become demonic is to maintain an old-fashioned reverence for the higher forces. This, alas, requires humility, which the modern condition finds almost unattainable.

What happened to Nietzsche happened to Germany as a whole. It became inflated beyond its means, thought it could control the world, and exploded. Whenever I see images of the bombing of Dresden I think of this narrative. Nietzsche had prefigured the fate of Germany: the loss of human boundaries and the influx of 'godlike' powers, followed by the demonisation of those powers in psychotic ways. The German people had ingested archetypal spirit and it proved to be a lethal dose. Nazi Germany felt entitled, by superhuman sanction, to rampage through the world bringing genocide, havoc and destruction. The Allied forces of opposition eventually contained this outbreak of evil, but Jung warns it could happen again. By swallowing forces that do not belong to the human realm, we do not become *Übermenschen* as Nietzsche had hoped but demons of darkness.

We have demolished the credibility of the gods and rubbed out their old names, but the psychic factors to which those names point are still alive. The gods are far from dead, they are merely hidden from our awareness. In this regard, I think of a bumper sticker I saw recently in heavy traffic: '"God is dead" – Nietzsche. "Nietzsche is dead" – God'. Our enlightenment has been an endarkenment. It has been a false enlightenment, and we need to move to a new level of knowledge in an effort to protect our humanity against further assault from the dark forces. The key to this shift to a higher level is, paradoxically, for us to adopt a lower position and admit our humility and ignorance in the face of greater forces. This is hard to achieve when our educated intelligence tells us the gods are fictions and spirit a creation of our imaginations. We have to overcome this prejudice and return to a traditional view of the world, in which humanity can find its rightful place as an instrument of the divine, not as a would-be god who inflates and becomes demonic. We either humble ourselves before the gods or become humiliated by them.

The poet sings the warning song

In times such as ours, the challenge is not to succumb to hubris like Nietzsche or the Nazis, or to atheism like Marx or Freud. These are pitfalls along the way and we too easily fall into them. The true task at the end of the demise of religious order is to ask: 'Where is the god-principle to be found, after the death of God?' The notion that God or gods can disappear is an illusion of our making; we must know where they are now. In lines that have been made famous by frequent citation, Friedrich Hölderlin wrote:

> and what are poets for in a destitute time?
> But they are, you say, like the wine-god's holy priests,
> Who fared from land to land in holy night. (ll. 122–4)[32]

The role of the poet in 'destitute times' is to keep the memory of the gods alive, to inspire people to reimagine them, and find the courage to believe in them anew. The wine of ecstasy has been lost to formal religious life and now artists and poets are the 'holy priests' who are forced to take on this spiritual task, because religion has abandoned it to formulaic ritual and convention. However, this is easy to say and difficult to do. While Hölderlin recognised the need for the poet to track the gods, he was not successful in his own personal attempt to keep on track with the gods.

Tragically, like Nietzsche after him, Hölderlin observed the collapse of God and the gods and went mad. Seventy-five years before Nietzsche grappled with this crisis, and a hundred and thirty years before the Nazi catastrophe, Hölderlin was the embodiment and harbinger of what I would call the German national psychosis. What we find in Nietzsche and the Nazis was already in preparation in Hölderlin's life and work. There is a consistent development in German thought and philosophy, indicating that a disaster was waiting to happen in the national psyche.

In Hölderlin's elegy 'Bread and Wine', which I will explore, we find this sequence: the collapse of the gods, the dark night of the soul, the failure to develop a new relationship with the gods, and the 'thundering of the gods' into the psyche, where they trample and destroy the fragile human frame. Those who become aware of the death of the gods, and bring this tragic news to humanity, inhabit a psychic space which is full of danger. Unless poets and philosophers find a genuine alternative to the collapsed religious dispensation, they are liable to be torn apart by the savage gods whom they have not been able to accommodate. Being a poet, philosopher or depth psychologist comes with a moral and spiritual burden: it is not enough to announce 'God is dead' without showing the future course of the god-principle.

Hölderlin went mad but we do not know enough about his life to understand why. Freudians have claimed that his schizophrenia was due to intense emotional turbulence in early childhood.[33] However a Jungian approach might argue that he fell victim to a distinctly Germanic form of hubris. As Jung put it, 'Germany is a land of spiritual catastrophes.' Throughout Hölderlin's life he was at odds with the human and preferred the company of gods. 'Man is a god when he dreams,' he wrote in his novel *Hyperion*. He opened his psyche to the gods, but they split him apart – that is my own sense of why he went mad.

In his poem 'Bonaparte', Hölderlin writes:

> But this young man's spirit,
> The quick – would it not burst
> Any vessel that tried to contain it?[34]

No human vessel can contain the gods. If we try to hold them, they disintegrate the mind. Hölderlin knew this in his poetry, as an intellectual idea, but such knowing did little to protect him from the onslaught. What separates madness from health is whether or not we can find an appropriate container to hold these powers. Although they have fallen into the psyche, Jung insists we should objectify them as soon as possible, so they are not so close to us that they burn us up.[35] We need to recognise their eternal nature apart from our human nature. This separation of cosmic power from personal power is crucial, and only the cultivation of a spiritual attitude is able to carry us to safety and sanity.

It may have been with a degree of wishful thinking that Hölderlin penned these lines in his hymn, 'As on a Holiday':

> And the deeply shaken heart, sharing
> The suffering of the stronger god,
> Will endure the raging storms when he approaches.[36]

The approach of the 'stronger god' is not something that humanity can resist, unless we develop a religious attitude which separates the god from our humanity. Although he was trained as a Christian theologian but later abandoned his faith, Hölderlin seemed unable to maintain a religious attitude before the gods. He managed to put the Christian God to one side, like so many in Germany, but to the nature gods, and to the lower pantheon, he fell mightily into inflation. Hölderlin abruptly cut off this remarkable poem with a fierce reproach to himself. It is as if he recognised his own hubris and knew that it would be severely punished:

> My shame!
> And let me say at once:
> That I approached to see the Heavenly,
> And they themselves cast me down, deep down
> Below the living, into the dark cast down
> The false priest that I am, to sing,
> For those who have ears to hear, the warning song.[37]

Hölderlin's is a 'warning song' indeed. His poetry at the turn of the nineteenth century is a warning to humanity that it is in for a monstrous time. Although we elevate ourselves to the level of the Most High, the effect of such elevation is that we are thrown down, 'deep down', into the depths and made less than human. The Lucifer story haunts the background of this poem. The fact that this fierce reproach should end the poem is a sign that the creativity of the poet has acted in a compensatory way to his conscious idealism. He thinks of himself as at one with the gods, but his muse thinks differently. However, despite his eventual madness, there is much value in Hölderlin's poetry, as he struggled with the religious crisis of our times and the collapse of the sacred order.

Suffering and awareness

Hölderlin's argument in 'Bread and Wine' is that although we are 'urged on by a fire that's divine' (l. 40), we are unable to face this source and shield ourselves from it. But in vain we conceal what is 'deep within us' (l. 37). He does not seek to condemn the human race for its retreat from divine light, for in the words of this poem: 'Each of us goes toward and reaches the place that he can' (l. 46). We do what we able to and make the best of things, but we go wrong when we leave the gods out of the equation because they seem foreign to reason. By neglecting to keep faith with the gods, we face the wrath of punishment, since the point of our existence has been denied. We are prone to forget the Creator, and when we do so, the order that binds the universe comes unstuck. Hölderlin reminds us of our spiritual responsibility:

> But where are the thrones and the temples, where are the vessels
> Brimming with nectar, the songs delighting the gods?
> Where, then, where do they shine, the oracles winged for far targets?
> Delphi sleeps, and where echoes great Destiny now? (ll. 59–62)

We are too concerned with what is near at hand and we neglect the desires that are 'winged for far targets'. We forget that our desires have a spiritual origin and we live as if we are the creators of our own destinies. To live properly we need to take into account the more-than-human, and if we ignore this dimension we inhibit our desires and make happiness impossible. Hölderlin asks: 'Where does Fate suddenly break forth, full of omnipresent/Joy, thundering out of clear air over our eyes?' (ll. 63–4). We have lost the glory of the gods, the majesty of fate and the high horizons. We inhabit a flat, self-centred and low-level existence and the gods are forgotten, until they come thundering against us, like the hunter Wotan and his entourage: 'Thundering come the gods' (l. 119).

When we fail to reach for the gods, they have to 'thunder' down to us, so they can express themselves and break down our defences. We force the gods to invade us in a destructive manner, emerging from our own shadows. This is a terrifying prospect and hardly makes the human mind more likely to open its boundaries to the gods, since our instinct is to protect ourselves against attack. The attempt of the gods to restore balance can make the human shield itself even more, as Hölderlin writes:

> At first the gods come unperceived. Children try to get
>   Near them. But their glory dazzles and blinds and
> Awakens fear. (ll. 73–5)

When the gods crash through the barriers we are so dazed we don't see them as gods. They remain 'unperceived' since the conscious life is so removed from the numinous background, which is foreign to it. Their light is dazzling and only children notice them, since in their wonder and openness they are closer to the numinous than adults.

The gods awaken fear in adults and this is not such a bad response, since scripture claims that 'the fear of the Lord is the beginning of wisdom'.[38] We know that a god is near only because our freedom is curtailed. Hölderlin argues that humanity persists in this non-recognition of the gods because we have no access to what is taking place:

> Such is man; when the wealth is there, and no less than a god in
>   Person tends him with gifts, blind he remains, unaware.
> First he must suffer. (ll. 87–9)

He strikes a prophetic note which is to be the keynote of depth psychology a hundred years later. The only way humanity can recognise the gods, see them for what they are, is through suffering. Humanity will not voluntarily submit to the gods because we are content to be locked inside the envelope of reason. It is only when we are wrenched out of our comfort zone that we see reality for what it is. Much psychosis in human experience is precisely about the gods invading the human domain. The gods are reappearing in our time and suffering is the primary site of their unveiling.

Building a new vessel

We will have to work with diligence to build the moral strength to withstand this assault of the gods. They will keep coming at us, in menacing ways, until we are able to revere and contain these forces:

> The human vessel is weak and cannot always contain them,
>   Only at times can our kind bear the full impact of gods.
> Ever after our life is a dream about them. But perplexity
>   And sleep assist us: distress and night-time strengthen,
> Until enough heroes have grown in the bronze cradle
>   With hearts as strong as the gods, as it used to be. (ll. 113–18)

Interior strength needs to be found, else the gods will sweep us away with their intensity and blinding light. The ego is an unworthy container of the gods and if it tries to hold them it will be blown to pieces in schizophrenia. The ego's task is not to control the gods but to serve them and act as their instrument.

Hölderlin keeps arguing in this poem that a new vessel is needed to contain the gods. What then is the new vessel? The poet does not know; he seems in a quandary and confused about this. He would like to announce a new dispensation, a renewed church or temple, but he cannot. Running through the poem, which is in part an elegy on the passing of Christianity in Europe, is the theme that Christianity can no longer hold the divine for us. It has become too institutionalised, too human and limited. It offers the 'bread and wine' of the poem's title, but these do not transform us. We receive them, and we remain the same. We have made God too familiar and known, and the devastating, life-changing power of God no longer reaches us. We have killed off God by recreating him in our own image.

Hölderlin hints in the poem that it could have been existential isolation and loneliness which later drove him to madness. He could not share his knowledge of the living spirit with other human beings. He writes:

> No man could bear life so intense on his own;
> Shared, such wealth gives delight and later, when bartered
>   with strangers,
> Turns to rapture. (ll. 66–8)

It is in sharing our spiritual perceptions that community is created and cultures are formed. The horror that the gods bring, their wrath or dread, can 'turn to rapture' when we share this communion with 'strangers'. Indeed, others are no longer strangers when such rituals are shared. The message of the spirit is universal and the more it can reach the world, by means of culture and ritual, the more we can be assured that the rapture of spirit, rather than its terror, will be experienced.

We must invite the gods to enter our psychic space, but not identify with them. Our task is to hold onto our humanity while we welcome the gods back into our lives – our sanity and that of civilisation depends on this subtle balancing act. If we let the gods into our lives, they won't have to crash down the barriers to get inside. If we provide a front entrance, with ritual, decorum and beauty, they won't have to break through in the form of epidemics, disease and malaise. What humanity needs is a middle place between the flatland of rationality and the sublime realm of the gods. This is the symbolic role of the church or temple: they provide the meeting place between two worlds. Without a meeting place, a spiritual *temenos*, we fall prey to humanism and rationality on the one side, and to archetypal possession and godlikeness on the other. The first gives rise to banality, boredom and materialism. The second leads to the psychoses of Hölderlin and Nietzsche, and – on a different scale – to the murderousness of fascism and terrorism.

Moreover, humanism points the finger of blame at archetypal possession, fascism and other fanatical ideologies and says, 'Look what happens when we give in to spirit.' It sees these distorted social formations as the natural fruits of the spirit, thus bolstering its own egoic defences. When humanistic forces succeed in their war against spirit-possessed terror, they feel more convinced than ever that the gods are tyrants and generate nothing other than *Sturm und Drang*, a tempestuous struggle. This is the vicious circle in which modernity is caught, oscillating between a rationality that is boring and unproductive, and an irrational expression of archetypal forces which is positively insane. When the irrational forces are put back in place, the dynamics of spirit are banished and surrounded with an aura of shame.

Towards the turning

Hölderlin's 'Bread and Wine' inspired the German philosopher Martin Heidegger to write one of his most evocative essays on the spirit in the modern age. Heidegger's 'What Are Poets For?' is a meditation on the direction humanity must take if we are to win back the sacred and not allow ourselves to be overtaken by brutal forces. Heidegger knew about these brutal forces, because he himself had become a member of the Nazi party as Hitler rose to power and fascism seduced the nation into a frenzy of enthusiasm.[39]

After the defeat of Germany, and in response to Hölderlin's question about the usefulness of poets, Heidegger reflected in 1950:

The Storm Gods and the German Psychosis | 189

> The world's night is spreading its darkness. The era is defined by the god's failure to arrive, by the 'default of God'... The default of God means that no god any longer gathers men and things unto himself. The default of God forebodes something even grimmer, however. Not only have the gods and the god fled, but the divine radiance has become extinguished in the world's history. The time of the world's night is the destitute time, because it becomes ever more destitute. It has already grown so destitute, it can no longer discern the default of God as a default.[40]

Heidegger is alarmed that our darkness is not perceived as darkness, because we are too busy patting ourselves on the back for bringing about the triumph of science, technology and logic. In the artificial light of our materialism and the floodlit shopping malls and highways, we do not notice our spiritual darkness. The default of God is not seen because our ego has filled the vacant spaces left by the absence of God. Our ego has swollen to fill the void, just as Nietzsche had advocated. The loss of divine radiance is no longer perceived as a problem, because human industry is so frenetic that we do not pause long enough to sense the emptiness in our lives. If ignoring the darkness has become the norm, then the absent God is the void in us that we pretend not to see. By this reading, the God-shaped hole is God.

Heidegger claims we cannot move out of the cycle of darkness unless individuals explore the abyss and discover for themselves that there is something more to life than what society or technology offers. He argues that only individuals, acting on their conscience and spiritual need, can see through the lie of modernity, because the social institutions have vested interests in keeping us asleep while they continue to rush towards the illusory goals of wealth, progress and secularisation. Heidegger says that the hand of destiny waits for individuals to blow the whistle on modernity – and this is what he refers to as *the turning*:

> Long is the time [of darkness] because even terror, taken by itself as a ground for turning, is powerless as long as there is no turn with mortal men. But there is a turn with mortals when these find their way to their own nature.[41]

All this may seem odd coming out of Heidegger's mouth. He began his career as an existentialist who wanted to get rid of metaphysics and ban such words as *Geist* or spirit, and *Seele* or soul. But it seems that the suffering of war had served, among other things, to change this philosopher's mind. It was French philosopher Jacques Derrida who commented, in his groundbreaking work *Of Spirit*, that Heidegger began to break his own rules after the Nazi catastrophe: 'Heidegger often spoke not only of the word "spirit" but, sometimes yielding to the emphatic mode, in the name of spirit.'[42] Heidegger had experienced something of a 'turning' himself, and Derrida too, in his late career, turned towards the sacred in a way that was totally uncharacteristic of his early career.[43] Derrida admits that his own and Heidegger's turn to the sacred must seem 'anachronistic' and 'provocatively retro' to many readers, especially academics. He does not apologise for the way spirit has reappeared in philosophy: 'Spirit returns,' he writes, 'and the word "spirit" starts to become acceptable again.'[44]

It seems that all this 'thundering of the gods' upon human lives has awoken philosophy, at least, to the reality of the sacred. 'Hammer them, and they will yield' could be the motto of our times. However I take Heidegger's point that terror, 'taken by itself', is not a ground for turning. But this bolsters the idea that suffering continues to be the royal road to the sacred. The world's darkness has to be overcome by individuals who see through the pretence of modernity. As Heidegger puts it: 'In the age of the world's night, the abyss of the world must be experienced and endured.'[45] When mortals are able to endure that abyss, they might then be 'touched by presence, the ancient name of Being'.[46]

What philosophers call the abyss is what depth psychologists call the unconscious; it is the same thing. The lesson is similar in either case: if we are able to face the darkness of the unconscious, we might bear witness to the enlivening forces of our being. As Jung, echoing Goethe, put the same idea, modern humanity 'stands before the Nothing out of which the All may grow'.[47] Society shrinks away from the abyss in horror, yet it is precisely this encounter which will win back the spirit to our soulless culture.

The makeweight in the scales is the individual, acting on conscience and need. Only the individual can remind society that its supposed 'enlightenment' is a form of darkness. The individual has to move counter to society's repressions and renew our contact with the gods. Heidegger can have the last word: 'The gods who were once there ... return only at the right time, that is, when there has been a turn among men in the right place, in the right way.'[48]

CHAPTER 9

Spirituality, Medicine, Health

> It is far more the urgent psychic problems of patients, rather than the curiosity of research workers, that have given effective impetus to the recent developments in medical psychology and psychotherapy.
>
> Jung[1]

The changing landscape of health

Spirituality in medicine and health is a booming industry. The graphs that track publication activity in this area in the last few years show a steep upward curve, and developments are described as 'exponential'.[2] There is a lot of international excitement about this 'new' field, but spirituality in the health context is fraught and controversial. Until relatively recently, the *Diagnostic and Statistical Manual of Mental Disorders* referred to spirituality as a likely source of mental illness rather than as a cure for illness. Psychiatrists and therapists are generally wary of spirituality, and perhaps this is fair enough and to be expected, given that the term is used loosely today. It has become something of a buzz word and now seems to cover a multitude of mental states, some of which are of dubious status.

What some refer to as their 'spirituality' can be a form of neurosis or a maladaptation to reality, as Freud argued. He referred to the longing for religious experience as the 'universal obsessional neurosis of humanity'.[3] Even Jung doubted the validity of a range of 'religious' states and said that when patients start talking about spirituality the therapist ought to be wary that it does not announce an imbalance: 'When a prophet appears at a moment's notice [in the consulting room], we would be better advised to contemplate a possible psychic disequilibrium.'[4] As a popular saying has it, 'Those who talk to God are spiritual, but those to whom God talks back are schizophrenics.'

This sums up the complex and fraught relations between spirituality and mental health. If the job of the therapist is to ground disturbed patients in the real, it is to be expected that spirituality is not a welcome guest in the clinic. But it has to be said that not all forms of the spiritual are pathological, and some kinds of spirituality bring people to fuller health and a renewed relationship with reality.[5] However it is also true that our concepts of health and illness are constructed by social values and historical conditions, and these are subject to change and even reversal. Such reversal is evident, for instance, in the statement on the official website of the Royal College of Psychiatry in the UK: 'Spirituality involves a dimension of human experience that psychiatrists are increasingly interested in, because of its potential benefits to mental health.'[6]

What was regarded with suspicion twenty or thirty years ago is being viewed with new eyes today. Note, however, the pragmatic element here: spirituality is only of value if we can discern practical 'benefits' emerging from it. This is still a long way from religious spirituality, which is concerned with the spirit not because of what it does for *oneself* but what it does for others and for the Absolute Other.

We are living in a time in which notions of normality, health and illness are undergoing rapid change. The tables are being reversed, and even 'normality' is viewed with some suspicion. Jung foreshadowed this when he boasted: 'Show me a sane man and I will cure him for you.'[7] Today the spiritual is being included in the inventory of things that constitute the new normality. We are emerging from a long period of materialism and rationality, and just as our age is referred to as 'postmodern', so it could be argued it is 'post-secular' as well.[8] We live in an era in which it is not uncommon for people to talk about their search for spiritual meaning, just as they might talk about personal relationships or psychological issues.[9]

New wine of the spirit

However, the *spiritual* is radically different to what it was in the past. In more stable and conservative times, spirituality was felt to be the living core of religious life. Today it is felt to be the living heart of the individual and the location of spirituality has shifted from tradition to experience. This shift from formal religion to individual experience began with the sixteenth century Reformation and continues into our time. The effect has been that experience has been elevated above tradition, and 'spirituality' has been elevated above religion. On present trends, established traditions will be displaced and take a secondary role in society.

In the context of health and wellbeing, this has placed chaplains and pastoral care workers in an awkward situation because 'spirituality' has gone mainstream, which means it has been taken up by secular professionals and carers. In particular, nurses have seized the initiative on the spiritual dimension of health care, and books in this field have emerged from every corner of the globe.[10] A computer search on 'spirituality and nursing' in my university library yields over seventy recent acquisitions in this category alone, and journal articles are even more plentiful. This 'spirituality revolution', as I once called it,[11] has left some representatives of churches feeling without a current social context. It seems that there is 'new wine' of the spirit which cannot be poured into the old wineskins of traditional religions.[12]

Personally I believe that the new spirituality can be accommodated by the traditional faiths, but only if they are prepared to place experience before dogma, and individual encounters with God before the rules and regulations of religion. The approach needed today can be summed up by the phrase 'religion without religion', which has been used extensively by postmodern philosophers and revisionist thinkers.[13] Experience needs to be foregrounded and doctrine placed in the background, and it seems to me that clergy and chaplains who have a natural feeling for this kind of ministry know exactly what is required, and often do it well.

The key elements of this kind of chaplaincy are compassion for the suffering of others, love of humanity and intuitive understanding of the presence of a God who may not be recognised or named as 'God', especially by those who suffer in secular and humanist contexts rather than traditional religious ones. If clergy have the ability to recognise, with Jacques Derrida, that 'secularisation is only a manner of speaking',[14] and that those who suffer need to bring their suffering into a spiritual understanding no matter how 'nonreligious' they are, the way is open to a new kind of ministry. The national body of chaplains and pastoral carers which was called the Australian Association of Health and Welfare Chaplains has recently changed its name to Spiritual Care Australia. They do not want to be left out of the 'spirituality revolution' simply because they are tied to religious institutions.

Historical tensions

But I have noted a tone of despondency in some chaplains and church workers who feel they have no role to play in the new world in which religion no longer holds any special purchase on the spirit. In an essay significantly titled 'Old Religion, New Spirituality and Health Care', Carlton Brown, a hospital chaplain in Canada, wrote:

> The health care literature shows an increasing interest in 'spirituality' in health care. 'Religion' appears to be falling into disfavour because of its rigid boundaries, while 'spirituality' is seen as more creative and transcendent of boundaries. Unfortunately, chaplains and perhaps pastoral counsellors, too, are more frequently seen as 'religious' rather than spiritual. Health care is enjoying a spiritual revival, not a religious one, and its growth is being championed by a multi-disciplinary team of health care professionals, which excludes chaplains and pastoral counsellors.[15]

I understand his point of view, but feel these views could be too pessimistic. In my experience, secular health workers, doctors and nurses are willing and prepared to include church, synagogue or temple chaplains in their health and recovery programs. The only point of tension between these cultures is when church-related workers show rigidly doctrinal or fundamentalist tendencies, and are not receptive to the fluidity and diversity of modern experience. Nevertheless, some in the chaplaincy areas see themselves sidelined by cultural change and marooned by history.

I sense the return of an historical rivalry between patriarchal religions and matriarchal spiritualities. Since so many in the health field, and especially in nursing, are women who practise their intuitive, feminine versions of spirituality, we may well be seeing the contemporary echo of an ancient conflict between male religions and female spiritualities. Those who practised non-Christian spiritualities were once branded as 'witches' by those who feared them most. Today nurses are keen to point out that the so-called witches who were burnt at the stake were practising the arts of herbalism and 'women's healing knowledge' in a time in which men dictated the terms. It would not surprise me if health care and medicine were to become the modern theatre in which this historical tension is revived and expressed. However the tables have turned in our era, and the patriarchal traditions can no longer exert their authority over unorthodox activities. Instead, they have to find their place in the range of options in a pluralist landscape and if necessary adopt a subsidiary role.

The spiritual was once bracketed as religious and controlled by male institutions, but in the postmodern world it is increasingly seen as an entirely natural element of human psychology. It is no longer classified as supernatural, or needing patriarchal endorsement or a revelation from on high to legitimate it. Spirituality is viewed as individualistic and diverse, and not requiring the institutional infrastructure or tradition that once strove to spread the good news to people. Perhaps the word 'spirituality' is at fault and needs to be changed, because it carries historical associations of supernatural intervention, and it suggests a dualism between body and spirit, or mind and nature, which is no longer meaningful in a world which tries to treat the human being in terms of a holistic paradigm of body, mind and spirit. But spirituality remains the favoured term, despite its historical legacy of supernaturalism and dualism. It behoves our health care professionals and medical experts to re-educate themselves regarding the new discourses on spirituality and health. This area must be taken seriously as an important dimension of experience and not left to the margins, where it can be exploited by right-wing religious fanatics or by the commercial forces of the New Age and popular culture.[16]

If spirituality gathers on the margins, it is because the mainstream has been unable to include the spiritual, which has been split off and treated as eccentric. This gives spirituality a certain freedom to find its own voice, but it often means it is at the edges of respectability, where shonky activities take place. The world today seems full of dubious offerings, including retreats, workshops, books, tapes and programs, which operate under the general rubric of 'spirituality in health and wellbeing'. Some of these offerings are barely disguised exercises in manipulation, indoctrination and money-making. It is best for all concerned if the spiritual element is taken into the mainstream and treated with respect, in which case it can also be treated with a critical eye and reasoned discernment. We pay a real price for spirituality now being severed from the parent tree of religion, where it was once checked by morality and often conducted for charitable rather than commercial purposes. What we do know is that the spiritual will not go away. If it continues to be rejected by institutional authorities, it will proliferate at the margins of society where it can do as much evil as good by virtue of it being split off and unregulated.

Wisdom and medicine

Most of our health care professions and the discourses that support them have been shaped by a secular and humanist paradigm that has ignored the spiritual. Therefore many health care workers have had to do their spiritual training by themselves, or with small groups of like-minded people. Often it is a matter of individual discretion and self-tuition rather than professional training as such. As mentioned, nurses seem to have taken the leadership in this regard, but overall it seems to be a grassroots or even an underground movement, not something that has been delivered in professional trainings. In times of cultural transition, the individual worker is often ahead of the policy and curriculum designers, who may be working from old or out of date assumptions about health and wellbeing. As a result, the discourses on spirituality have been grassroots and have taken the official institutions by surprise.

The Western model of health is in a difficult situation at present and is not coping well with the radical changes. Many in the community are turning away from conventional medicine towards so-called complementary medicine, whose sources are found in the East or in the pagan and pre-Christian West.[17] The internal healing capacity of the body-mind-spirit is new to the Western mainstream, but not new to the East, or to Western gnosticism, alchemy, wicca or hermeticism. In the same way that some chaplains are reconstructing themselves as workers in the non-religious field of spirituality, so a great many medical practitioners are retraining in non-Western medicine, especially in Chinese, Japanese and Indian healing systems, to meet the new demand for a holistic approach to health. Professionals in all fields are learning to change and adapt to new values emerging with the spirit of the time. But it has been hard for the medical schools and training programs to reconstruct themselves overnight. It is not simply a matter of adding 'spirituality' to the existing body of knowledge and stirring it in.[18] The whole point of spirituality, and the holistic paradigm that it supports, is that it challenges everything we know, especially if our knowledge is based on dualistic or mechanistic assumptions that holism does not support.

Jung's problematical reputation

Jung is a contender for the status of grandfather of spirituality in mental health. Other contenders for this category would be William James in America and Rudolf Otto in Germany, who opened up the discourse about the healing power of the numinous. Many scholars and writers in spirituality studies today do not seem to understand Jung's central place in the field, and this is possibly because of his obscure standing in academia in general and psychology in particular. When psychology uprooted itself from philosophy and the humanities and tried to convince itself that it could be a pure science, philosophical psychologists like Jung and his cohort got left out of the picture. As psychology formed itself as a hard science, and got rid of everything that seemed mystical or vague, Jung was banished from the discipline and refused entry to the carefully guarded fortress.

But ironically, now that every discipline in the health sciences, including psychology and psychiatry, struggles to include spirituality within its intellectual horizons, researchers are reinventing the wheel rather than going back to the pioneers who were controversial figures in the past. Perhaps it is less painful to reinvent the wheel than it is to admit that the discipline made some bad decisions and got things wrong when it operated under a purely rational and reductive paradigm.

It is somewhat strange to see hundreds of new books and articles produced today in spirituality and health with few or none looking back to the early days of the field. There is a sense that spirituality is a new area without a history, and researchers rush forward with excitement believing that everything lies ahead. Perhaps they are fearful of looking back in case they don't like what they find. While it now seems possible to turn to spirituality in a serious way, there is still work to be done about repairing the damage of the past. For instance, Harvard psychiatrist Gregg Jacobs is the author of *The Ancestral Mind*, which concerns itself with spirit, soul and ancient sources of wisdom in the psyche.[19] For all the world it looks like a replica of Jung's researches of the 1930s. But Jung does not rate a mention in this research, even though it is very close to his work. Psychiatrists are wary of making any connection with a famous or perhaps infamous psychiatrist like Jung, who was discredited by his profession precisely because he turned to spirituality. Somehow, a stain remains on the past and new researchers don't want to face it. If the field has amnesia, it could be due to the desire to protect itself from a wound, but it has to deal with these wounds if it is to have integrity.

Meaning and spirit in healing

Jung was one of the first of the modern medical practitioners to publicly criticise the medical model and argue that its limitations had to be overcome:

> In the course of the nineteenth century medicine had become, in its methods and theory, one of the disciplines of natural science, and it cherished the same basically philosophical assumption of *material causation*. For medicine, the psyche as a mental 'substance' did not exist, and experimental psychology also did its best to constitute itself a psychology without a psyche.[20]

Jung introduced into medicine the idea that the doctor has a responsibility to bring meaning or spirit into a patient's life. But this was the last thing medicine wanted to hear at the time. It saw itself as a child of natural science and shared its assumption of material causation. To science, meaning seemed insubstantial, ambiguous and elusive. How could such a thing influence the healing of neurosis, much less the organic diseases of the body? The old paradigm assumed that the body was a machine, and we can understand its working parts in purely chemical and physical terms. Jung could see this was a flawed argument, and would eventually have to be replaced by a more holistic point of view. For his trouble, Jung was treated as a 'witch doctor' who possessed primitive or outmoded views on medicine. But it was medicine itself that was out of date, and in the eighty years or so since Jung made these pronouncements his criticisms have been vindicated.

The official motto of the Royal College of Psychiatrists is 'Let Wisdom Guide', but this reads ironically in view of the current state of general psychiatry. The medical and healing professions have forgotten, or rather intentionally renounced, their roots in the spiritual origins of healing, origins which in our Greek heritage go back to the temples of Asclepius, the 'Divine Physician', and to the dream incubation chambers of Cos, Pergamon and Epidaurus. The healing professions are suffering from a form of amnesia, and are called to remember what they have forgotten through centuries of rationality and neglect. Important recent books are urging the professions to remember their ancient background, for instance, John Swinton's *Spirituality and Mental Health Care: Rediscovering a 'Forgotten' Dimension*.[21] Culturally we are at a turning point where we need to take a detour back to the past to gather up what has been lost from our scientific model, which has privileged a purely rational kind of knowing.[22]

Re-shamanising medicine

What has been lost to our knowledge is wisdom, which is broader and more comprehensive than rational science. Wisdom teaches that there are forces at work in life that are greater than rational motivations and larger than the biological laws of cause and effect. Wisdom introduces us to the view that consciousness is not limited to the human being but extends beyond the ego and includes forces that we have not yet imagined. In the past, such forces were mythologised as gods, angels and spirits. These forces have the capacity to heal and make us whole, which is why medicine has historically been linked with religion, cosmology and shamanism. Along with medicine, religion may be forced to remember its ancient heritage if it is to remain relevant in a new holistic paradigm, in which spirit can no longer be separated from the body.

The ministry of Jesus, from which the churches have radically departed, was focused on healing the sick.[23] For hundreds of years healing was part of the Christian church's business, but as medicine separated from religion, founding itself on materialistic laws, the churches pulled away from healing and focused on worship and ritual. As Brian Inglis has argued, priests eventually attended patients 'only for spiritual consolation', and with prayers 'designed to supplement treatment, not to supersede it'.[24] If we think of indigenous or tribal societies, the spiritual leader of the group was also the 'medicine' man or woman who was trained in the knowledge of spirit and body. There was no separation of these social functions, which in the West split apart into religion and medicine.

What we are made to realise as we move toward a more holistic model of health is that 'religion and medicine find their common roots in ancient understandings of disease and healing'.[25] If this is the case, then the way to the future is to return to the past and explore what has been lost. Illness and disease has historically been seen in a much larger and broader context than Western medicine has allowed. Illness is not just about the body and its 'chemicals' or physical laws, but about the forces and functions of the psyche or soul. As Carlton Brown puts it: 'Shamanism attributed illness to a loss of soul-power [and] both the ancient Greeks and the biblical Jews frequently attributed disease to a disfavoured God.'[26] By making adjustments to the reality of the spirit, by seeing what needed attention in the subtle or invisible realm, healing could take place and patients could be cured. In the temples of Asclepius, the priest would pay attention to the dreams of the patient and carefully observe what spirit or force was asking for attention in the symbolic patterns of dreams. If these internal suggestions were respected and acted upon by the patient, a form of healing could take place.

Most of this wisdom has been lost, but it can be recovered, albeit in a new way and using a language that is scientific rather than mythological. Instead of speaking of gods or spirits, we might speak, following Freud, of drives of the psyche, or, following Jung, of archetypes of the unconscious. Our language will have to remain poetic and open to some extent, to grasp the subtle nature of mental forces, but we will need to recognise that the spiritual dimension requires a language that changes with the spirit of the times. Because our time remains scientific, the language of spiritual healing will have to appear as scientific, even if, to some people, Jung's theory of archetypes seems just as *mystical* as the theory of gods and spirits that it seeks to replace or update. But some reappropriation of the nonrational side of experience will need to take place. The main difference between modern and ancient spiritualities is that modern systems will need to view their spiritual models through metaphorical rather than literal eyes. The spiritual forces themselves are unknowable, and any attempt to know them will necessarily happen in a metaphorical way with a limited life-span.

In fact, one way to discern shonky spiritual systems today is to ask whether they take themselves literally or not. If the answer is yes, then we are in the presence of quackery or indoctrination. This is the great danger of New Age appropriations of ancient spiritual systems, such as shamanism, healing technologies and divinatory codes. The New Age advocates are right to be interested in these ancient systems, but utterly wrong to bring them into the modern period in a literal or untransformed way. Everything has to be discovered anew, and the spiritual knowledges of the past have to encounter, and be transformed by, modern science and reason. Only then are they acceptable to modern consciousness and only then are we justified in using them in the modern context. Otherwise, critics can justifiably identify such activities as examples of cultural regression.

Spirituality cannot be controlled

When I notice the resistances that some in the health professions put up to spirituality, I often feel that the nonrational is being confused with the *irrational*. The nonrational is not supernatural or occult but is an entirely normal and natural element of human experience. The irrational, on the other hand, is contrary to rationality and potentially dangerous and disruptive to mental and physical health. These distinctions were made by Rudolf Otto in *The Idea of the Holy*.[27] We need an appreciation of life beyond or outside rational motivations, to understand the field of spirituality and its potential to heal or 'make whole' the injured or diseased psyche.

It is the rational approach to life and healing that causes some physicians to dismiss spirituality and regard it as lunatic or fringy. The haste with which some dismiss this matter in the clinical setting is often justified as a desire to protect the client from delusional ideas. As London psychiatrist Andrew Powell concedes:

> Patients' attempts to talk about their spiritual beliefs and concerns are often met with incomprehension and mistrust. Sometimes the chaplain will be called in but frequently the patient will be advised not to dwell on such matters, or else will find those experiences dismissed as delusions or hallucinations.[28]

But such dismissal, designed to protect the client from delusions, might express a desire to protect the profession from the incursion of spirituality into its precinct. This might represent a challenge that is too hard to cope with, given the model upon which the profession is founded. Andrew Powell continues:

> The psychiatrist, frequently beleaguered and trying to maintain an emergency service with pitifully inadequate resources, relies first and foremost on medication, second on social support networks, third on psychological interventions where deemed appropriate and least of all on spiritual sources of strength. On top of that, he or she is three times less likely to hold a religious faith than the patient.[29]

There is often a gap between the assumptions and values of the health professional and the spiritual demands of the client, and this has been called the 'spirituality gap'.[30] We can see from the above sketch of a typical approach from a practising psychiatrist how difficult it is to bring the spiritual aspect into Western medicine. Spirituality appears to be operating on a different level and is alien to the values of contemporary practice. To make matters worse, the hospital chaplain is sometimes as confused and beleaguered as the psychiatrist, especially if he or she has not understood the difference between formal religion and spirituality.

Professional therapists, like professionals everywhere, prefer to be in control of a situation, and are reluctant to allow a meeting to drift off into areas of the unknown. Freud pointed out that therapists do not like to be 'exposed' by their clients or found wanting. Freud talked of 'the feeling of repulsion in us which is undoubtedly connected with the barriers that rise between each single ego and the others'.[31] How much more must this 'feeling of repulsion' arise when clients try to take therapists into the unchartered waters of the spirit? When professionals sense they are losing control, they are likely to pull back and steer the conversation in a different direction. In this way, clients may be deprived of exploring spiritual questions. We have to face the fact that most therapists are not trained in spiritual matters, and are often 'flying blind' in this realm. However this is a flaw in our system of knowledge, and not necessarily a personal failing of individual practitioners.

Spirituality as the meaning that quickens

What is spirituality in the context of mental health? Spirituality is the experience of connectedness with a transcendent meaning or force. This does not have to be as grand as it sounds. We do not have to be a special prophet or genius to discover the transcendental world. We simply have to make a 'good enough' connection with something meaningful, so that the spirit in us is justified and feels content. There has to be some kind of acknowledgement of a higher power or authority in our lives, and when this is achieved we can acquire a new sense of identity and a new energy is at our disposal. The rest takes care of itself, since an outlet is found for our libido, and we can get on with living *sub specie aeterni*, or under the aspect of eternity. When we achieve the right relationship to eternity, we know how to live in time and space. But without the eternal connection, time and space appear meaningless, and we cannot stand a meaningless life. As Nietzsche said, 'If we have our own why in life, we shall get along with almost any how.'[32] While spirit might sometimes be seen as the instigator of suffering, it is true that without spirit our suffering cannot be endured. Without the sense that our suffering is meaningful, it is hard to put up with it. We become demoralised and numbed to others, the world and to ourselves.

The sick patient is searching for a personal connection with spiritual meaning. In Jung's view, 'A psychoneurosis must be understood, ultimately, as the suffering of a soul which has not discovered its meaning.'³³ Lack of meaning can make us physically sick and mentally disturbed. 'Meaning' may seem inconsequential to some, and they may refer to it as fantasy or fiction. But Jung is convinced that the role of spiritual meaning has been hugely underestimated in the approach to disease:

> But 'meaning' is something mental or spiritual. Call it a fiction if you like. Nevertheless this fiction enables us to influence the course of the disease far more effectively than we could with chemical preparations. Indeed, we can even influence the bio-chemical processes of the body. Whether the fiction forms itself in me spontaneously or reaches me from outside via human speech, it can make me ill or cure me. Fictions, illusions, opinions are perhaps the most intangible and unreal things we can think of; yet they are the most effective of all in the psychic and even the psychophysical realm.³⁴

Jung goes on to describe this 'fiction' as a 'healing fiction' and 'the meaning that quickens'.³⁵ It quickens the body, mind and spirit because the person feels connected to the world and no longer shut off inside an alienated ego. The meaning that quickens is the bread by which the soul is nourished, and by which the state of crippling alienation is overcome. Such meanings might seem illusions to the rational mind, and even to the mind of the sick person who hungers for them, but they act as a balm to the soul and a cure to our search for justification and purpose.

Spirituality as a wild zone

Spirituality is a cry for hope in the midst of despair and chaos. With so much collapsing in today's world, with the demise of traditions and structures that were central to life in the past, including moral norms and ethical guidelines, authority figures, religious institutions, youth clubs, family networks and social supports, many people are turning to 'spirituality' to find something solid, secure and reliable in their lives. And why not? The winds of change are howling in the streets, and people seek solace in the spirit, and communion with forces beyond the ephemeral forms that are collapsing. It has always been the case that when a social order is crumbling, the people seek, by way of compensation, to make a new pact with the forces of eternity, forces beyond time.

Some people want to define spirituality according to a definite set of meditation practices, religious rituals or exercises, and while these are undoubtedly helpful in our pursuit of the spiritual they must not be seen as essential. We are forever trying to put things into formulas and rules. But I believe the seeking of the spiritual is a personal choice, and we cannot pin it down to any one tradition or code. It is best that we are not too prescriptive about it, and that our definitions are general and broad. For me, spirituality is not merely something we do when we are being self-consciously spiritual. It is the pursuit at all times – and not just at meditation or prayer times – of *a particular attitude* towards ourselves, the world and others. The attitude is one of reverence, awe and openness to mystery. The spiritual attitude impels us to search for connectedness, and this search intensifies when we live in disconnected times such as now. There are many kinds of connection, but spiritual connection seeks a relationship with something greater than ourselves, something that links us to the cosmos, but also to what is most genuine and true in ourselves.

Spiritual connectedness need not express itself in otherworldly ambitions, in a longing to live in the heavens, to fly above the world or a desire for death. Spirituality, if grounded in reality and a love of life, can arise through our connections with others, society, nature and existence. This connectedness can restore flow and meaning to lives, make us feel part of a whole, connect us to our ancestry and family line, enrich us by restoring faith in community, ground us in our particular time and place, and alleviate the pain of being isolated, lonely and apart. These are precious and life-giving gifts, and it is little wonder that spiritual achievements have been associated through the ages with such symbols as gold, treasure, living water, the elixir, flow, joy, delight, bliss – in fact, every imaginable metaphor has been attributed to the achievement of connectedness with the spirit.

A client-led recovery of the spiritual

According to recent medical research, it is often the suffering patient who brings the question of spirituality into the clinical setting.[36] The person suffering from a neurosis, mental illness, addiction or compulsive disorder tentatively expresses the barely formed view that a lack of 'spiritual' meaning in his or her life might have something to do with their malady and feeling of despair. In our non-religious era, people often have inadequate language to express this feeling of spiritual absence, but they grope towards it, using their intuition and whatever resources they can find, whether these are drawn from organised religion, popular music, movies, conversations or the New Age movement. The attempt by suffering patients to express their illness in terms of a spiritual malaise is a problem that Jung first noted in his 1932 essay 'Psychotherapists or the Clergy', but we are only becoming aware of this matter today.

Spirituality has arisen as a major item on the agenda of health and healing professions not because university professors have had conversion experiences, but because suffering clients want to bring this vague and often ill-formed concept into the therapeutic setting. Today we can speak of a client-led or grassroots recovery of the spiritual dimension in health and healing.[37] It is a sign that civilisation is in transition, that men and women 'do not live by bread alone'. The client-centred therapist has to learn to go along with this drift into spiritual discourse, even if he or she does not fully comprehend its meaning. If the spiritual has been raised as part of the healing process, there should be some acknowledgement that this element has crept into the professional setting, even if it makes both parties embarrassed because of their secular groundings.

If the health professional happens to belong to a particular religious tradition, he or she must, I believe, resist the temptation to turn the client into a new recruit, or to treat the disturbance as a sign that some particular religion is lacking. Postmodern spiritual hunger cannot always be nourished by traditional religious solutions.[38] We live in fragmented, pluralist and diverse times, and we can no longer assume that one spiritual solution fits all problems. There has to be receptivity to the particular case, a sensitivity that reaches out to the suffering patient and empathises with their condition and search.[39] But if 'spirituality' is suddenly being discussed across disciplines and in conferences and research seminars, it is because clients and patients are bringing questions of spiritual meaning into the clinical setting, often to the bafflement of professionals. We are in the midst of a revolution from below, and it is often from below that real change takes place.

We must not assume that this interest in the spiritual is a marginal activity of sick individuals in need of healing. This hunger afflicts not only the patients in clinics and counselling rooms, but society as a whole. Beneath the broken promises of secular society – its promises of wealth, happiness and fulfilment – is a pervasive sense that life is not as meaningful as it once seemed to be. Prior to modernity, people had religion to help them make sense of the bigger picture. Today, without religion, people are taking matters into their own hands, and the phenomenon of 'spirituality' is a response to disillusionment, an attempt to go in search of meaning and find the vision that adds depth and purpose to life.

It is not true that an unfortunate few are spiritually afflicted and the rest of us are healthy. To the extent that we are cut off from the reality of spirit and its healing capacity, we are all diseased at this level. Patients take these painful journeys of the spirit not only because their personal lives lack meaning but because modern consciousness as a whole lacks meaning. The mentally afflicted are the involuntary pioneers of a new dispensation, the human experiments, as it were, in which a new picture of reality is being forged.

The art of spirituality in a clinical setting

Jung felt that meaning or spirit cannot be imposed on the patient from above as an act of religious manipulation, but must be discovered with the client in the process of the therapeutic encounter. It is certainly not the job of professionals (be they medical doctors, psychiatrists, psychologists, counsellors or nurses) to foist their particular beliefs upon patients and suffering people. The task in therapy is to listen to the spiritual needs of the client, and in this art of listening we have to become acutely aware of the difference between religion per se and the religious attitude in the soul, as Jung explains through the example of his own practice history:

> During the past thirty years, people from all the civilized countries of the earth have consulted me. Many hundreds of patients have passed through my hands, the greater number being Protestants, a lesser number Jews, and not more than five or six believing Catholics. Among all my patients in the second half of life – that is to say, over thirty-five – there has not been one whose problem in the last resort was not that of finding a religious outlook on life. It is safe to say that

every one of them fell ill because he had lost what the living religions of every age have given to their followers, and none of them has been really healed who did not regain his religious outlook. This of course has nothing whatever to do with a particular creed or membership of a church.[40]

If there is an imposition of belief from outside, the individual religious attitude may not be realised and may even be thwarted or undermined. The important task of the therapist is to bring to birth the religious attitude that is most 'therapeutic' for this particular suffering soul. This means that one's own prejudices and beliefs have to be bracketed out in the therapeutic encounter, and one has to resist the desire to pass on to the patient one's own cherished worldview. This becomes all the more acute in the case of therapists who have a religious belief of their own, and who are keen to 'share' it with their clients. The good therapist does not impose, but draws out from the client what needs to be brought into consciousness. To put it in Jung's words: 'If the doctor wants to guide another, or even accompany him a step of the way, he must feel with that person's psyche.'[41]

Jung is a complete relativist on this point. He does not believe that only one source of the holy can have a healing influence. He does not subscribe to the view, for instance, that only Jesus can give the salvation we need. Jung believes that the numinous can derive from countless sources and religious traditions, from mythologies, cosmologies, esoteric systems, arts and sciences. He believes that the numinous is present, at least potentially, in everyday experience, and can be felt and made known through meaningful coincidence, synchronicity and a symbolic relationship with the facts of the world. He does not believe that institutions of faith or creedal doctrines should regulate the spiritual experience but that such experience should occur spontaneously, as we engage in life with depth and commitment.

My hope is that the health care professions can emphasise spirituality and not organised religion. What needs to develop in the clinical context is an interest in what could be called a *generic spiritual attitude*. The clinical discussions need to draw the spiritual element out of a person, not impose it from above. This will allow the person to choose the pathway that is right for him or her. Therapy and consultation can help people find the courage to believe in an invisible level of support, but it is not up to the professionals to supply the specific language or tradition. This makes general acceptance of a generic spirituality all the more attractive and desirable in today's world, and especially important for professionals maintaining open and ethical conduct.

The aim is to find a large healing framework, which is potent enough to evoke a sense of the sacred but loose enough to allow variations on a theme. The professional's task is not to evangelise or proselytise but to encourage people to discover what is life-giving and creative in their experience of the world. Healing is achieved when the self connects to that which is 'more than' itself, but a therapist's belief system, however genuinely held, can act as a barrier to the healing forces within the client's immediate world. The key for professional practice is to use the patient's language, not our own, to access and mobilise the healing forces. This requires listening instead of preaching, and the results will be liberating rather than oppressive. The art of spirituality is the art of deep listening, of attunement to the Other within and beyond the self. This is spirituality in action, not only as a path for the patient but also as a clinical method for the carer.

CONCLUSION

The Numinous as a Source of Healing

Healing may be called a religious problem.
Jung[1]

Healing as reconnection

Viewing illness through a spiritual perspective, the process of healing is twofold. At one level the personality needs to connect with the unconscious and integrate with it into a broadened concept of self. We might call this linking back with lost or buried parts of the self. As this effort is being carried out in the name of personal development, there is a spiritual enterprise to attend to at the same time, which is linking with spirit.

What 'spirit' is in real terms, we do not know. It appears to be transcendent, and being transcendent it transcends our ability to know it with our minds. We can experience its presence in our lives, and in particular, we can experience its absence or loss when our lives get derailed. Spirit is not lost or buried like those parts of the self that have fallen into the unconscious because it was never conscious in the first place. But strangely, one might almost say magically, as we reach into the unconscious to bring up what has been lost, spirit tends to surface along with our lost parts. We get more than we counted on by reaching into the psyche and bringing up the parts that need to be restored to consciousness. In this way, our psychological and spiritual work seem to go hand in hand.

The absence of spirit often generates a longing to reconnect with spirit, but this longing can be interrupted by our ego if it has become defensive, hardened or rational in its orientation. An overly intellectual attitude, and a demand for proof or reason, can kill off the life of the spirit and prevent us from experiencing its healing field. In our highly intellectualised world this is a persistent danger. Jung is uncompromising in his view that Western intellectualism is hugely responsible for the proliferation of neuroses:

> Anyone who cherishes a rationalistic opinion ... has isolated himself psychologically and stands opposed to his own basic human nature. This contains a fundamental truth about all neuroses, for nervous disorders consist primarily in an alienation from one's instincts, a splitting off of consciousness from certain basic facts of the psyche. Hence rationalistic opinions come unexpectedly close to neurotic symptoms. Like these, they consist in distorted thinking, which takes the place of psychologically correct thinking. The latter kind of thinking always retains its connection with the heart, with the depths of the psyche, the tap-root.[2]

This reminds me of Patrick White's remark in his classic novel *Riders in the Chariot*, where he has his central character announce that 'the intellect has failed us'.[3] The intellect has failed not only because it is limited and narrow in its operations, but because we have relied too heavily on it. It makes a great instrument but a lousy master. Our education system places too much emphasis on intellect, which is unreliable and likely to convince us that God and gods do not exist, that all that exists is what we can see, that rationality can define reality – all toxic and dangerous positions when it comes to the care of the soul. We think of ourselves as wise and clever to have rejected the ancient world of beliefs and superstitions, but when we are landed with a neurosis or madness for throwing out what is essential to the psyche we need to revise our views.

At the basis of healing is the persistent idea of reconnection. Reconnection is healing, because through reconnection a link is established to something greater than ourselves, and the energy of life can move freely again. This is a powerful idea since it reminds us of the meaning of the word religion, based on the Latin *religio*, derived from *ligare* ('bind, connect'), and *re* ('again'). Religion means to 'reconnect' or 'bind again', and this meaning was made prominent by St Augustine. It is a pity that this great word has become so debased in our time, to become synonymous with, on the one hand, dreary or moralistic church sermons, and on the other, terrorist organisations hell-bent on destroying civilisation as we know it. But the original meaning of 'religion' is 'reconnection', and that is precisely the sense in which Jung uses it in relation to the healing of mental illness. The ego has become alienated from spirit and soul, and if the ego can risk a reconnection, patients are often healed of their maladies or illnesses.

The numinous as a healing field

In a remarkable letter to P. W. Martin in London, Jung wrote, in English:

> The main interest of my work is not concerned with the treatment of neuroses but rather with the approach to the numinous ... The fact is that the approach to the numinous is the real therapy.[4]

The 'real therapy' is not the doctor's words or ideas, not what he knows or what is conveyed to the patient through speech. It is not the medication or prescribed drugs, not chatting about problems, but this more mysterious and subtle factor: contact with the numinous. The numinous is a 'field' as I understand it, and it is a field that interacts with us all the time, if only we could see it. The transference to the analyst is effective only insofar as it conveys a sense of the numinous to the patient, in other words, insofar as it activates the internal healing capacity.

The problem with the theory of the healing power of the numinous is that it is unproved, invisible and subtle. Science as yet cannot get at it. Jung is willing to support it nevertheless, based on his experience as a psychotherapist. He borrowed the term *numinous* from Rudolf Otto, who rediscovered this term in 1923: 'Omen has given us "ominous",' says Otto, 'and there is no reason why *numen* should not give rise to the word "numinous".'[5] 'Numinous' is widely used today, but few realise its etymological connection with the sacred. The Latin *numen* refers to the nod or might of a deity, and numinous thus refers to the power of an *other* whom we might encounter in intuitive, reflective or critical moments.[6] Otto and Jung believe that the modern person living outside religion, and not only the traditional person living within a religion, can experience the numinous.

Healing through therapy is ultimately self-healing, although most of us have no way of knowing that. The 'self' that heals is not the usual or habitual self but something more mysterious, which is nevertheless part of ourselves. The healing process begins in earnest not when the patient has followed the cues of the analyst but when the patient has sensed the presence of an *other* at the core of his or her being. The idea of an objective spiritual presence at the core of our subjectivity is new to Western medicine, which tends to externalise the healing process, seeing it as the result of one's encounter with the doctor, or the result of medical interventions and pharmaceuticals. The inward healing presence is, alas, often absent in Western religions as well, where it is sometimes felt that only the saint or the monastic, and not the ordinary person, has access to spirit. If ordinary people claim this kind of experience they are treated with suspicion, or regarded as witches, blasphemers or frauds. In the West we have systematically downplayed the healing resources of the body-mind-spirit, which is why so many of us are at the mercy of the external forces of healing.

Let me say that we are not talking about miraculous cures through the spirit. Such might indeed happen, but if they occur it is due to the workings of the divine and not because we ask for a cure. On this point I have argued with some colleagues in the healing profession, including psychiatrists with interests in spirituality, who seem more concerned with cure than healing. But I am otherwise inclined: to me, healing is more important than cure, and by healing I mean a reconciliation within a person to the suffering that has befallen him or her, not necessarily a getting rid of the symptoms. Healing may lead to cure, but it may not. If the illness is still confined to the mental domain, there is more chance of a cure through contact with the numinous, in my view. However, if a neurosis has been somatised (converted from a psychological to a physical disorder) there could be less chance of a recovery, since once the body has taken on the illness, working with the mind or spirit might be less effective.

But how does this work? How does contact with the numinous bring about healing? In this regard, I have to concede, I work primarily with my intuition. I cannot produce empirical studies as I am not a scientist. But I am interested in metaphor and its powerful effects. I particularly like the metaphor that has emerged from theoretical physics about waves and particles, and I would like to apply this metaphor to healing and recovery from illness. In physics and chemistry this theory is called *wave-particle duality*.

The wave-particle paradox

Many of us imagine the human self to be a discrete entity, solid, formed and known. But this could be an illusion of our making, albeit a useful illusion, that allows us to act efficiently in the world. Researchers of the unconscious have found that the self has no definite boundaries, and that at its inner depths it trails off into mystery and the unknown. To borrow the metaphor from physics, what we had previously thought of as a solid entity may turn out to be a wave of infinite extension. Quantum physics discovered that the smallest elements of matter behave in one moment as particles and in another as waves. As particles, they are discrete and separate, and can be 'split' to release energy. As waves, they behave less like bits of matter and more like bands of light or energy, reaching out to eternity. They cannot be confined or boxed in but participate in an ocean of being, as it were.

This suggests a certain paradoxical instability at the heart of matter. Matter looks stable to the eye but, from the perspective of microphysics, the world is fluid, and uncertain, even bizarrely so. Einstein argued that all particles have a wave nature, and vice versa. Heisenberg, Max Planck and others refined and changed the theory. Needless to say, this discovery shattered the prevailing views of Newtonian physics, and its ramifications are still being felt today. As Brian Greene put it in *The Elegant Universe*, 'Matter has been dematerialized.'[7]

What has happened in physics has occurred in the parallel movement of Jung's analytical psychology. This is more than coincidence, because while he was a Swiss citizen and based in Zurich, Einstein befriended Jung and they had discussions about the nature of reality.[8] Einstein was discovering relativity in physics and Jung was discovering it in psychology. Like matter, the self is only relatively stable. At its depths, it too can lose its solid formation and appear as a wave or as a fluid process. The notion of applying the wave-particle duality to psychology is mine and not Jung's, but I think the metaphor holds if we think in terms of the healing experience of the numinous. As with the concept of matter in physics, I think we live simultaneously as waves and particles as psychological beings.

As particles, we are distinct beings, physical and discrete, each with our unique personality and makeup. As waves, we are not so individual. We are similar to each other, and participate in the cosmos in predetermined ways. As waves, we are spiritual beings, fluid, open-ended and connected to other waves. We are especially receptive to archetypal currents that course through us, which Jung identified as universal and collective. In his terms, the particle is the ego or conscious self, and the wave is the infinite expanse of the unconscious. 'The suprapersonal or collective unconscious,' writes Jung, 'is like an all-pervasive, omnipresent, omniscient spirit.' It represents 'an extension of man beyond himself; it means death for his personal being and rebirth in a new dimension as literally enacted in certain of the ancient mysteries'.[9] Rituals such as those of ancient Greece, in which rebirth in a new dimension was enacted, seek to lead us away from the particle to the wave, and such experiences are referred to theologically as grace, unconditional love or transcendence. The wave-like connection is precisely what we today call *spirituality*, namely, the capacity to feel connected to the cosmos and the entirety of life.

Soothed by waves
My contention is that as soon as we experience ourselves as waves, this has a healing effect on consciousness. When this connection is restored, we overcome ego-bound existence and

anxiety, and feel ourselves to be part of a larger whole. The ego's petty concerns and worries are dropped and we feel renewed. It is burdensome to be confined to the ego and to its tiny world. As Freud correctly observed, the ego is the 'seat of anxiety', and when we move outside the ego our anxiety – which can produce disease and neurosis – falls away. We are not designed to dwell all our lives in the ego, in its confining world. This has long been a part of human knowledge, which is why ritual and liturgy played such a huge role in people's lives in the past. Today we are more likely to seek out this experience of transcendence in a variety of secular ways, including music, drugs, sexuality, relationships, contact with nature and awe and wonder.

There is a core dimension in us that is not about material causation and mechanics but about the cosmos at large. I do not see this point of view as 'romantic' or far-fetched but as just realistic. There is a hidden dimension of our lives that is real and needs attention, especially in times of illness and despair. From a spiritual point of view, mental illness might be described as alienation from our source. Religions have long known this fact, and that is why the core rituals of religions are about *communion*, that is, binding back to the divine. But in a non-religious time, we still need to have the experience of communion, which restores the soul and vivifies the spirit. When we transcend ego boundaries in personal rituals, psychotherapy, art or meditation we return to the ocean of being and are restored. Jung felt that our meddling intellect gets in the way of our need for nonrational experiences of transcendence. We deny ourselves this release, and sometimes even feel embarrassed if we discover our need for such experiences.

The tranquillity that we experience as we walk beside the ocean, or the calm that descends as we look across a landscape, or move through a ferny gully, is related to the experience of the particle returning to the wave. The therapeutic effect of music or dance, which takes us outside the ego into 'waves' of sound and movement, is expressive of the joy experienced as we enter the wave. The word *ecstasy*, from the Greek *ekstasis*, or to be 'outside the self', points to the pleasurable experience of transcendence. The wave-like effect is what all religions seek in their rituals; in liturgy, prayer and ceremony, the isolated self is eclipsed and we participate in a relationship with forces beyond ourselves. Religions build communities in ways that secular society never can, because they reach beyond the façade of individuality and draw from the depths our longing to connect to our 'home', as Wordsworth called it. But it is hard to find our way home in a secular society which has no respect for our spiritual needs, and can only offer us religious substitutes, addictions or drugs to satisfy our craving.

The struggle to reach the waves

There is little doubt that, with the absence of 'official' forms of transcendence, the tried and true way to spiritual experience is suffering. If we cannot move beyond the ego and return to God through the cultural doorway of mythos (mythology), there is only the pathway through pathos (suffering). With culture committed to the ego rather than spirit, nature gets its revenge. Mental suffering is often the trigger to a religious conversion or a spiritual point of view. When life proceeds normally, and the task of social adjustment is successful, there may never arise the need or opportunity to find a relationship to a spiritual core. But when the normal self has been ruptured, the only option left, apart from running to others for help, is to seek reunion with the wave-like dimension at our core. By so doing, we turn to what is most profound in ourselves and ask it, implore it, to heal us, to close our wounds and grant us life. This is why many recovery programs, and methods of dealing with addictions, alcoholism, drug dependence, eating disorders, depression and anxiety, as well as techniques to deal with grief and trauma, find themselves moving into the spiritual domain, of which the AA movement is an example.[10]

Our society produces, and even encourages, the myth of the atomised, discrete, self-sufficient and autonomous ego, and that is the source of illness in our world. The socially adapted and healthy ego is generally not interested in humbling itself before the divine. It thinks of this as something odd, antiquated, even perverse. It does not make sense from the ego's point of view. Alas, that is why the ego must suffer, because it cannot come to the sacred any other way. In normal life, and in going about our business, we live a 'particle' existence. We behave like atomised entities, separate and autonomous, each concerned with his or her own self-interest or with a small family group. Beyond these narrow circles of concern, there is no interest in the cosmos at large or with God as an active agent in our lives. But as waves, we seek connection to that which is beyond the ego. We extend beyond the particular, breaking its boundaries, and reach out for eternity and the stars.

Thomas Berry wrote that ecological healing occurs when the world is no longer experienced as a collection of objects but as a communion of subjects.[11] This is the formula that underpins the creation of human community and it is the formula at the heart of the ecological vision. This is also the winning formula for psychological healing. Healing occurs when we no longer experience ourselves as isolated particles in a world of objects but when we experience ourselves as waves merging and interacting with other waves. Although I am too old to go to rave parties or trance dances, I imagine that this is the allure of such activities. The prison-house of the ego needs to be opened every now and then. The self may not realise its true nature, which releases bliss, until it experiences itself in relation to a larger subject. The self 'comes home' to itself when it glimpses the *other* who is its origin. Longing is fulfilled when we recover our belonging.

The oceanic feeling

We are emerging from an historical period in which our search for connection to this wave-like dimension has been represented as pathological or deluded. Modern society has invited us to seek a false security in the material world and this has amounted to a shift in the course of civilisation. We seek material security, but naturally we do not find it and cannot find it, since the search is self-defeating. But the longing for real – that is, spiritual – security is innate and this search continues despite the contrary impulses of society. Without true security we fall prey to nervous disorders, obsessions and illnesses. It seems that if we fail to care for the needs of the soul, we pay a price at both individual and collective levels.

Freud wrote about the wave-like experience in negative terms. He called it the 'oceanic feeling', but with a sneer. Unlike Jung, he feared the waves and saw them as tempestuous and dangerous. It is fascinating that Freud wrote his famous 1914 polemical tirade against Jung under the epigraph, *fluctuat nec mergitur* – 'tossed by waves, it does not sink'.[12] For him, only the particle – the distinct being, the ego – is the true human identity and our place of stability. The wave, which in Freud's polemic is associated with Jung, is constructed as the hostile opponent of the heroic particle. The Freudian particle has to bravely strive against the destructive Jungian wave to survive.

In a later work, *Civilization and its Discontents* (1930), Freud wrote about the oceanic feeling, which he saw as an unformed fluid state in which we are buoyed along by the current of being:

> The true source of religious sentiments [Father Romain Rolland claims] ... consists in a peculiar feeling. This feeling which he would like to call a sensation of 'eternity', a feeling as of something limitless, unbounded – as it were, 'oceanic'.

This feeling, he adds, is a purely subjective fact, not an article of faith.[13]

As a reductionist, Freud viewed the oceanic feeling as an expression of neurosis. He saw most attempts to lose the solidity of the ego as pathological, while both Jung and Nietzsche saw the Dionysian desire for loosening or *ekstasis* as a sign of spiritual rebirth. Freud conceded that 'there is only one state' in which such loosening cannot be 'stigmatized as pathological', and that is the state of love:

> At the height of being in love the boundary between ego and object threatens to melt away. Against all the evidence of his senses, a man who is in love declares that 'I' and 'you' are one, and is prepared to behave as if it were a fact.[14]

Apart from this exception, Freud believed that the oceanic feeling was negative for ego development, and it characterised the feeling that neurotic patients experience in states of regression. Freud distrusted the wave-like dimension of the psyche, and saw our longing for it as a symptom of our desire for incest, for returning to the womb. In the regressed state, we huddle in the womb like an embryo, buoyed up by the waves of amniotic fluid. He felt we should aim at all times to 'maintain clear and sharp lines of demarcation' and thus identify ourselves with our solid and separate egos. Interest in the oceanic state was suspect and all concern with altered states of consciousness was treated with disapproval by the pioneer of psychoanalysis.

Swimming or drowning

Freud believed that in states of mental disorder, the suffering person can be lost to the world of form and definition, and dropped into a formless chaos of undifferentiated life, where the boundary lines between the ego and the external world become uncertain.[15] This is why psychotic patients often report that they are 'at sea' and cannot distinguish the outlines of objects, such as chairs or tables, because their perception is blurred, and everything appears to be in a swirling chaos.

Psychosis plunges us into an oceanic void which precedes form, where everything is intermixed with everything else, and nothing can be perceived as separate from the chaotic stream. Jung would call this the descent (or *nekyia*) into the undifferentiated life of the collective unconscious. This is clearly not a state of cosmic consciousness, although it shares with spiritual experience the overriding sense that 'all things are one', that everything is connected and nothing is separate. However in psychosis this is far from a pleasant or elevating experience. It is deeply destructive and the ego seems to drown in the ocean of being, rather than be swept along blissfully by its current as in states of transcendental meditation or spiritual rebirth.

This is a vital point of difference that we need to make clear. What the mystic or guru experiences as a state of bliss can be experienced by the psychotic as a terrifying nightmare of disintegration. The waves of preconscious existence can be destructive, like a tsunami or tidal wave, but they can also bring healing if we relate to them in the right way. The ocean of being is the same ocean in madness and transcendence, but the difference between spiritual awakening and psychosis depends on the nature of the consciousness that encounters the ocean. Here we might learn from observations made by anthropologist Joseph Campbell in *Myths to Live By*:

> The difference [between the mystic and the schizophrenic] is equivalent to that between a diver who can swim and one who cannot. The mystic, endowed with native talents for this sort of thing and following, stage by stage, the instructions

> of a master, enters the waters and finds he can swim; whereas the schizophrenic, unprepared, unguided, and ungifted, has fallen or has intentionally plunged, and is drowning. Can he be saved? If a line is thrown to him, will he grab it? ... What I am saying is that our schizophrenic patient is actually experiencing inadvertently that same beatific ocean deep within that the yogi and saint are ever striving to enjoy; except that, whereas they are swimming in it, he is drowning.[16]

Jung warns that if the ego 'lacks any critical approach to the unconscious ... it is easily overpowered and becomes identical with the contents that have been assimilated'.[17] He says it is a 'psychic catastrophe when the ego is assimilated by the self'.[18] Jung insists that the ego must find a 'right relation' to the unconscious, and this involves, first of all, the ego preserving its integrity in the face of the ocean of being that makes up the collective unconscious.

If the ego is not properly formed, if it has been damaged by trauma or eclipsed by devastating inner or outer experiences, it is not in a fit state to make contact with the ocean of being. When the ocean comes towards it the ego will drown, because it needs to hold its integrity before the onslaught of the unconscious. If it can't hold its integrity it is lost in the water and becomes a subhuman fish swimming in the sea, or, more fatally, it dissolves into the ocean like an aspirin dropped in a tumbler of water. In states of psychotic depression or anxiety, dreams will indicate that the ego has been submerged under a wave, or lost to some distant galaxy or star. The metaphors will constantly change, but the message will be the same: an eternal force has obliterated the temporal personality. This becomes problematical, as I will explain, if the sufferer is a follower of a cult or creed which views such self-obliteration as a spiritual achievement.

Classic symptoms of such 'psychic dissolution' are inflation, depression, paranoia, mania, catatonia and bipolar disorder. In each of these states, the ego has been eclipsed and replaced by archetypal contents that substitute for the personality – the ego has been assimilated by the unconscious. In severe cases of psychosis, this may involve identifying oneself with an archetypal power or figure, in which the person claims to be Jesus, Caesar or Napoleon. Whoever the chosen figure is, it is apparent that the ego has been annulled by the unconscious, which has wiped out the human element and replaced it with an archetype that exerts a destructive impact.

Pathological spirituality

The negative effects of the ocean of being are not only found in psychotics who have entered into dangerous states and situations. Some risk-taking adventurers in search of mystical experiences can end up with the same disorders, as can those who engage in recreational drugs or binge drinking, or who experiment with hallucinogenics and altered states of consciousness. All can find themselves in deep water and unable to survive.

There are also people who misread Buddhism, Jung, Vedanta, the Upanishads or Christian or Jewish mystical writings and adopt a foolhardy attitude in their quest for a spiritual journey. The misreading may not be deliberate; rather, under the influence of a powerful impulse, the misreading is involuntary and unintentional. Perhaps they say their goal is enlightenment or wholeness, but interpret this to mean a loss of self in the ocean of being.

Typically, this is a Western misreading of Eastern spiritual goals. Such people are on a pathway of regression, and in this sense Freud was right to suspect mental illness at the core of some attempts at spiritual experience. Where Freud went wrong was in universalising this tendency, and refusing to see that some spiritual experience is authentic. Obviously discernment is needed to tell the difference between pathological and authentic spirituality.

Today, with so much ignorance and sentimentality attached to the spiritual domain, it is relatively easy to pass off pathology as spirituality. This is one reason why, in previous times, religious traditions insisted that every spiritual journey should be monitored by a spiritual director, who might be able to save us from the possibility of delusion or regression. But in the deregulated arena of today's spiritual experience, everyone considers him or herself a master of the way, and many do not submit to genuine teachers, who admittedly are hard to find. Instead, those who are hopelessly lost in the spiritual arena are themselves likely to pose as teachers, which gives a bad name to spirituality in society.

We can easily confuse a mental disorder with an experience of the spirit. Some seekers claim to be tired of living as mere egos and are impelled towards a new or bigger life. Where they go wrong is in assuming that the ego can be thrown aside and a new self taken on, like a new garment. If the ego is ditched in this way we do not become wise, mystical or spiritual but rather monsters of egotism and madness, as many stories of the lives of recent gurus attest. If the ego is not brought into a conscious relation to the sacred archetypal figures it is merely replaced by them, and this causes inflation, arrogance and megalomania. Strictly speaking, it is not their ego that has become huge but an archetypal figure that has seized control. The ego has been annulled, and it is the archetypal personality which gives the impression of 'egotism' by virtue of its arrogant display.

In therapy – if they seek it, and don't once there assume they are wiser than the therapist – such people need to be returned to their ordinary personality, which some might see as boring and not 'spiritual' enough. Analysts can have trouble with such patients, who might consider the analyst's attempt to ground them as an attack on their spiritual nature. They might see therapy as a form of brainwashing, a way of forcing adaptation to social norms. But therapy will show that the ego is smashed up in the unconscious, despite the fact that some around them complain of their 'egotism'.

Such victims might claim they have sacrificed their ego for the sake of a higher life in the Self. They have flung themselves into the unconscious and relied on the Self to save them, but the Self is not always able to save. What we encounter first in the unconscious are wild and primordial forces, aptly represented in myths and legends as dragons, monsters and demons. The Self may only come into being once the ego and the unconscious have interacted with each other and a dialogue has been established. The popular myth of the all-saving Atman or spiritual self can be destructive if people imagine they can abandon themselves to the unconscious without having to do any work to achieve psychic balance. We need a healthy respect for the unconscious and its ability to devastate. If we don't have this respect, we are devoured by the archetypes and forced to lead a less than human existence. There is a great difference between psychic disintegration and individuation.

The healing festivals of Dionysus

It is possible to see the relation between particle and wave in the experiences of the devotees of Dionysus. In many ways, Dionysus is the god who invites us to return to the source and immerse ourselves in the ocean of being. As Zurich analyst Verena Kast writes of the Dionysian festivals of ancient Greece:

> Those seized by Dionysus broke out of the conventional order to become part of a cosmic order; human beings became one with nature, social rank was obliterated, rivalries ceased. Torn out of their isolation, individuals

experienced prophecy and a momentary connection with the transpersonal Self.[19]

In the ancient festivals, the ego personality was momentarily eclipsed by a different order of being or, as Kast puts it, 'the devotees of the god experienced the Self through momentary forgetfulness of self'.[20] The Dionysian spirit is ecstatic and it brings release from the isolation of our individual selfhood. Dionysus lures us out of our shells into ecstatic communion with others and with nature. However, the enchantment that Dionysus offers can lead to intoxication, loss of control, excess and obliteration. This is why the god Dionysus was feared as well as revered. He personifies a primal wave that can engulf and obliterate the particle. The human element can be destroyed in a frenzy of elation and mania. He invites us to move out of our confined state, but the chaos of the primordial is the danger we face, which in the cult of Dionysus is symbolised by his companions, the maenads, whose name derives from mania and means possession or frenzy.

Walter Otto and Karl Kerenyi provide memorable descriptions of the ancient festivals of this god.[21] Dionysus was invoked by singing the dithyramb or ritual song. The wearing of the ritual masks of the god would invite Dionysus to enter the festivities and insinuate himself in the human throng. Women would gather in a circle, clap their hands, and sing and dance to the sound of drums and flutes. The dithyrambic choir would enter an altered state of consciousness, in which members lost their identities and acted as one. Describing this process of fusion with nature and life, Nietzsche wrote:

> So stirred by Dionysus, the individual forgets himself completely... In the Dionysiac rite, nature itself, long alienated or subjugated, rises again to celebrate the

reconciliation with her prodigal son, man. The mystical jubilation of Dionysus breaks the spell of individuation and opens a path to the maternal womb of being.[22]

This is a fascinating way of putting the relation between our particle- and wave-like natures. Note the reversal of Freud's notion that the particle should never be overcome. It is clear that Nietzsche's successor is Jung and not Freud. The alienation of the ego is overcome in an ecstatic ritual of unity and return, with strongly sexual and orgiastic elements in this celebratory rite. Nietzsche, Otto and Kerenyi emphasise that this is no mere orgy of sex, as Freudian readers might surmise. If anything, sexual union serves as a symbol for the higher union with the god. The participants in this ritual are experiencing a return to the primal condition for the sake of spiritual rebirth.

On the first day of this Greek festival, devotees would work themselves into a heightened state, in which some saw visions or discovered the gift of prophecy. The arrival of Dionysus was symbolised by the appearance of a ship from the high seas, indicating that Dionysus is a spirit which arises from the ocean of being. On the second day of the festival, Dionysus was ritually 'married' to the city in dancing, singing and celebration. On the third day, '[t]he souls of the dead returned and the prayer for the dead was recited. Everything that was dead in life, and everything that one wished were dead, returned to visit the living; all that was repressed and gone now reappeared'.[23]

In psychological terms, this festival represents a flooding of the conscious by the unconscious. Repressed longings, sexual urges, physical desires were given permission to announce themselves, everything lost was restored, and even the spirits of the dead were released into the city – indicating that this was an encounter with the collective and not merely with things suppressed in personal life. In a sense, Dionysus brings eternity back into time, and the waters of renewal are allowed to flood the dry land of our existence. The devotees of the god felt that their souls would become immortal by their participation in the god's eternal nature. The third day was the 'day of the dead', when the spirits of ancestors and forces of creation were brought up from the underworld.

It is important to note that the festivals were celebrated in March, after the thawing of the winter cycle and the coming of the spring. Otto indicates that the festival was primarily about renewal and healing and it was celebrated in this spirit, not as a destructive festival of madness or death. But he points out that not all participants were renewed or healed. Some women (these festivals were primarily organised by and for women) went mad and were led too far into the unconscious, never to return to sanity or society. In Euripides' *The Bacchae*, some women lost their bearings and were discovered days later almost dead from exhaustion on the far side of Mount Parnassus.[24] There were rituals to contain such victims of ecstasy: a ring of women from the nearby village would form a protective ring around those who were lost to a state of trance, symbolising an attempt to provide order or containment around them. The message emerging from *The Bacchae* is that the Dionysian spirit is vital to our existence, but only as much of it should enter our lives as can be matched by our ability to achieve reintegration and balance.

The contemporary relevance of Euripides' *The Bacchae* is extraordinary. Some of us can be transformed by our contact with ecstasy but some of us can be destroyed. As Verena Kast notes: 'Ecstasy carries us beyond our limits, killing our normal personality. It can fragment us so that we do not know how, or if, we are going to return.'[25] Not only are participants in danger of being overcome but onlookers are liable to be destroyed if their interest is inauthentic or voyeuristic – those who remain closed to the archetypal wave can be overwhelmed by it if we do not approach it with reverence and sound mind. In Euripides, the fate of Pentheus is the most famous case in this regard. King Pentheus is an enemy of Dionysus, opposed to the festivals and fearful of their frenzy. At the same time he is curious about them, and, disguised in women's clothing, he attempts to spy on the maenads at their rituals. He is mistaken for a wild beast and set upon by his own mother, who tears him apart.

The fate of Pentheus is echoed in the death of Orpheus, as found in Aeschylus's play *Bassarids*. This figure of Greek myth, the player of sublime music, refused to worship any of the gods except Apollo. Early one morning he went to the oracle to salute his god at dawn but was torn to pieces by the maenads for not honouring his previous patron, Dionysus. These myths indicate that holding back from the forces of Dionysus can destroy an ego which refuses to allow these forces into its life. To repress, judge and withhold is to invite the lethal powers of the unconscious, and one can be consumed by them.

But the important point emerging from the Greek festivals is that we need to achieve an appropriate connection with the wave-like dimension. As Kast puts it, we need to find a balance between fusion and individuation:

> The Dionysian ritual signifies entry into a symbiosis rather than individuation. We often hear that mystics are able to establish a symbiosis with the divine without ceasing to individuate, having found a good rhythm between symbiosis and individuation. This balance can be explained psychologically by the fact that the more defined the ego boundaries are, the greater their permeability is.[26]

The maintaining of both our boundaries and our openness to the numinous are not mutually exclusive. We gain the most beneficial relation to the numinous if we have secure ego boundaries in place. There is a belief today that if we drop our boundaries and inhibitions, all will be revealed and we will be enlightened. But the spiritual process of healing does not work this way. If we drop everything and run into the sea, we will most likely be engulfed. Only a mature person who respects their limitations and has an appropriate fear of the ocean is able to be permeated by the divine. We need to allow the water to flow through and over us, without having our lives washed away.

Finding a balance between particle and wave

When I was a undergraduate in the 1970s, many young adults in my peer group were experimenting with their receptivity to the wave, which in those days was called 'cosmic consciousness'. However it occurred to me that a more appropriate term might have been cosmic *unconsciousness*. Sometimes the wave they tried to ride was their last. One thing I noticed was a tendency towards dangerous or unhealthy relations with the 'cosmos'. The notion that one can trust the wave and give in to its healing powers has to be compensated by a dose of reality. The 'soft' idea of letting go and surrendering to the other has to be balanced by the 'hard' idea of making sure the ego is in a fit state to let go, or that other people are around to provide backup and support. The ego can only give itself over to the unconscious if it has the right attitude, and if it does not secretly wish to destroy itself in the infinite. I saw several of my friends destroy themselves by drugs, meditation and sexual excess. It seemed that they harboured a death wish, although they said they were hungering for the embrace of the cosmos. I was not convinced by the rhetoric, and had read enough Freud to make me aware that the death wish can operate in an autonomous way, and may disguise itself as a desire for altered states.

According to Freud, everyone harbours a death wish, and we have to be careful how this might manifest. If the ocean proves destructive it may not be the fault of the ocean, and we may not be able to curse it for ruining our lives. Rather we have to face the destructiveness in our nature, and examine why we went to the ocean in the first place to drown ourselves in its watery chaos. Today there is a popular repulsion towards the ego, partly as a reaction to our society's obsession with it. Too many of us are prepared to give the ego away at a moment's notice, to sacrifice it for a higher cause, but in so doing we lose the part that keeps us grounded in reality. We have to monitor this impulse in ourselves, and make sure this anarchic streak is not what we are calling our 'spirituality'.

The transpersonal psychologist Ken Wilber has explored the differences between spirituality and self-destruction, especially in *Up from Eden* and *The Atman Project*.[27] Wilber points out that a negative attachment to the unconscious can disguise itself as spiritual experience, and we are seeing borderline personality disorders misrepresented as mystical conditions in which the ego is supposedly 'transcended'. Wilber argues that spirituality cannot be allowed to stand in for, or take the place of, psychological development. Spirituality is about adjustment to the needs of the spirit, and the normalising project is about adjustment to society and the ego. Both spirit and society are vitally important.

Wilber points out that it is typical for some of us, especially those dazzled by New Age ideas, to confuse failed development of the ego with transcendence of the ego. The higher and lower levels of development have one feature in common: in both, the *nonegoic* is the dominant element of our experience. In the authentic spiritual state, the ego is transcended by a higher order of integration, in which the ego learns to serve and nurture the entire personality. However in the case of psychopathology, the ego has not been fully 'born' into the world. Wilber's thesis is that we are unable to tell the difference between spiritual development and infantile regression, and to the inexperienced eye the transcendence of ego and the pre-egoic condition look the same. Wilber calls this the 'Pre/Trans Fallacy', in which we confuse the pre-rational with the trans-rational, and he claims this is widespread.[28] Many cannot tell them apart, which is why a pathological person can parade as a spiritual guru and get away with it for a time. But those of us who secretly or openly despise the ego have to be made aware that it has an important role to play and needs to be treated with respect.

Finding a right relation to the unconscious is finding the middle path between extremes. On the one hand, the normal ego is inclined to deny the reality of the ocean – what ocean, I don't see one? This leads to typical debunking positions such as rationalism, cynicism, intellectualism, scientism and so on, all of which are attempts to convince oneself that the unconscious does not exist. On the other hand, we must avoid drowning in the ocean in order to give oneself over to the cosmos. This leads to false humility, depression, melancholia, catatonia and bipolar disorder. The corollary of this is where the ego attempts to swallow the ocean in an act of assimilation. This leads to arrogance, triumphalism, identification with archetypal figures, inflation and mania. A right relation to the ocean can be found when we respect both the otherness of the ocean and the integrity of the ego, and attempt to get them into dialogue. This dialogue is what many experience symbolically as they engage in surfing, bodyboarding and so on.

We have to learn to live beside and with the ocean of being and not let it overwhelm us. If we learn to attune ourselves to the wave-like dimension, we can allow ourselves experiences of unity and harmony, and these can have a positive effect on our state of mind, our nervous system, immune system and mental condition. The numinous can heal the body and psyche, but we have to enable this to happen. By experiencing the more-than-human, we are released from our ego-bound state and returned to a deeper sense of our humanity, from which the water of life flows. It is contact with the non-human, the dimension beyond time, that makes us human again, and allows us to be restored so we can live another day and meet the challenges before us.

For its part, the wave does not set about to extinguish the particle. Or to use theological language, the gods do not set out to destroy their creation. William Blake believed that 'eternity is in love with the productions of time'.[29] If this is true, we should feel this love as we attempt to approach the eternal dimension. The wave of eternity may even need the humble particle, because without it it has no way of entering time and space or incarnating into the world.

Bibliographical Note

All references to the works of Jung in the *Collected Works* are to paragraph numbers, not to page numbers. References to the *Collected Works* will be indicated by the essay title, original date of publication, followed by *CW*, and the volume number. Such references are to *The Collected Works of C. G. Jung*, translated from the German by R. F. C. Hull, edited by Herbert Read, Michael Fordham, Gerhard Adler and William McGuire, and published by Routledge in London and in America by Princeton University Press, 1953–1992.

All references to the works of Sigmund Freud in the *Standard Edition* are to page numbers. References to the *Standard Edition* will be indicated by the essay title, original date of publication, followed by *SE* and the volume number. Such references are to *The Standard Edition of the Complete Psychological Works of Sigmund Freud*, translated from the German and edited by James Strachey, in collaboration with Anna Freud and assisted by Alix Strachey and Alan Tyson, and published in London by The Hogarth Press, 1953–1975.

With regard to the Bible, several editions and translations have been consulted and compared, including *The English Revised Version* (1885), *The Revised Standard Version* (1952), *The Jerusalem Bible* (1966), and *The New International Version Study Bible* (1995).

Endnotes

Opening Epigraphs

C. G. Jung, 'Commentary on "The Secret of the Golden Flower"' (1929), *CW*, vol. 13, para. 54.

Sophocles, *Antigone*, in H. D. F. Kitto (trans) and Edith Hall (ed.) *Antigone; Oedipus the King; Electra* (Oxford: Oxford University Press, 1998), from the Chorus, part 6.

C. G. Jung, 'The State of Psychotherapy Today' (1934), *CW*, vol. 10, para. 367.

Introduction

1   Albert Kreinheder, *Body and Soul: The Other Side of Illness* (Toronto: Inner City Books, 1991), pp. 16–17.
2   David Tacey, *Edge of the Sacred: Jung, Psyche, Earth* (Einsiedeln, Switzerland: Daimon, 2009).
3   Edward Tylor, *Primitive Culture: Researches into the Development of Mythology, Philosophy, Religion, Art and Custom* (1871), (New York: Gordon Press, 1974), p. 3.
4   John Caputo, *On Religion* (London: Routledge, 2001).
5   *The Holy Bible*, Proverbs 29:18.
6   Sigmund Freud, *The Future of an Illusion* (1927), in *The Standard Edition of the Complete Psychological Works*, vol. 21 (London: The Hogarth Press, 1953).
7   G. K. Chesterton, *Orthodoxy* (1909), (Rockville, MD: Serenity Publishers, 2009), p. 25.
8   ibid.
9   Fritjof Capra, *The Turning Point: Science, Society, and the Rising Culture* (London: HarperCollins, 1982).
10 *The Holy Bible*, Psalms 118:22.

Chapter 1 Gods and Diseases

1   Alfred Ziegler, *Archetypal Medicine* (Dallas: Spring Publications, 1983), p. 14.
2   T. S. Eliot, 'Burnt Norton' (1935), *Collected Poems* (London: Faber, 1965), p. 190.

3   C. G. Jung, 'Commentary on "The Secret of the Golden Flower"' (1929), in *The Collected Works of C. G. Jung*, vol. 13, para. 54 (London: Routledge, 1968).
4   ibid.
5   John Swinton, *Spirituality and Mental Health Care: Rediscovering a 'Forgotten' Dimension* (London: Kingsley, 2001).
6   C. G. Jung, letter to P. W. Martin (1945), in Gerhard Adler (ed.), *C. G. Jung Letters*, vol. 1 (Princeton: Princeton University Press, 1973), p. 377.
7   C. G. Jung, 'Archetypes of the Collective Unconscious' (1934/1954), *CW*, vol. 9, part 1, para. 50.
8   C. G. Jung, 'Freud and Jung: Contrasts' (1929), *CW*, vol. 4, para. 780.
9   *The Holy Bible*, Matthew 18:1.
10 Kreinheder, op. cit., pp. 51–2.
11 Ziegler, op. cit., p. 5.
12 Louise L. Hay, *Heal Your Body: The Mental Causes for Physical Illness and the Metaphysical Way to Overcome Them*, fourth edition, (Carlsbad, CA: Hay House, 1988).
13 C. G. Jung, 'The State of Psychotherapy Today' (1934), *CW*, Vol. 10, para. 361.
14 ibid.
15 C. G. Jung, *Memories, Dreams, Reflections* (1963) (London: Fontana, 1995), p. 201.
16 ibid.
17 ibid., pp. 211–12.
18 C. G Jung, *The Red Book: Liber Novus*, Sonu Shamdasani (ed.), (New York: W. W. Norton, 2009).
19 ibid. p. 360.
20 Susan Sontag, *Illness as Metaphor* (New York: Vintage Books, 1977), p. 3.
21 Susan Sontag, *Illness as Metaphor; and AIDS and its Metaphors* (New York: Picador, 1990).
22 Susan Sontag, *Illness as Metaphor*, op. cit., pp. 55–56.
23 ibid., p. 57.
24 Friedrich Nietzsche, *Twilight of the Idols* (1888), trans. R. J. Hollingdale (London: Penguin, 1994), p. 12.
25 Susan Sontag, *Illness as Metaphor*, op. cit., p. 46.
26 Mircea Eliade, *The Sacred and the Profane* (New York: Harcourt Brace, 1959), p. 203.
27 Albert Kreinheder, op. cit., p. 37.
28 ibid., p. 38.

29 ibid., pp. 52–3.
30 ibid., p. 51.
31 ibid., p. 37.
32 ibid., p. 59.
33 ibid.
34 ibid., p. 48.
35 ibid., p. 59.
36 ibid., p. 68.
37 ibid., p. 49.

Chapter 2 The suffering of Spiritual Rebirth

1 Arnold van Gennep, *The Rites of Passage* (1908), (Chicago: University of Chicago Press, 1960).
2 Mircea Eliade, op. cit., p. 187.
3 See Vicki Grieves, *Aboriginal Spirituality: Aboriginal Philosophy: The Basis of Aboriginal Social and Emotional Wellbeing*. Discussion Paper No. 9 (Darwin: Cooperative Research Centre for Aboriginal Health, 2009). This work by an Aboriginal writer can be downloaded for free at: http://www.crcah.org.au/publications/downloads/DP9-Aboriginal-Spirituality.pdf
4 Eliade, op. cit., p. 190.
5 ibid., p. 188.
6 I should point out that in my discussion of initiation and rites of passage I am limited by cultural protocols to speak only of the experiences of men. According to Aboriginal custom in Australia, I am not able to speak of 'women's business', as this is offensive to tribal law. As a Westerner, I am tempted to give the other side of the story, and discuss initiations for women and girls, but this would be a violation of Aboriginal law.
7 C. G. Jung, 'Basic Postulates of Analytical Psychology' (1931), *CW*, vol. 8, para. 673.
8 C. G. Jung, *Memories, Dreams, Reflections* (1963), (London: Fontana, 1995), p. 216.
9 C. G. Jung, 'Concerning Rebirth' (1940/1950), *CW*, vol. 9, part 2, para. 224.
10 Deborah Bird Rose, 'Consciousness and Responsibility in an Australian Aboriginal Religion', in W. H. Edwards, (ed.), *Traditional Aboriginal Society: A Reader* (Melbourne: Macmillan, 1987), p. 260.
11 In this book, I use the word 'self' in two contexts: to refer to the normal human personality, I use it without capitalisation, and to refer to the image of the God within, I capitalise it.
12 C. G. Jung, *Aion* (1951), *CW*, vol. 9, part 2, para. 42.

13 Pontifical Council for Culture and Pontifical Council for Interreligious Dialogue, *Jesus Christ: The Bearer of the Water of Life: A Christian Reflection on the 'New Age'* (Vatican, Rome: 2003), located at: http://www.vatican.va/roman_curia/pontifical_councils/interelg/documents/rc_pc_interelg_doc_20030203_new-age_en.html
14 A. D. Hope, 'An Epistle from Holofernes' (1960), *Selected Poems* (Sydney: Angus & Robertson, 1992), p. 56.
15 William Wordsworth, 'Ode: Intimations of Immortality' (1807), in Margaret Ferguson, Mary Jo Salter and Jon Stallworthy (eds.), *The Norton Anthology of Poetry*, fifth edition (New York: W. W. Norton, 2005), pp. 796–801, lines 58–65.
16 See James Hillman, '*Anima Mundi*: The Return of the Soul to the World' (1982), in *The Thought of the Heart and the Soul of the World* (Dallas: Spring Publications, 1992).
17 C. G. Jung, *Modern Man in Search of a Soul* (1930), (London and New York: Routledge, 2004).
18 Lynne Hume, *Ancestral Power: The Dreaming, Consciousness, and Aboriginal Australians* (Melbourne: Melbourne University Press, 2002).
19 Linda Leonard, *Witness to the Fire: Creativity and the Veil of Addiction* (Boston: Shambhala, 1989).
20 John Keats, letter to George and Tom Keats (22 December 1818), in Jane Campion, (ed.), *Bright Star: The Complete Poems and Selected Letters* (London: Vintage Books, 2009), p. 492.
21 David Tacey, *Patrick White: Fiction and the Unconscious* (Melbourne: Oxford University Press, 1988).

Chapter 3 The Midlife Crisis as Spiritual Interruption

1 Elliott Jaques, 'Death and the Midlife Crisis', *International Journal of Psychoanalysis* (1965) no. 46, pp. 502–14.
2 C. G. Jung, 'The Stages of Life' (1930–31), CW, vol. 8, para. 772.
3 ibid., para. 773.
4 ibid., para. 764.
5 David Tacey, 'Homoerotic Desire and the Fathering Spirit', in *Remaking Men: Jung, Spirituality and Social Change* (London and New York: Routledge, 1997), pp.131–48; also David Tacey, 'Homoeroticism and Homophobia in Heterosexual Male Initiation', in Robert Hopcke (ed.), *Same-Sex Love and the Path to Wholeness* (Boston and London: Shambhala, 1993), pp. 246–61.
6 See Chapter 6.
7 Jung's sustained exploration of the incest motif can be found in *Symbols of Transformation* (1912/1952), CW, vol. 5.

8   Robert Hopcke, 'Homophobia and Analytical Psychology', in *Same-Sex Love*, op. cit., pp. 68–87.
9   C. G. Jung, 'The Stages of Life', op. cit., para. 773.
10 ibid., para. 767.
11 ibid., para. 766.
12 ibid., para. 788.
13 ibid., para. 764.
14 Joseph Campbell, *Myths to Live By* (New York: Bantam, 1972).
15 C. G. Jung, 'The Stages of Life', op. cit., para. 787.
16 ibid., para. 792.
17 ibid., paras. 790 and 794.
18 Robert Forman, *Grassroots Spirituality* (Boston: Academic Imprint, 2004).
19 C. G. Jung, 'The Stages of Life', op. cit., para. 793.
20 ibid., para. 794.
21 Plotinus, *Enneads* III, 8:x, in John Gregory (ed.), *The Neoplatonists* (London: Kyle Cathie, 1991), pp. 40–1.
22 Plotinus, *Enneads* VI, 4:xiv, in Gregory, ibid. p. 130.
23 ibid., p. 6.

Chapter 4 Cancer Phobia as a Doorway to Soul

1   Susan Sontag, *Illness as Metaphor*, op. cit., p. 66.
2   C. G. Jung, letter to Rudolf Jung (1956), in Gerhard Adler, (ed.), and R.F.C. Hull (trans.), *C. G. Jung Letters*, vol. 2 (Princeton: Princeton University Press, 1975), p. 297.
3   Russell A. Lockhart, 'Cancer in Myth and Dream: An Exploration into the Archetypal Relation between Dreams and Disease' (1977), in *Words as Eggs: Psyche in Language and Clinic* (Dallas: Spring Publications, 1983), pp. 57–8.
4   C. G. Jung, 'The State of Psychotherapy Today' (1934), *CW*, vol. 10, para. 361.
5   C. G. Jung, 'In Memory of Sigmund Freud' (1939), *CW*, vol. 15, para. 68.
6   Donald Kalsched, *The Inner World of Trauma: Archetypal Defenses of the Personal Spirit* (London and New York: Brunner-Routledge, 1996).
7   C. G. Jung, *Aion*, op. cit., part 2, para. 40.
8   C. G. Jung, 'Psychology and Religion', op. cit.
9   ibid., para. 72.
10 ibid., para. 12.
11 ibid.
12 ibid.

13   ibid.
14   ibid., para. 19.
15   ibid., para. 21.
16   ibid., para. 22.
17   ibid., para. 26.
18   ibid., para. 12.
19   ibid., para. 74.
20   ibid., para. 26.
21   ibid.
22   ibid., para. 28.
23   ibid., para. 79.
24   C. G. Jung, 'The Stages of Life', op. cit., para. 764.

Chapter 5 Sexuality and the Sacred

1   Joseph Campbell, in Joseph Campbell and Bill Moyers, *The Power of Myth* (New York: Doubleday, 1988), p. 236.
2   C. G. Jung, 'Psychotherapy and a Philosophy of Life' (1943), CW, vol. 16, para. 181.
3   C. G. Jung, 'The Relations Between the Ego and the Unconscious' (1928), *CW*, vol. 7, para. 206.
4   ibid., para. 206.
5   ibid.
6   ibid.
7   ibid., para. 214.
8   C. G. Jung, 'On the Nature of the Psyche' (1947/1954), *CW*, vol. 8, para. 420.
9   Pope Benedict XVI, *Deus Caritas Est*, the first encyclical letter of the Pontiff (2006), which can be found at: http://www.vatican.va/holy_father/benedict_xvi/encyclicals/documents/hf_ben-xvi_enc_20051225_deus-caritas-est_en.html
10 C. G. Jung, *Symbols of Transformation* (1912/1952), *CW*, vol. 5.
11 C. G. Jung, 'The Relations Between the Ego and the Unconscious', op. cit., para. 214.
12 ibid., para. 206.
13 ibid.
14 ibid.
15 ibid., para. 213.
16 ibid., para. 206.
17 ibid.
18 ibid., para. 214.
19 William Shakespeare, *The Tempest*, act 4, line 158.

20 Jung, 'The Relations Between the Ego and the Unconscious', op. cit., para. 211.
21 ibid., para. 217.
22 See Charles Taylor, *A Secular Age* (Cambridge, Mass.: Harvard University Press, 2007).
23 Jung, 'The Relations Between the Ego and the Unconscious', op. cit., para. 216.
24 ibid., para. 215.
25 ibid.
26 ibid., para. 216.
27 ibid.
28 ibid., para. 219.
29 On the topic of 'implicit spirituality' see David Hay, *Why Spirituality is Difficult for Westerners* (Exeter: Imprint Academic, 2007).
30 C. G. Jung, 'The Relations Between the Ego and the Unconscious', op. cit., para. 216.
31 Victor Frankl, *Man's Search for Ultimate Meaning* (New York: Basic Books, 2000), p. 70.
32 C. G. Jung, 'The Relations Between the Ego and the Unconscious', op. cit., para 216.
33 Sigmund Freud, letter to Jung (22 April 1910), in William McGuire (ed.), *The Freud/Jung Letters* (Princeton: Princeton University Press, 1974), p. 310.
34 Sigmund Freud, letter to Jung (18 February 1912), in *The Freud/Jung Letters*, ibid., p. 485.
35 C. G. Jung, *Memories, Dreams, Reflections* (1963) (London: Fontana, 1995), p. 173.
36 ibid., p. 174.
37 William James, *Pragmatism* (1907), (Cambridge, Mass.: Harvard University Press, 1978), p. 14.
38 C. G. Jung, *Memories, Dreams, Reflections*, op. cit., p. 175.
39 ibid., p. 173.
40 C. G. Jung, 'Psychology and Religion' op. cit., para. 77.
41 ibid., para. 81.
42 ibid., para. 79.
43 C. G. Jung, *Memories, Dreams, Reflections*, op. cit., p. 173.
44 ibid., p. 174.
45 ibid.
46 ibid.
47 ibid., p. 175.
48 ibid.

49 ibid., p. 176.
50 Janine Burke, *The Gods of Freud: Sigmund Freud's Art Collection* (Sydney: Random House, 2006).
51 See Freud's study on religion, *The Future of an Illusion* (1927), *SE*, vol. 21.
52 Sigmund Freud, 'On the History of the Psycho-Analytic Movement' (1914), *SE*, vol. 14, p. 43.
53 C. J. Jung, *Memories, Dreams, Reflections*, op. cit., p. 192.

Chapter 6 Incest, Child Abuse and Alcoholism
1 *The Holy Bible*, John 3:5.
2 Sophocles, *Oedipus Rex*, in H. D. F. Kitto (trans.), and Edith Hall (ed.), *Antigone; Oedipus the King; Electra* (Oxford: Oxford University Press, 1998).
3 C. G. Jung, *Symbols of Transformation* (1912/1952), *CW*, vol. 5.
4 Jeffrey Masson, *Freud: The Assault on Truth: Freud's Suppression of the Seduction Theory* (London and New York: Routledge & Kegan Paul, 1994).
5 Sigmund Freud, 'The Aetiology of Hysteria' (1896), *SE*, vol. 3.
6 Masson, op. cit., p. xix.
7 Paul Kugler, 'Childhood Seduction: Physical and Emotional', in *Spring 1987* (Dallas, Texas), pp. 40–60.
8 Jane O'Hare and Katherine Taylor, 'The Reality of Incest', in J. H. Robbins and R. J. Siegel (eds), *Women Changing Therapy* (New York: Haworth Press, 1983).
9 David Tacey, 'Incest, Society, and Transformation: An Australian Perspective', in *Psychological Perspectives* (Los Angeles, California), no. 23, 1990, pp. 16–31.
10 Alice Miller, *Banished Knowledge: Facing Childhood Injuries* (London: Virago, 1991), and Milton Klein, *An Amazing Grace* (New Orleans: University Press of the South, 2004).
11 Robert Stein, 'On Incest and Child Abuse', in *Spring 1987* (Dallas, Texas), p. 65.
12 Rex Wild and Patricia Anderson, *Little Children are Sacred* (2007), (Darwin: Northern Territory Government), available at: http://www.nt.gov.au/dcm/inquirysaac/pdf/bipacsa_final_report.pdf
13 *The Holy Bible*, the Revised Standard Version, Proverbs 29:18.
14 Christopher Koch, *The Year of Living Dangerously* (London: Michael Joseph, 1978), p. 236.
15 Stein, op. cit., p. 64.
16 ibid., p. 65.
17 *The Holy Bible*, John 3:3.

18 John 3:5.
19 John 3:5–6.
20 John 3:7–8.
21 John 3:9.
22 John 3:10.
23 C. G. Jung, *Symbols of Transformation*, op. cit., para. 226.
24 C. G. Jung, 'The Symbolic Life' (1939), in *CW*, vol. 18.
25 Jung, *Symbols of Transformation*, op. cit., para. 226.
26 Jung, 'The Symbolic Life', op. cit., para. 649.
27 Baldwin Spencer and Francis Gillen, *The Arunta: A study of a stone age people* (London: Macmillan, 1927).
28 Mircea Eliade, op. cit., p. 64.
29 William James, *The Varieties of Religious Experience* (1902), (New York: Penguin, 1982), p. 387.
30 ibid., p. 388.
31 Robert Johnson, *Ecstasy: Understanding the Psychology of Joy* (San Francisco: Harper & Row, 1989).
32 ibid., p. 21.
33 A report of the Turning Point Drug and Alcohol Centre of Melbourne, quoted by Kate Hagan, 'Huge rise in risky drinking', *The Age* (4 August 2010) p. 3.
34 A report of the Australian Institute of Criminology, quoted by Ari Sharp, 'Alcohol primary cause of Aboriginal violence', in *The Sydney Morning Herald* (9 April 2010), p. 8.
35 C. G. Jung, letter to William G. Wilson (1961), in Gerhard Adler, (ed.), and R.F.C. Hull, (trans.), *C. G. Jung Letters*, vol. 2, op. cit., pp. 624–25.
36 *Alcoholics Anonymous*, third edition, (New York: Alcoholics Anonymous World Services, 1976).
37 Thich Nhat Hanh, *Living Buddha, Living Christ* (New York: Riverhead Books, 1995), p. 37.
38 *The Sunday Missal* (Sydney: HarperCollins, 1998), p. 446.
39 Thich Nhat Hanh, op. cit., p. 62.

Chapter 7 Depression, Self-Harm and Suicide
1 Thomas Moore, *Care of the Soul* (New York: HarperCollins, 1992), p. 63.
2 Richard Eckersley, *Well and Good: How We Feel and Why it Matters* (Text: Melbourne, 2004).
3 C. G. Jung, *Memories, Dreams, Reflections*, op. cit., p. 99.
4 C. G. Jung, 'The Philosophical Tree' (1945), *CW*, vol. 13, para. 335.
5 Sigmund Freud, 'Mourning and Melancholia' (1915), *SE*, vol. 14, (London: The Hogarth Press, 1953), pp. 243–58.

6   Once again I point out that my discussion of the tribal initiations is limited to the male experience. In Aboriginal culture there is a strict protocol about gender and sacred knowledge, and since I am a man I can only speak about men's business. This frustrates our Western demand to look at both genders, but as a person from central Australia, I have to respect indigenous views.
7   Ronald M. Berndt, *Australian Aboriginal Religion* (Leiden: Brill, 1974).
8   See Luigi Zoja, *Drugs, Addiction and Initiation: the Modern Search for Ritual* (Boston: Sigo Press, 1989).
9   Ian Keen, *Knowledge and Secrecy in an Aboriginal Religion* (New York: Oxford University Press, 1994).
10 Mircea Eliade, op.cit., p. 190.
11 Tom Beaudoin *Virtual Faith: The Irreverent Spiritual Quest of Generation X* (San Francisco: Jossey-Bass, 1998), pp. 77–8.
12 Joseph Chilton Pearce, *The Biology of Transcendence: A Blueprint of the Human Spirit* (Rochester, Vermont: Park Street Press, 2002), p. 53.
13 Eckersley, op. cit., pp. 176–77.
14 T. K. Hamilton and R. D. Schweitzer, 'The Cost of Being Perfect: Perfection and Suicidal Ideation in University Students', *Australian and New Zealand Journal of Psychiatry* (2000), vol. 34, pp. 829–35.
15 See David Hay, *Something There: The Biology of the Human Spirit* (London: Darton, Longman & Todd, 2006).
16 Eliade, op. cit., p. 188.
17 See also Mircea Eliade, *Rites and Symbols of Initiation: The Mysteries of Birth and Rebirth* (1956), (New York: Harper, 1975).
18 Various conversations with Charles Ilyatjari have been recorded in Robert Bosnak, *Tracks in the Wilderness of Dreaming* (Boston: Delacorte Press, 1996).
19 Pers. comm., June 1997.
20 David Mowaljarlai, *Yorro Yorro: Everything Standing Up Alive* (Broome: Magabala Books, 1993).
21 Pers. comm., November 1996.
22 James Hillman, *Suicide and the Soul* (New York: Harper & Row, 1973), p. 146.
23 *The Gospel According to Thomas*, Gilles Quispel et al. (eds.) (New York: Harper & Row, 1959), Saying 70, p. 41.

Chapter 8 The Storm Gods and the German Psychosis

1   Friedrich Hölderlin, 'Bread and Wine' (1801), in *Poems of Friedrich Hölderlin*, (trans.) James Mitchell (San Francisco: Ithuriel's Spear, 2004) p. 13, line 119.

2   C. G. Jung, 'Commentary on "The Secret of the Golden Flower"' (1929), *CW*, vol. 13, para. 54.
3   C. G. Jung, 'After the Catastrophe' (1945), *CW*, vol. 10, para. 410.
4   Sigmund Freud, letter to Jung (22 April 1910), in William McGuire (ed.), *The Freud/Jung Letters*, op. cit., p. 310.
5   For a succinct study of the psychology of projection, see C. G Jung, 'The Shadow' (1951), *CW*, vol. 9, part 2, paras. 13–19.
6   John Lindow, *Norse Mythology: A Guide to the Gods, Heroes, Rituals, and Beliefs* (Oxford: Oxford University Press, 2002).
7   Anthony Faulkes (trans. and ed.), *Edda* (London: Everyman, 1996).
8   C. G. Jung, 'Wotan' (1936), *CW*, vol. 10, para. 373.
9   ibid., paras 373–4.
10 ibid., para. 388.
11 C. G. Jung, 'The Role of the Unconscious' (1918), *CW*, vol. 10, para. 17.
12 See Andrew Samuels, 'Jung, anti-semitism and the Nazis', in *The Political Psyche* (London and New York: Routledge, 1993), pp. 287–316.
13 C.G. Jung, 'Wotan', op. cit., para. 387.
14 ibid., para. 384.
15 W. B. Yeats, 'The Second Coming' (1920), in *W. B. Yeats: Selected Poetry*, Timothy Webb (ed.) (Harmondsworth: Penguin, 1991), p. 124, lines 3–4.
16 Jung, 'Wotan', op. cit., para. 397.
17 ibid., para. 389.
18 ibid., para. 391.
19 C. G. Jung, 'Psychology and Religion', op. cit., para. 25.
20 Friedrich Nietzsche, *Beyond Good and Evil* (1886), (Harmondsworth: Penguin, 1982).
21 C. G. Jung, 'After the Catastrophe', op. cit., para. 431.
22 C. G. Jung, 'Answer to Job' (1952), *CW*, vol. 11, para. 556.
23 C. G. Jung, 'The Phenomenology of the Spirit in Fairytales' (1945/1948), *CW*, vol. 9, part 1, para. 454.
24 Friedrich Nietzsche, 'The Madman', Aphorism 125, in *The Gay Science* (1887), second edition (New York: Frederick Ungar Publishing, 1960), pp. 167–9.
25 C. G. Jung, *Nietzsche's* Zarathustra: *Notes of the Seminar Given in 1934–1939*, James L. Jarrett (ed.), two volumes (Princeton: Princeton University Press, 1988).
26 Friedrich Nietzsche, *Thus Spoke Zarathustra* (1885), R. J. Hollingdale. (trans. and ed.), (Harmondsworth: Penguin, 1983), p. 23.
27 ibid., p. 42.
28 ibid., p. 104.
29 C. G. Jung, 'Psychology and Religion', op. cit., para. 145.

30 *The Holy Bible*, Genesis 3:5.
31 *The Holy Bible*, Matthew 4:9.
32 Hölderlin, 'Bread and Wine', op. cit., p. 13. Line numbers of this poem will be quoted in the text.
33 Jean Laplanche, *Life and Death in Psychoanalysis*, Jeffrey Mehlman (trans.) (Baltimore: Johns Hopkins University Press, 1976).
34 Friedrich Hölderlin, 'Bonaparte' (1799), in *Friedrich Hölderlin: Poems and Fragments*, Michael Hamburger (trans.) (London: Routledge & Kegan Paul, 1966), p. 5.
35 On the need to personify and objectify the gods, see C. G. Jung, *Memories, Dreams, Reflections* op. cit., p. 211.
36 Friedrich Hölderlin, 'As on a Holiday' (1803), in *Friedrich Hölderlin: Poems and Fragments*, op. cit., p. 177.
37 ibid.
38 *The Holy Bible*, Psalm 111:10.
39 Julian Young, *Heidegger, Philosophy, Nazism* (New York: Cambridge University Press, 1997).
40 Martin Heidegger, 'What Are Poets For?' (1950), in Albert Hofstadter (ed.), *Poetry, Language, Thought* (New York: Harper Colophon, 1975), p. 91.
41 ibid., p. 93.
42 Jacques Derrida, *Of Spirit: Heidegger and the Question* (Chicago: University of Chicago Press, 1989), pp. 1–2.
43 Jacques Derrida, 'Faith and Knowledge: The Two Sources of Religion at the Limits of Reason Alone' (1996), in Jacques Derrida and Gianni Vattimo (eds.), *Religion* (Stanford: Stanford University Press, 1998).
44 Jacques Derrida, *Of Spirit*, op. cit., p. 23.
45 Martin Heidegger, op. cit., p. 92.
46 ibid., p. 93.
47 C. G. Jung, 'The Spiritual Problem of Modern Man' (1928/1931), CW, vol. 10, para. 150.
48 Martin Heidegger, op. cit., p. 92.

Chapter 9 Spirituality, Medicine, Health
1 C. G. Jung, 'Psychotherapists or the Clergy' (1932), CW, vol. 11, para. 488.
2 See Harold G. Koenig, Linda K. George, David B. Larson, and Michael E. McCullough, 'Spirituality and Health: What We Know, What We Need to Know', *Social and Clinical Psychology* (2000), vol. 19, no. 1, pp. 102–16.
3 Sigmund Freud, *The Future of an Illusion* (1927), SE, vol. 21, p. 43.
4 C. G. Jung, 'The Relations between the Ego and the Unconscious' (1928), CW, vol. 7, para. 263.

5   Harold G. Koenig, *Spirituality in Patient Care* (Philadelphia and London: Templeton Foundation Press, 2002).
6   Royal College of Psychiatry, 'Spirituality and Mental Health' (2009), located at: http://www.rcpsych.ac.uk/mentalhealthinfo/treatments/spirituality.aspx
7   C. G. Jung, quoted in Andrew Samuels, *The Plural Psyche* (London and New York: Routledge, 1989), p. 109.
8   John Caputo, *On Religion* (London: Routledge, 2001).
9   Robert Forman, *Grassroots Spirituality* (Boston: Academic Imprint, 2004).
10 Barbara Stevens Barnum, *Spirituality in Nursing: From Traditional to New Age*, second edition (New York: Springer, 2003); Carolyn Cooper, *The Art of Nursing* (London: W. B. Saunders, 2001); Judy Harrison, *Spirituality and Nursing Practice* (Avebury, UK: Aldershot, 1993); William McSherry, *Making Sense of Spirituality in Nursing and Health Care Practice*, second edition (Philadelphia: Jessica Kingsley Publications, 2006); Susan Ronaldson (ed.), *Spirituality: The Heart of Nursing* (Melbourne: Ausmed Publications, 1997).
11 David Tacey, *The Spirituality Revolution* (Sydney: HarperCollins, 2003; London and New York: Routledge, 2004).
12 *The Holy Bible*, Matthew 9:17 – 'Nor do people put new wine into old wineskins; if they do, the skins burst, the wine runs out, and the skins are lost.'
13 See John Caputo, *The Prayers and Tears of Jacques Derrida: Religion without Religion* (Bloomington: Indiana University Press, 1997).
14 Jacques Derrida, 'Epoché and Faith: An Interview with Jacques Derrida' (2000), in Yvonne Sherwood and Kevin Hart (eds.), *Derrida and Religion: Other Testaments* (New York: Routledge, 2005), p. 32.
15 Carlton Brown, 'Old Religion, New Spirituality and Health Care', in Augustine Meier, Thomas St James O'Connor, and Peter VanKatwyk (eds.), *Spirituality and Health: Multidisciplinary Explorations* (Ontario: Wilfrid Laurier University Press, 2005), p. 192.
16 See David Tacey, *Jung and the New Age* (London and New York: Routledge, 2001).
17 Andrew Powell, 'Soul, Consciousness and Human Suffering', *Journal of Alternative and Complementary Medicine* (1998), vol. 4, no. 1, pp. 101-108.
18 Eugene Peterson, *Subversive Spirituality* (Grand Rapids: Eerdmans, 1997).
19 Gregg Jacobs, *The Ancestral Mind* (New York: Viking, 2003).
20 C. G. Jung, 'Psychotherapists or the Clergy', op. cit., para. 490.

21 John Swinton, op. cit.
22 Fritjof Capra, op. cit.
23 See Amanda Porterfield, *Healing in the History of Christianity* (Oxford: Oxford University Press, 2005).
24 Brian Inglis, *Natural Medicine* (Glasgow: William Collins Sons, 1979), pp. 23–4.
25 Brown, op. cit., p. 191.
26 ibid., p. 191.
27 Rudolf Otto, *The Idea of the Holy*, John W. Harvey (ed.) (1923), (London: Oxford University Press, 1958), p. 1.
28 Andrew Powell, 'Spirituality, Healing and the Mind', *Spirituality and Health International* (2005), vol. 6, no. 3, p. 167.
29 ibid.
30 David Tacey, 'The Spirituality Gap: Credibility and Supernaturalism', in *The Spirituality Revolution*, op. cit., pp. 199–214.
31 Sigmund Freud, 'Creative Writers and Day-Dreaming' (1908), *SE*, vol. 9, p. 153.
32 Friedrich Nietzsche, *Twilight of the Idols* (1888, Harmondsworth: Penguin, 1992), p. 121.
33 C. G. Jung, 'Psychotherapists or the Clergy', op. cit., para. 497.
34 ibid., para. 494.
35 ibid., para. 498.
36 Simone M. Roach, *Caring from the Heart: The Convergence of Caring and Spirituality* (New York: Paulist Press, 1997).
37 John Swinton, op. cit.
38 Thomas Moore, *Care of the Soul* (New York: HarperCollins, 1992).
39 Helen Orchard (ed.), *Spirituality in Health Care Contexts* (Philadelphia: Jessica Kingsley, 2001).
40 C. G. Jung, 'Psychotherapists or the Clergy', op. cit., para. 509.
41 ibid., para. 519.

Conclusion

1 C. G. Jung, 'Psychotherapists or the Clergy', op. cit., para. 523.
2 C. G. Jung, 'The Soul and Death' (1934), *CW*, vol. 8, para. 808.
3 Patrick White, *Riders in the Chariot* (New York: Viking, 1961), p. 264.
4 C. G. Jung, Letter to P. W. Martin (1945), in Gerhard Adler (ed.), *C. G. Jung Letters* vol. 1 (Princeton: Princeton University Press, 1973), p. 377.
5 Rudolf Otto, op. cit., p. 7.
6 See David Tacey and Ann Casement (eds.), *The Idea of the Numinous: Contemporary Jungian and Psychoanalytic Perspectives* (London and New York: Routledge, 2006).

7   Brian Greene, *The Elegant Universe* (New York: Vintage, 1999), p. 104.
8   Joseph Cambray, *Synchronicity: Nature and Psyche in an Interconnected Universe* (College Station, TX: Texas A & M University Press, 2009).
9   C. G. Jung, 'The Role of the Unconscious', op. cit., para. 13.
10 Oliver Morgan and Merle Jordan, *Addiction and Spirituality* (St Louis: Chalice Press, 1999).
11 Thomas Berry, *The Dream of the Earth* (San Francisco: Sierra Club Books, 1988), p. 2.
12 Sigmund Freud, 'On the History of the Psychoanalytic Movement' (1914), *SE*, vol. 14, p. 7.
13 Sigmund Freud, *Civilization and its Discontents* (1930), *SE*, vol. 21, p. 64.
14 ibid., p. 66.
15 ibid.
16 Joseph Campbell, *Myths to Live By* (New York: Viking, 1972), pp. 215–16, 226.
17 C. G. Jung, *Aion*, op. cit, part 2, para. 23.
18 ibid., para. 24.
19 Verena Kast, *Joy, Inspiration and Hope* (College Station, TX: Texas A & M University Press, 1991), p. 6.
20 ibid., p. 8.
21 Walter Otto, *Dionysus: Myth and Cult* (Dallas: Spring, 1981); and Karl Kerenyi, *Dionysus: Archetypal Image of Indestructible Life* (Princeton: Princeton University Press, 1976).
22 Friedrich Nietzsche, *The Birth of Tragedy*, Shaun Whiteside (trans.) (1872), (London: Penguin, 1993), p. 97.
23 Verena Kast, op. cit., p. 121.
24 Euripides, *The Bacchae*, in D. Grene and R. Lattimore (eds.), *The Complete Greek Tragedies* (Chicago: University of Chicago Press, 1960).
25 Verena Kast, op. cit., p. 122.
26 ibid., p. 120.
27 Ken Wilber, *Up From Eden: A Transpersonal View of Human Evolution* (Boston: Shambhala, 1986); and *The Atman Project: A Transpersonal View of Human Development* (Wheaton, IL: Quest Books, 1980).
28 Ken Wilber, *The Atman Project*, ibid., p. 58.
29 William Blake, 'The Marriage of Heaven and Hell' (1793), in Geoffrey Keynes (ed.) *Blake: Complete Writings* (London: Oxford University Press, 1976), p. 151.

Index

Aboriginal communities: alcoholism in 15, 138–40, 141–42, 143; impact of European colonisation on 14–15, 139; incest/child sexual abuse 15, 130–31; initiation rites 50–53, 53, 54–56, 152–54, 155–56, 164; self-harm in 151–52, 163–64; spirituality of 13–14, 19–20, 22, 40, 63, 138–39, 143, 152; suicide in 163–64
Aboriginal Dreaming 14, 15, 20, 55, 142
adolescence 156–57
affirmations 35
Africa, initiation rites 155–56, 157
afterlife 81–84
agape 104, 124
Alcoholics Anonymous 142–45, 224, *see also* recovery programs
alcoholism 137–38; in Aboriginal communities 15, 138–40, 141–42, 143; as substitute for transcendence 138–42
ancestor spirits 53–54
androgyny 76
angels 38
anima 74–75
anima mundi 62
animism 13–14, 54–55
animus 75–76
Anthropos 64, 76
anxiety disorders 18, 221–22
Apocalypse 172
archetypal medicine 20, 27–30; and the metaphor 32–34
archetypes 25–26, 47, 54, 60, 63, 175, 176, 229; father archetype 102–3; and Germany 168–69, 172
Arrernte tribe 13
Asclepius 40, 202, 203–4
Australia: alcohol abuse 15, 138–40, 141–42, 143, *see also* Aboriginal communities

authenticity 161, 164
autobiography of author 17–20

Beaudoin, Tom 157–58
befriending of illness 47–48, 49
Berry, Thomas 224
'Bill W' 142
Blake, William 239
blame, of person for illness 36, 42
body piercing 155, 157–59
Body and Soul: The Other Side of Illness (Kreinheder) 44–48
boundaries, and the numinous 235–36
brain, right/left brain thinking 12–13
'Bread and Wine' (Hölderlin) 181, 183–88
Brown, Carlton 196, 203
Buddhism 58, 124, 144–45
Burke, Janine 117–18

Campbell, Joseph 99, 227–28
cancer: cancer phobia case study (Jung) 197–98; as growth gone wrong 87–88; and Kreinheder 44; and psychological theories 42
celibacy 124, 129
change, resistance to 46
chaplains 194, 195, 196, 206
Chesterton, G. K. 16
child motif 67
child sexual abuse: in Aboriginal communities 15, 130–31; and Freud 125–28; metaphors 32; and symbolic images 129–32
children, spirituality of 185
Christ, the 54, 58
Christianity 64, 124, 165, 182, 186; and Germany 170–71, 172; healing ministry 203, *see also* Jesus
circumcision 153
Cognitive Behavioural Therapy (CBT) 150–51

collective unconscious 54, 58, 221, 227; Germany 170
complementary medicine 199
connectedness 207, 209–10; and healing 215, 217, see also waves
conversion 33
'cosmic consciousness' 236
creation stories 64
credibility 30–31
criminality, and spirituality 134–37
cure 219, see also healing
cutting (self-harm) 51, 155, 157–59

darkness, spiritual 179, 189
death: and afterlife 81–84; death wish 236–37; and healing 44–45; metaphors of 52–53; and rebirth 154, 155; and spirituality 80–82
depression 146–51; in Aboriginal communities 15; of author's mother 17–18, see also self-harm; suicide
Derrida, Jacques 190, 195
diseases see illness
divine love 103–5
dreams 57, 96–97, 203–4, 228; hysterical neurosis case study 109–11; and midlife 74, 75, 76, 77–78
drugs: in initiation rituals 155–56; and pathological spirituality 229
Dyer, Wayne 35

Eastern spirituality 229; Buddhism 58, 124, 144–45
Eckersley, Richard 160–61
ecstasy 223, 234
ego 15, 63–64, 228, 229, 237–38; and anxiety 221–22; and midlife 78; and neurosis 89, 90; and non-ego 70–74; and the Self 57, 58, 64–66; and spirit 38; and spiritual initiation 53, 54, 55, 56; and stages of life 60, 62; surrender of 55–56, 144–45; transformation of 72–74, 78
Einstein, Albert 220–21
elders 79, 80
Eliade, Mircea 43–44, 51, 52–53, 139, 141, 157, 162
enlightenment 14, 179
epilepsy 18
eros 105, 112, 113, 115, 118, 119, 120, 124
Euripides 234, 235
exile 64–67
existentialism 21

'false memory syndrome' 126
father archetype (*senex*) 102–3, 129–30
father/daughter relationship case study 99–112
Frankl, Victor 112
Freud, Sigmund 15, 21, 37, 41, 43, 60, 106, 107, 193, 229; and the death wish 236–37; and incest 122–28; 'oceanic feeling' 225–27; and the sacred 112–20; and self-esteem 151; on therapists 206–7

gender identity, and midlife 73–76
Germany, national psychosis 167–74
Gillen, Francis 138
God-principle 112, 116, 180, 181
gods 9–11; death of God (Nietsche) 177–78; and Germany 167–74; West's failure to acknowledge 174–77
Gospel of Thomas 165
Greece, ancient 28, 40; Dionysus 141–42, 173, 231–36
Greene, Brian 220
guilt, and illness 36

Hay, Louise 35
healing 29–30, 48, 214; and death 44–45; and incest 131; and meaning 201–2, 207–8; non-Western 199; and the numinous 215–28, 236–39; and religion 203–4; spiritual roots of 40–41; and surrender 144–45; women's 197
healthcare: and Jung 199–202; and spirituality 192–99, 202–8, 210–14
Heidegger, Martin 188–91
Hendricks, Gay 35
Hicks, Jerry 35
Hillman, James 20, 164–65
Hinduism 124
Hitler 169, 170, 173, 188, see also Nazi Germany
Hölderlin, Friedrich 167, 176, 180–88
homecoming 64–67
homosexual imagery 77
Hope, A. D. 59
hospital chaplains 194, 195, 196, 206
humanism 188

illness: and the spirit 26–27, 31; wisdom of 46–47, 203–4
Illness as Metaphor (Sontag) 41–44
Ilyatjari, Charles 163–64

images, translation of symptoms into 37–40
incarnation 60
incest 102, 121–22, 226; in Aboriginal communities 15, 130–31; and Freud 122–28; and Jung 122–25, 134–35; metaphors 32, see also child sexual abuse
incest imagery 77
indigenous cultures: and healing 40; initiation rites 34, 50–53, 152–54, 155–56, 164
indigenous influence 13–15
individuation 55, 58, 65–67
Inglis, Brian 203
initiation: and depression 148–49; initiation rites in indigenous cultures 34, 50–53, 152–54, 155–56, 164; and Jungian thought 53–56
intellectualism, and neurosis 216–17, 222
'intuitive method' (Jung) 37
intuitive thinking 11–13
irrational, the 205

Jacob story 38, 153
Jacobs, Gregg 200
James, William 113–14, 140, 199
Jaques, Elliott 68
Jesus 29, 178; healing ministry 203; Nicodemus story 121, 132–35, see also Christianity
Jocasta 122
Johnson, Robert 141
Judaism 64
Jung, Carl Gustav 20, 21–22, 26, 41, 43, 138, 142, 191; and archetypal medicine 27, 28–29, 30–31, 36–40; on cancer 88; cancer phobia case study 91–98; and depression 149–50; and Einstein 220–21; and the end of life 80–82; and German national psychosis 167–77; hysterical neurosis case study 100–112; and incest 122–25, 134–35, 136; and initiation rites 53–56; and meaning 201–2, 207–8; and midlife transition 68–69, 70, 71, 73, 78, 79–80; on neurosis 88–90, 216; and Nietsche 177–79; and primordial thinking 82–83; and the sacred 112–20; and the Self 54, 56–59, 64–66; spirituality and health 193, 194, 199–202, 207–8, 212–14, 217–18, 225, 226, 227, 228

Kast, Verena 231, 232, 234, 235
Kerenyi, Karl 232, 233
Klein, Milton 127
knowing, and illness 33–34
Koch, Christopher 131
Kreinheder, Albert 9, 33, 44–48
Kugler, Paul 126

left brain thinking 12–13
libido 104, 105, 108, 111, 120; and incest 124–25, 128, 135, 136
life: spiritual meaning of 62–64; stages of 60–62, 68–69, 70–72, 80–82, 85
Lockhart, Russell 87–88
logos 16, 17
Lucifer 178, 182

Martin, P.W. 217
Masson, Jeffrey 125, 126, 127
matriarchy, and spirituality 196–97
meaning, and healing 201–2, 207–8
medicine see healing; healthcare
men, and midlife 73–75
mental health: and pathological spirituality 229–31; and spirituality 192–208, 210–14
mental reprogramming 35
metaphor: of death 52–53; for diseases 29, 30, 32–34, 37; as illness 41–44
midlife crisis 67, 68–70; and gender identity 74–76; and the 'non-ego' 70–72; and resistance to transformation 77–78; and secular society 78–80; and sexual identity 76–77; transformation without cultural support 72–74
Miller, Alice 127
'mind over matter' 35
monotheism 20–21
Moore, Thomas 20, 146
Mowaljarlai, David 164
mysticism 16–17; of indigenous peoples 13; pathological 229–31
mythos 11–12, 16, 17

Nazi Germany 167–70, 171, 173, 174, 179, 181, 188, see also Hitler
negative thinking 35–36
neurosis 87; as arrested development 88–90; cancer phobia case study 91–98; as distorted religious interest 104–5; hysterical neurosis case study

100–112; and intellectualism 216–17, 222; symptoms 29
New Age 23, 198, 204, 210, 237
Nhat Hanh, Thich 144
Nicodemus story 121, 132–35
Nietzsche, Friedrich 21, 42, 71, 173, 177–80, 181, 207, 226, 232–33
'non-ego' 70–72, 73
non-religious people 43–44
nonrational, the 205
numinous, the 55; and boundaries 235–36; and children 185; and healing 30, 215–28, 236–39
nurses, and spirituality 194–95, 196–97, 198–99

'occultism' 115–16
'oceanic feeling' (Freud) 225–27
Oedipus 122
old age 79, 80–82
openness, importance of 48
Otto, Rudolf 199, 205, 218
Otto, Walter 232, 233, 234

paganism, Germany 168–71
Plato 76
particles 222, 224, 225, 233, 236–39; waves and particles metaphor 219–21
pathological spirituality 229–31
patriarchy, and religion 196–97
Pearce, Joseph Chilton 159–60
personification, of unconscious contents 39–40
philia 124
physics 220–21
Pitjantjatjara tribe 13, 163
Plato 60, 61, 64
Plotinus 84–85
polytheism 20–21
positive thinking 34–36
Powell, Andrew 205–6
'Pre/Trans Fallacy' (Wilbur) 238
primordial thinking 82–84
projection: and Nazi Germany 168; religious 176–77
psyche, the 22, 175; and depression 147–48; and rebirth 136–37; and stages of life 60, 62
psychoanalysis 21
psychosis 227, 229; in Aboriginal communities 15
psychosomatic medicine 34–36, 43

quantum physics 220–21

rapture 187
rationality 82–83
reason 95–98
rebirth 18, 33, 34, 51, 52–53, 160, 226; and child sexual abuse 129, 131, 132; and incest 121–22, 123, 124–25, 128, 136–37; and the Nicodemus story 121, 132–35; and suicide 154
recovery programs 223–24, *see also* Alcoholics Anonymous
Red Book, The (Jung) 39–40
reincarnation 61, 81
relativity 220–21
religion 176, 217; and alcohol 140–41; and neurosis 103–5; and the non-religious 109–12; and patriarchy 196–97; and sexuality 124, 130–31
resistances 77–78, 91–92
responsibility, for illness 36, 96
right brain thinking 12
Rose, Deborah Bird 55
Royal College of Psychiatrists 193, 202

sacred forces 9–10, 11, 14
sacrifice, and spiritual development 88
St Theresa of Avila 105
Sardello, Robert 20
Satan 178
schizophrenia 90, 186, 193, 227–28; of Holderlin 181; of Nietsche 178
second ego 78, 79
secularism 72, 78–80, 195
'seduction theory' (Freud) 125
Self, the 54, 56–59; and child sexual abuse 129; and ego 64–66
self-destruction, and spirituality 236–37
self-esteem 151–52, 162
self-harm 146, 155–59; in Aboriginal communities 152, 153–54; metaphors 32; psychology of 51, *see also* depression; suicide
senex (father archetype) 102–3, 129–30
sexual identity, and midlife 76–77
sexuality: and the father/daughter relationship 99–112; and Freud and Jung 112–20; and religion 124, 130–31
shamanism 40, 203, 204
Socrates 21
somatisation 34, 101, 219
Sontag, Susan 41–44, 86
soul 62, 93–95, 98; 'loss of' 152

source, returning to 84–85
Spencer, Baldwin 138
spirit 215–16; and diseases 26–27, 31; and ego 38; and healing 40–41; repression of 112–16
Spiritual Care Australia 195
spiritual development, and sacrifice 88
spirituality: and criminality 134–37; Eastern 58, 124, 144–45, 229; and healthcare 192–99, 202–8, 210–14; individual experience 194–95; Jung and mental health 193, 194, 199–202, 207–8, 212–14, 217–18, 225, 226, 227, 228; and matriarchy 196–97; and nursing 194–95, 196–97, 198–99; pathological 229–31; practical nature of 15–17; and self-destruction 236–37; uncontrollable nature of 205–7; as a wild zone 208–10; and young people 159–60
Stein, Robert 129–30, 131
subtle forces 25–26
suffering 223
suicide 146, 152–53; in Aboriginal communities 15, 56, 163–64; as a collective problem 163–64; and Jungian psychology 164–66; metaphors 32; and young people 161–63, *see also* depression; self-harm
surrender 55–56, 144–45
Swinton, John 202
symptoms: in depression 151; understanding of 36–40, 47–48; value of 45

Tao 57
tattooing 157–59
transcendence 221, 222, 223
transference 105–8
transformation 30, 32, 33, 34, 38, 48, 55; and incest 13, 124–25; resistance to 77–78; young people's expectation of 159–60
turning, the (Heidegger) 190–91
Tylor, Edward 14

unconscious, the 35, 37, 39, 57, 60, 62, 72, 83, 90–91, 94–95, 105, 114–15, 122, 131–32, 215, 220, 228–29, 231, 238; collective unconscious 54, 58, 170, 221, 227
university education, of author 12–13, 20

Warlpiri tribe 13
waves 221–29, 233, 236–39; waves and particles metaphor 219–21, *see also* connectedness
West, the: failure to acknowledge gods 174–77; and spirituality 15–17
White, Patrick 216
wholeness 67, 76
Wilber, Ken 237, 238
Wilson, William 142
wisdom: of illness 46–47; and medicine 198–99, 202–4
witches 197
women: and midlife 75–76; spirituality 196–97
Wordsworth, William 61
'world soul' 62
Wotan (Odin) 168–69, 171–72, 173–74

Yeats, William Butler 172
Yolngu people 130
young people: development of personality 69–70; and self-harm 146, 155–59; and spirituality 159–60; suicidal impulses 160–63

Zarathustra 177, 178
Ziegler, Alfred 25, 33–34